LANDLORDS AND TENANTS IN IMPERIAL ROME

LANDLORDS AND TENANTS IN IMPERIAL ROME

by Bruce W. Frier

PRINCETON UNIVERSITY PRESS

Published by Princeton University Press, Princeton, New Jersey

In the United Kingdom: Princeton University Press, Guildford, Surrey

Library of Congress Cataloging in Publication Data will be found on the last printed page of this book

Publication of this book has been aided by a grant from the National Endowment for the Humanities

This book has been composed in Linotype Janson

Clothbound editions of Princeton University Press books are printed on acid-free paper, and binding materials are chosen for strength and durability

Printed in the United States of America by Princeton University Press, Princeton, New Jersey

HERRN UNIV.-PROF. DR., DR. H. C. MULT.

MAX KASER

UND

DEM INSTITUT FÜR RÖMISCHES RECHT

DER UNIVERSITÄT SALZBURG

IN HERZLICHER FREUNDSCHAFT

DARGEBRACHT

Contents

Contents

List of Plan and Plates

The plan was drawn by Mr. Robert Bailey, following Beccati; the author would like to thank him and Prof. John Humphrey for their generous help. All photographs were taken by the author in September 1978, with the kind permission of the Sopraintendenza di Ostia.

Foreword

PROFESSOR FRIER's book could not have come at a more crucial time for legal history, law, and jurisprudence. For legal history it signals, I hope, a revival of interest in Roman law, a topic which has almost disappeared from view in America and is struggling for survival in Europe. For American law it comes at a time when the winds of change are blowing strong in the area of urban landlord and tenant law but when the course these changes ought to take is by no means clear. For jurisprudence it comes at a time when interest is once again keen in the mechanisms by which legal systems develop, but when the comparative knowledge which is necessary to develop a general theory of legal development is becoming increasingly difficult to obtain. It is a remarkable tribute to Professor Frier's capacities that as a classicist he is nonetheless able to speak to three diverse concerns normally associated with the legal profession.

The sad state of Roman law studies is well known. In the United States, Roman law has virtually disappeared from the university curriculum, as a result of the death, retirement or return to Europe of an extraordinary group of scholars whom the chaos of the war brought to our shores. While the subject is still taught in many of the great law schools of Europe, it has suffered badly as a result of the curriculum reforms of the late sixties and early seventies, and new names in the field are disturbingly few.

We could dismiss these developments as simply the reflection of the lack of scholarly discipline of the age. Roman law is difficult. Learning it requires command of a language that fewer and fewer Americans and Europeans have, mastery of a formidable scholarly apparatus written in virtually every Western language, and persistence with detail and legal imagination, qualities that are rarely found in combination in any age. But I think the decline of the study of Roman law must be attributed to causes deeper than its difficulty. The last generation of scholars of Roman law, for all their greatness, did not, on the whole, speak to this generation. Their minds had been formed by teachers in the pandectist tradition. They were systematic, rule-oriented, and analytical. Unlike the nineteenth-century pandectists, however, they had learned from the philologians of the late nineteenth and early twentieth centuries the critical importance of establishing the text. Because of the peculiar way in which most of Roman law has been transmitted to us, the last generation of scholars of Roman law had to devote great energy to establishing what was the text of the classical jurists and what the work of Justinian's Byzantine compilators.

With the legal realist movement in America and with the advent of sociological jurisprudence on the Continent somewhat later, much of the jurisprudential underpinning of this effort was removed. Lawyers became far more concerned with the way in which law and society interact, and the average student and professor of modern law can have no more than "academic" interest in the study of an abstract scheme of rules from a time long past. Unless legal historians respond to these developments by investigating the interaction of law and society in the past, they will have no students and nothing to say to their colleagues.

At the same time, I am convinced that the effort to reconstruct society and law of the past is crucial not only for the professional survival of legal historians, but also for the advancement of our own knowledge of the present. No theory of law and society can begin to have any generality unless it can account for the evidence of the past, and the modern reformer who wishes to use law for the purpose of social engineering is likely to do as much damage as good if he changes the rules inherited from the past without an adequate appreciation of how they came to be there in the first place or if he changes rules without an adequate knowledge of how other societies deal with similar problems. If today's legal historian, then, can show how law and society interacted in the past, he will have a considerable contribution to make to the ongoing debate about the relationship between law and society.

Showing how law and society interacted in the past is, however, a formidable undertaking. We know remarkably little about how rules of law, particularly private law, reflect our own social patterns and affect those patterns, although the data for such research is close at hand. It is much more difficult to ask these questions about societies long gone where statistical data is unavailable and where we are limited to the inferences we can draw from evidence which was compiled and which survives for reasons quite unrelated to the questions we are asking.

The first question that I pose of Professor Frier's book is, then, in my capacity as a legal historian: has he, despite the evidentiary barriers, been able to reconstruct both the social stuff of Roman urban lease and the law surrounding it in such a way that the material can be used either for comparison with our own situation or for the purpose of generalizing about the relationship between law and society? In my view he has succeeded in doing so, and the achievement is all the more remarkable, when one considers that it has never been attempted before. That Frier was able to do this is a reflection not only of his perspicacity in seeing that this was the crucial question, but also of his familiarity with the archeological and literary evidence on which his study of the social stuff of Roman urban lease is based. Until one realizes, as Professor Frier has now convincingly demonstrated (Chapters I-III), that the Roman legal sources which talk of urban lease are overwhelmingly concerned with the *cenacula* of upper-class tenants, and not with the *meritoria* of the urban poor, no study of the interaction of Roman lease law and Roman society can be made.

When Professor Frier moves from the social stuff of

Roman landlord-tenant law to the law itself (Chapter IV), he is moving to more familiar ground. His contribution here consists in recognizing, as not all scholars have, that the juristic texts on rental of a thing distinguish between urban and rural tenancies, and that there was a distinct body of law applying to each. The discussion of the juristic rules on urban lease is necessarily detailed and to some extent traditional. But Professor Frier has a sure hand with the texts of the Digest, and his delicate handling of the interpolation question (normally found at the beginning of the discussion of each text) nicely summarizes the work of the best of the previous generation of scholars while at the same time avoiding the endless battles in which some of them engaged. While the discussion is technical, as any careful discussion of a legal topic must be, it should be understandable to anyone familiar with the basic terminology and problems of modern residential landlord-tenant law, and it is critical to what follows.

Professor Frier does not make the direct comparison between the Roman law he has thus unfolded and modern European or American law. In the case of the latter, despite the difference in fundamentals (a Roman lease was a contract, not a conveyance, and the tenant had no right to possession but only to contract damages), there are striking similarities between the issues with which Roman landlord-tenant law dealt and those dealt with in our law prior to the recent reforms, and also striking similarities in result. These similarities can hardly be due to the influence of one legal system on another, and those who seek causes of these similarities will have to look to something more basic—perhaps it lies in the essentially upper-class nature of the Roman law and of, until quite recently, our own.

In his last two chapters, Professor Frier attempts to sketch out the implications of his findings for the theory of the interaction of law and society. While these are the most tentative chapters in the book, they are also the most exciting. The Roman jurist, like the common law judge until quite recently, rarely appealed to policy directly. The purpose and effect of the juristic enterprise must be inferred from the scheme of decisions that they have left us and what we know of the social situation in which they operated. Professor Frier's conclusion that the jurist eschewed any effort to solve the "housing problem" of imperial Rome must clearly be correct in the light of the surviving sources. That within the context of upper-class residential leases they sought to balance the interests of landlord and tenant in such a way as to continue an adequate supply of housing for upper-class tenants is certainly a plausible reading of the evidence, and a conclusion that has important ramifications not only for our understanding of how the jurists operated but also for the way that professionals whose function it is to transmit and apply the law resolve the conflict between the social interests that the typical lawsuit represents.

Where the legal professional today takes this material depends, of course, on his bias. As a legal historian, I am encouraged that so fruitful a study of the interaction of law and society in a time long past could be done. As a professor of property law, I am puzzled by the remarkable similarities between Roman law and our own, and think that my understanding of the course of development of the latter has been improved. As a legal theoretician, I am reminded both of the dangers of drawing too swiftly the conclusion that there is social prejudice in a body of law and also of how pervasive and intractable the problem of balancing of competing interests is.

CHARLES DONAHUE, JR.
Cambridge, Massachusetts

Preface

THIS BOOK is concerned with the genesis, purposes, and achievement of early imperial Roman jurisprudence: how the law "got there," what it accomplished. I have taken urban lease law as a specific illustrative theme.

The choice of this theme requires explanation. In 1972-1973, I was (thanks to a grant from the American Council of Learned Societies) a guest in Boalt Hall, the California Law School in Berkeley. There I studied Roman law while auditing classes in Common Law. Perhaps due to this "confrontation," I became, in that year and after, increasingly uneasy about modern discussions concerning the relationship of Roman jurisprudence to its social and economic base; these discussions had, so I felt, confined themselves mainly to the superficial. Therefore, in the following years, I began to hunt for a topic which would allow me to examine at least a part of this broader subject.

The topic had to fulfill certain conditions:

(1) It had to be of self-evident social importance. Preferably, it should concern an area of law with which most modern readers would have parallel experience. Further, its limits had to be both clear and not excessively broad;

(2) The relevant juristic sources had to be well preserved and, if possible, free from the taint of excessive interpolation. Despite the recent decline of *Interpolationskritik*, this sort of criticism is still apt to hinder and distract even patient laymen;

(3) The social problem had to be clearly attested in nonjuristic sources—if possible, through both literature and archaeology; such independent evidence would offer a basis for assessing the social character of the law;

(4) The social problem should be one which remained

by and large constant and uniform throughout the period of classical Roman law. More complex problems associated with social and economic change would introduce additional variables which would make study that much more difficult;

(5) Finally, for rather more pragmatic reasons, the topic had to be comprehensible and interesting both to classicists and to legal historians; this was especially important as regards the United States, where knowledge of Roman law has probably reached its all-time nadir.

In 1974, acting on a suggestion from my friend Charles Donahue of the Michigan Law School, I began to interest myself in urban tenancy. I soon realized that the topic was ideal. It centered on the city of Rome, whose housing was relatively well known not only from numerous references in ancient literature, but also from the excavations at Ostia; indeed, Ostian housing had recently been the subject of a full-length study by James Packer. The ancient sources gave little reason to believe that the broad contours of the market for rental housing had significantly altered from the first century B.C. to the third century A.D., although the *quality* of housing was somewhat affected by early imperial technological advance (particularly the "concrete revolution") and the *number* of upper-class tenants also seems to have increased gradually.[1] Furthermore, classical jurists had for the most part lived in or near Rome, vividly reflect its social life in their decisions, and usually seem to refer specifically to Rome's judicial system. Finally, the relations between landlord and tenant in a metropolis constitute a subject with which most modern readers can readily identify.

There is, of course, already substantial scholarship on urban tenancy in Rome, although not from a specifically

[1] However, Mario Torelli believes that this view may be oversimplified, and that close examination of the archaeological evidence might reveal a social change in urban life that had direct bearing on the changes in urban lease law. If he is correct, a possible line of future research has been opened.

legal viewpoint. My first task was to extract from this scholarship a workable "model" of Rome's rental market. This model is the subject of my article (substantially completed by mid-1975) in the *Journal of Roman Studies* for 1977. My model brought out the point that legal sources on urban lease mainly concern a form of rental associated with the upper-class "tier" of the market. This hypothesis was the starting point for my consideration of Roman lease law.

In order to facilitate my study, the National Endowment for the Humanities awarded me a fellowship for study in Europe during the academic year 1976-1977, at the American Academy in Rome and at the Institut für Römisches Recht, University of Salzburg. In Rome I had the opportunity to reexamine the remains of Ostia. In Salzburg, especially under the extraordinarily kind and patient tutelage of Prof. Max Kaser, the book took on its present form:[2] a study of what may fairly be called upper-class rental housing in early imperial Rome. The book was broadly conceived, ranging from the physical aspects of such housing (Chapter I), through the economic and social characteristics of the rental market (Chapter II), to the private law which came to regulate this market. In Chapters III-VI, this body of law is progressively set out from various points of view. Chapter III provides what I believe to be an adequate sociological justification for the upper-class character of Roman lease law. In the following chapter, which is inevitably swollen out of all proportion to its fellows, Roman lease law is presented systematically, in an analytical fashion.[3]

[2] I completed this book in midsummer of 1978, and have referred to subsequent bibliography only sparingly.

[3] Chapter IV presupposes the reader's general familiarity with Roman private law and its procedural system. Readers lacking such knowledge might consult, as the need arises, books such as W. W. Buckland, *A Textbook of Roman Law* (3d ed. 1966), and A. Berger, *Encyclopedic Dictionary of Roman Law* (1953). All extended Latin quotations in Chapter IV and elsewhere are translated into English in Appendix B below; the raised letter at the end of each quotation serves as a reference.

Chapter V then discusses the major individual and social interests protected by Roman lease law, as well as the law's probable effect on its social base. In Chapter VI, I discuss the likelihood that Roman lease law was constructed with an eye to its social utility.[4]

This definition of theme deliberately excludes two related topics. First, I have abandoned a projected chapter on Egyptian house leases; it was simply not possible to integrate them with the context. I must however emphasize that the papyri are ripe not only for renewed legal study, but also for sociological treatment. (Appendix A discusses a recently published "eviction notice" from Oxyrhynchus.) Second, I also abandoned my original intention to include a chapter on the legal treatment of lower-class housing at Rome; it must never be forgotten that such housing probably accommodated upwards of 90 percent of Rome's free population. Unfortunately, this subject does not really belong in a book otherwise preoccupied with private law; the law concerning the lodging houses of the urban poor was mostly of a criminal, administrative, or regulatory nature—intended above all to maintain the facade of public order.

One final observation. In this book I argue that the relationship between Roman law and Roman society was far closer than most modern legal historians would have us believe. To a certain extent, however, this assertion is possible precisely because of the topic I have chosen. My topic,

[4] My sociological viewpoint in Chapter VI (and elsewhere) is a modified version of the American functionalism associated with Talcott Parsons and others; for an account, see W. E. Moore, in *A History of Sociological Analysis* (ed. T. Bottomore and R. Nisbet, 1978) 321-361. (Much modern criticism of this view was exploded in P. Sztompka's excellent *System and Function*, 1974.) For the functionalist view of law, see J. Stone, *Social Dimensions of Law and Justice* (1966) 643-651. In general, I have referred to sociological literature mainly to make clear my own attitudes, but have tried not to multiply bibliography. The best introduction in English to legal sociology is L. M. Friedman, *The Legal System: A Social Science Perspective* (1975).

as it emerged, involved certain special conditions; among them were the following: the upper-class rental market in Rome is a well-known, readily distinguishable, and rather highly institutionalized sector of Roman society. The lease of housing within Rome was in general emphatically and repeatedly characterized by contemporaries as a social problem, i.e. "some piece of social behaviour that causes public friction and/or private misery and calls for collective action to solve it."[5] On the other hand, the upper-class rental market apparently did not involve any organized conflict between conscious social groups, nor did it (for that or other reasons) undergo any evident institutional change during the classical period of Roman jurisprudence. As a social institution, the upper-class rental market related mainly to specific portions of Roman private law, namely one part of *locatio conductio* and the interdict *de migrando*. In turn, these portions of private law pertained to the rental market and to it alone. The procedural and social factors determining the incidence of litigiousness in Roman society gave to the jurists, through the judicial system, clear and relatively full (although non-statistical) information on the functioning of the upper-class rental market. With regard to upper-class rental housing, private law was left virtually without competition from other forms of law; thus, the primary and almost the sole legal method for social management of the rental market was "a grievance-remedial instrument (recognition of claims to enforceable remedies for grievances, actual or threatened)."[6] By virtue of their geo-

[5] P. Worsley *et al.*, *Introducing Sociology* (1970) 51. The key point is recognition of the problem as a *social* problem.

[6] R. S. Summers and C. Howard, *Law: Its Nature, Functions and Limits* (2d ed. 1972) 21, cf. 23-24; R. Summers, *California Law Review* 59 (1971) 733-751, at 736. Summers distinguishes four other types of law: penal law; administrative or regulatory law; redistributive law (especially for taxes and largess); and law "facilitating and effecting private arrangements." This last type of law, which creates "freedom of contract," intrudes somewhat into our framework; the others do so only marginally.

graphic, social, and legal position, the jurists were readily able to observe, at least passively, the effects of their rules within the judicial system and the upper-class rental market.

These conditions, taken together, appear to have considerable significance. They make the type of relationship I am looking for both likelier to have occurred and likelier to be identifiable. On the whole, it would be fair to suppose that if we could not show Roman law and Roman society to have been structurally related in the area of urban lease, then we probably could not show a close relationship anywhere. However, it remains to be seen whether and how the degree of closeness may be altered when one or more of these conditions is relaxed; and for the present I assert nothing positive concerning areas of Roman law not under examination.

This is part of the reason why I feel that, despite the apparent novelty of my typically American "realism," I have probably left the field of Roman law little different from how the English novelist Iris Murdoch once described it: "There are certain areas of scholarship, early Greek history is one and Roman law is another, where the scantiness of evidence sets a special challenge to the disciplined mind. It is a game with very few pieces, where the skill of the player lies in complicating the rules. The isolated and uneloquent fact must be exhibited within a tissue of hypothesis subtle enough to make it speak. . . ."[7]

This study of Roman lease law could not have been completed without help from many sources. My home university and department granted me a sabbatical; the National Endowment for the Humanities underwrote a portion both of my sabbatical and of the costs for publishing this book. Princeton University Press, its managing editor Mrs.

[7] Iris Murdoch, *The Nice and the Good* (Amer. ed., 1968) 176. Her hero, a Romanist, is writing a book entitled *Puzzle and Paradox in Roman Law*. With his concerns, compare F. Wieacker, *SZ* 94 (1977) 355-358, which in criticizing recent scholarship reads almost like a program for the present book.

Joanna Hitchcock, its in-house editor Jennifer Sparks, and its two anonymous readers handled my manuscript with care and dispatch, providing many useful suggestions. Several colleagues read my text and offered advice on it; they are Charles Donahue of the Michigan Law School (and now of Harvard), Alan Watson of the University of Edinburgh, Ramsay MacMullen of Yale University, and Mario Torelli of the Università di Perugia. Prof. Donahue also agreed to write a Foreword. The Sopraintendenza of Ostia allowed me to explore, measure, and photograph the buildings mentioned in Chapter I. Two of my graduate students, Robin Graham and Susan Martin, helped with the index and the proofs. To all these individuals and organizations I was and remain deeply grateful.

My relationship with the Institut für Römisches Recht in Salzburg was a particularly fruitful one. Professor Max Kaser received me as a guest and student; he read and criticized my manuscript in both draft and final forms, he used it as a basis for several meetings of his seminar, and he unfailingly encouraged my research even when it seemed to diverge from traditional canons of interpretation. The other participants in the Institut also allowed me, in long and interesting conversations, to draw on their learning; they include Professors Wolfgang Waldstein, Theo Mayer-Maly, and Karl Hackl, and my great-souled office mate Dr. Alfons Bürge from Zurich. The staff of the Institut assisted my research in every possible way. To all my Austrian friends I offer this book as the inadequate repayment of an abiding debt.

B. W. F.
July, 1979

Abbreviations

In citing scholarship on Roman law, I have followed the now standard abbreviations employed by Max Kaser in *Das Römische Privatrecht*, with a few variations and additions. Outside Chapter IV, I have tended to use slightly fuller abbreviations. Classical sources have been cited by the customary abbreviations of their names and works.

ACIR	*Atti del Congresso Internazionale di Diritto Romano*, Roma 1933 (2 vols.; Pavia 1934)
Albertario (E.), I-VI	Emilio Albertario, *Studi di Diritto Romano* vols. I-VI (Milan 1933, 1941, 1936, 1946, 1937, 1953 respectively)
ANRW	*Aufstieg und Niedergang der Römischen Welt* vols. I-II, ed. H. Temporini (Berlin and New York, since 1972); cited by volume and fasicule number
APal.	*Annali del Seminario Giuridico dell' Università di Palermo*
Atti Acad. Pont.	*Atti dell' Accademia Pontaniana* (Naples)
Atti Perug.	*Atti del Seminario Romanistico Internazionale* (held in Perugia, Spoleto, and Todi, 1971; Perugia 1972)
B., Basilica	*Basilicorum Libri LX*, ed. G. E. Heimbach *et al.* (Leipzig 1833-1870), cited by volume and page; new edition begun by H. J. Scheltema *et al.* (The Hague, since 1953), with text (*BT*) and scholia (*BS*) separate (each cited by page)

Beseler (G.), I-V	Gerhard von Beseler, *Beiträge zur Kritik der Römischen Rechtsquellen* vols. I-IV (Tübingen; 1910, 1911, 1913, 1920 respectively); vol. V (Leipzig 1931)
Betti (E.), *Ist.* I, II	Emilio Betti, *Istituzioni di Diritto Romano* vols. I and II.I (Padua 1942, 1960 respectively; both volumes reprinted)
Biondi (B.), *DRC*	Bianco Biondi, *Il Diritto Romano Cristiano* vols. I-III (Milan 1952, 1952, 1954 respectively)
Bull.	*Bullettino dell' Istituto di Diritto Romano* (Rome; since 1940 Milan); vol. 42 (1934) = n.s. 1; vol. 62 (1959) = 3d ser. 1
Bull. Comm.	*Bullettino della Commissione Archeologica Communale in Roma* (Rome)
C., CJ.	*Codex Iustinianus* (*Corpus Iuris Civilis*, vol. II ed. P. Krüger; often reprinted)
Cannata (C.A.), *Colpa*	Carlo Augusto Cannata, *Per lo Studio della Responsibilità per Colpa nel Diritto Romano Classico* (Milan 1967/1968)
CIL	*Corpus Inscriptionum Latinarum* (Berlin), cited by volume and inscription number
CJ	*The Classical Journal* (now from Boulder, Colorado)
Cod. Theod.	*Codex Theodosianus*, ed. T. Mommsen and P. M. Meyer; 4th ed. (Berlin 1962)
Coll.	*Collatio Legum Mosaicarum et Romanarum* (in *FIRA* II 541-589)
CPh	*Classical Philology* (Chicago)
D.	*Digesta* (*Corpus Iuris Civilis*, vol. I ed.

	T. Mommsen and P. Krüger; often reprinted); an Italian edition in two volumes was edited by P. Bonfante *et al.* (Milan 1918, 1931 respectively)
Daube (D.), *Rom. Law*	David Daube, *Roman Law: Linguistic, Social and Philosophical Aspects* (Edinburgh 1969)
FA	*Fasti Archaeologici: Annual Bulletin of Classical Archaeology* (Florence)
FIRA I-III	*Fontes Iuris Romani Anteiustiniani* 2d ed. vol. I (*Leges*; ed. S. Riccobono, 1941/1968), vol. II (*Auctores*; ed. I. Baviera and I. Furlani, 1940/1964), vol. III (*Negotia*; ed. V. Arangio-Ruiz, new ed. with appendix 1968), all from Florence (vol. III is also cited with arabic volume number and document number)
Fr. Dos.	*Fragmentum Incerti Auctoris Quod Vulgo Dositheanum Dicitur* (in *FIRA* II 615-621)
Frag. Vindob.	*Ulpiani ex Libris Institutionum Fragmenta Vindobonensia* (in *FIRA* II 305-306)
Frezza (P.), I, II	Paolo Frezza, *Le Garanzie delle Obbligazioni* vol. I: *Le Garanzie Personali*, vol. II: *Le Garanzie Reali* (Pavia 1962, 1963 respectively)
Fs. Felgentraeger	*Festschrift für Wilhelm Felgentraeger* (Göttingen 1969)
Fs. Hanausek	*Abhandlungen zur Antiken Rechtsgeschichte: Festschrift für Gustav Hanausek* (Graz 1925)
Fs. Kaser	*Festschrift für Max Kaser zum 70. Geburtstag* (Munich 1976)
Fs. Lewald	*Festschrift Hans Lewald* (Basel 1953)

Fs. Steinwenter	*Festschrift Artur Steinwenter* (Graz-Cologne 1958)
Fs. Wenger, I-II	*Festschrift für Leopold Wanger* vols. I-II (Munich 1944, 1945 respectively)
GrunhZ.	*Zeitschrift für das Privat- und Offentliche Recht der Gegenwart* (publ. Grünhut, Vienna)
Hägerström (A.), I-II	Axel Hägerström, *Der Römische Obligationsbegriff* vols. I-II (Uppsala-Leipzig 1927, 1941 respectively)
Horak (F.)	Franz Horak, *Rationes Decidendi* vol. I (Aalen 1969)
Index	*Index: Quaderni Camerati di Studi Romanistici* (Naples)
Inst.	*Iustiniani Institutiones* (*Corpus Iuris Civilis*, vol. I ed. P. Krüger; often reprinted)
Iura	*Iura: Rivista Internazionale di Diritto Romano e Antico* (Naples)
Journ. Soc. Arch. Hist.	*Journal of the Society of Architectural Historians* (Louisville, Kentucky)
JRS	*Journal of Roman Studies* (London)
Kaser (M.), *RPR*² I-II	Max Kaser, *Das Römische Privatrecht* 2d ed., vols. I-II (Munich 1971, 1975 respectively)
Kaser (M.), *RZ*	Max Kaser, *Das Römische Zivilprozessrecht* (Munich 1966)
Kaufmann (H.)	Horst Kaufmann, *Die Altrömische Miete* (Cologne-Graz 1964)
Kunkel (W.)	*Römisches Privatrecht, auf Grund des Werkes von Paul Jörs in 2. Aufl. Bearb. von Wolfgang Kunkel* 3d ed. (Berlin-Göttingen-Heidelberg 1949)

Kunkel (W.), *Herkunft*[2]	*Herkunft und Soziale Stellung der Römischen Juristen* 2d ed. (Graz-Vienna-Cologne 1967)
Lab., *Labeo*	*Labeo: Rassegna di Diritto Romano* (Naples)
Lenel (O.), *EP*	Otto Lenel, *Das Edictum Perpetuum* 3d ed. (Leipzig 1927; repr. Aalen 1956)
Lenel (O.), *Paling.*	Otto Lenel, *Palingenesia Iuris Civilis* vols. I-II (Leipzig 1889; repr. Graz 1960)
Levy (E.), *Konk.* I-II	Ernst Levy, *Die Konkurrenz der Aktionen und Personen* vols. I-II.1 (Berlin 1918, 1922 respectively)
Levy (E.), *VL*	Ernst Levy, *West Roman Vulgar Law: The Law of Property* (Philadelphia 1951)
Liebs (D.), *Konk.*	Detlef Liebs, *Die Klagenkonkurrenz im Römischen Recht* (Göttingen 1972)
Longo (G.), *Ric.*	Giannetto Longo, *Ricerche Romanistiche* (Milan 1961)
LQR	*Law Quarterly Review* (London)
MAAL	*Memorie della Classe di Scienze Morali e Storiche dell' Accademia dei Lincei* (Rome)
MAAR	*Memoirs of the American Academy in Rome* (Rome)
Maroi (F.), I-II	Fulvio Maroi, *Scritti Giuridici* vols. I-II (Milan 1956)
Mayer-Maly (T.), *LC*	Theo Mayer-Maly, *Locatio Conductio* (Vienna-Munich 1956)
Medicus (D.)	Dieter Medicus, *Id Quod Interest* (Cologne-Graz 1962)

Mél. Lévy-Bruhl	*Droits de l'antiquité et sociologie juridique: Mélanges Henri Lévy-Bruhl* (Paris 1959)
Michel (J.)	Jacques Michel, *Gratuité en droit romain* (Brussels 1962)
Not. Scav.	*Notizie degli Scavi di Antichità* (Rome)
Opusc. Arch.	*Opuscula Archeologica* (Lund)
PBSR	*Papers of the British School in Rome* (London)
Pernice (A.)	Alfred Pernice, *Labeo: Römisches Privatrecht im Ersten Jahrhundert der Kaiserzeit* vol. I (1873), vol. II 1/2 (2d ed. 1895/1900), vol. III.I (2d ed. 1892), all from Halle; repr. Aalen 1963
Perozzi (S.), I, II	Silvio Perozzi, *Istituzioni di Diritto Romano* 2 vols.; 2d ed. (Florence 1928; repr. 1949)
Rabel (E.), IV	Ernst Rabel, *Gesammelte Aufsätze* vol. IV (Tübingen 1971)
Rabel (E.), *Grdz.*	Ernst Rabel, *Grundzüge des Römischen Privatrechts*, 2d ed. (Darmstadt 1955)
RE	*Paulys Realencyclopädie der Classischen Altertumswissenschaft*, ed. G. Wissowa, W. Kroll, K. Mittelhaus, K. Ziegler (Berlin), cited by article and column number
Riccobono (S.), I, II	Salvatore Riccobono, *Scritti di Diritto Romano* 2 vols. (Palermo 1957/1964)
RIDA	*Revue internationale des droits de l'antiquité* (Brussels); 1st ser. from 1948, *RIDA*[3] = 3 ser. from 1954
RIL	*Rendiconti dell' Istituto Lombardo di Scienze e Lettere* (Milan)

Riv. It.	*Rivista Italiana per le Scienze Giuridiche* (Turin, since 1947 Milan); new ser. since 1926, again since 1947
RPAA	*Rendiconti della Pontificia Accademia di Archeologia* (Rome)
Schipani (S.)	Sandro Schipani, *Responsibilità "ex Lege Aquilia," Criteri di Imputazione e Problema della "Culpa"* (Turin 1968/1969)
Schulz (F.)	Fritz Schulz, *Classical Roman Law* (Oxford 1951)
Schulz (F.), *Principles*	Fritz Schulz, *Principles of Roman Law* (Oxford 1936), trans. from *Prinzipien des Römischen Rechts* (Munich-Leipzig 1934)
Scr. Ferrini Mil.	*Scritti in Onore di Contardo Ferrini Pubblicati in Occasione della sua Beatificazione* 4 vols. (Milan 1947-1949)
SD	*Studia et Documenta Historiae et Iuris* (Rome)
Siber (H.)	Heinrich Siber, *Römisches Recht in Grundzügen für die Vorlesung*, vol. II: *Römisches Privatrecht* (Berlin 1928)
Solazzi (S.), I-IV	Siro Solazzi, *Scritti di Diritto Romano* vol. I (1955), vol. II (1957), vol. III (1960), vol. IV (1963), all from Naples
St. Albertario	*Studi in Memoria di Emilio Albertario* 2 vols. (Milan 1953)
St. Betti	*Studi in Onore de Emilio Betti* 5 vols. (Milan 1962)
St. Biondi	*Studi in Onore di Biondo Biondi* 4 vols. (Milan 1965)
St. Bonfante	*Studi in Onore di Pietro Bonfante* 4 vols. (Milan 1930)

St. De Francisci	*Studi in Onore di Pietro de Francisci* 4 vols. (Milan 1956)
St. Donatuti	*Studi in Memoria di Guido Donatuti* 3 vols. (Milan 1973)
St. Grosso	*Studi in Onore di Giuseppe Grosso* 6 vols. (Turin 1968-1974)
St. Riccobono	*Studi in Onore di Salvatore Riccobono* 4 vols. (Palermo 1936)
St. Volterra	*Studi in Onore di Edoardo Volterra* 6 vols. (Milan 1971)
Stud. M. Kaser	*Studien im Römischen Recht: Max Kaser zum 65. Geburtstag* (Berlin 1973)
Symb. Lenel	*Symbolae Friburgenses in Honorem Ottonis Lenel* (Leipzig 1935)
Synt. Arangio-Ruiz	*Synteleia Vincenzo Arangio-Ruiz* 2 vols. (Naples 1964)
SZ	*Zeitschrift der Savigny-Stiftung für Rechtsgeschichte*, Romanist. Abt. (Weimar): kan. = kanonist. Abt.
TR	*Tijdschrift voor Rechtsgeschiedenis = Revue d'Histoire du Droit = The Legal History Review* (Haarlem, since 1950 Groningen)
Watson (A.), *Obl.*	Alan Watson, *The Law of Obligations in the Later Roman Republic* (Oxford 1965)
Wieacker (F.), *Textst.*	Franz Wieacker, *Textstufen Klassischer Juristen* (Göttingen 1960)
ZVgl. RW	*Zeitschrift für Vergleichende Rechtswissenschaft* (Stuttgart)

LANDLORDS AND TENANTS IN IMPERIAL ROME

I

Upper-Class Apartment Housing in Ostia and Rome

EXCAVATIONS at Ostia, the port city of Rome, have revealed, in the course of the past century, a pattern of urban housing which literary sources also associate with Rome of the High Empire: sturdy four- and five-story apartment blocks (*insulae*), constructed primarily in brick and concrete with vaults or wooden raftering, and a high density of settlement—in short, an urban pattern perhaps distinguishable from Rome's only by the much smaller size of Ostia (ca. 20,000-35,000 inhabitants).[1] An understanding has also emerged of the relationship between the social structure of Ostia (well-known from inscriptions) and the types of housing uncovered by excavations.[2]

The Ostian excavations have in part merely confirmed what was already known from literary sources. Thus, the stately homes of the Ostian governing classes[3] are perhaps

[1] On Ostia's population, see J. E. Packer, *The Insulae of Imperial Ostia*, *MAAR* 31 (1971) 65-71 (the figures involve many guesses); on the relation of Ostia's housing pattern to Rome, *ibid.* 74-79. This book, which contains most earlier bibliography, is henceforth cited by the author's last name only. *Insulae* are referred to by the "addresses" in G. Calza *et al.*, *Scavi di Ostia* vol. I (1953); e.g. Casa di Diana (I, iii, 3-4).

[2] See B. W. Frier, *JRS* 67 (1977) 27-37 (and literature there cited); compare Packer pp. 71-72.

[3] E.g. the Domus della Fortuna Annonaria (v, ii, 8), built ca. A.D. 150-200: cf. A. G. McKay, *Houses, Villas and Palaces in the Roman World* (1975) 78 (bibliography at n. 110); the Domus del Tempio

only smaller and less costly versions of the houses of wealthy Roman senators and knights. Into the category constituted by these mansions can be placed as well a number of large and luxurious apartments, which display the same generous proportions and also the same tendency to orient major rooms in loose, functional groups around an interior court.[4] Within such houses and luxury apartments, the rich and powerful of Ostia encountered one another in circumstances of worldly ease.

Nor has lower-class housing occasioned much surprise, although to be sure archaeologists have tended to ignore these humble structures and concentrate instead on the better-built and thus better-preserved housing of the upper classes.[5] Nonetheless, the plan of Ostia displays a great numerical preponderance of lower-class housing: not only large and relatively well-constructed tenements like the Caseggiato degli Aurighi (III, x, 1),[6] but also numerous smaller and more anonymous structures. A typical example is III, i, 12-13: a Trajanic construction consisting of two rectangular "rooms," each ca. 115 sq. m. and each subdivided by flimsy partitions into two or three tiny "apartments." The use of temporary partitions is very characteristic of lower-class housing at Ostia; it occurs also on the mezzanine floor of the Insula degli Aurighi, on the ground

---

Rotondo (I, xi, 2-3), built ca. A.D. 225 (Packer pp. 155-157, plan: p. 99); the Casa delle Muse (III, ix, 22), built ca. A.D. 128 (Packer pp. 173-177, plan: p. 185); in general, G. Becatti, *Case Ostiensi* (1948).

[4] E.g. the handsome apartments in the Insula di Giove e Ganimede (I, iv, 2), built ca. A.D. 120-140 (Packer pp. 134-139, plan: p. 95).

[5] This is perhaps the reason why the impression of Ostian housing in such books as R. Meiggs, *Roman Ostia* (2d ed. 1973) 235-251, is so favorable. In these pages I have largely ignored shops, which, however, also housed a good portion of the Ostian population; see G. Girri, *La Taberna* (1956) 37-43.

[6] Built ca. A.D. 140-150 (Packer pp. 177-182, plan: p. 106). Packer's description of the "Second Floor" (more properly, the mezzanine floor) refers to the "later tufa block walls" dividing upstairs rooms (p. 181), and these are clearly visible in his plate LXVI, fig. 188.

floor of the slum-like Caseggiato del Temistocle (v, xi, 2),[7] and on the first floor of the Casa di Diana (I, iii, 3-4).[8] Because such partitions are easily swept away in the ruin of a building, their existence tends to be ignored by archaeologists. Nonetheless, even the surviving walls confirm an impression of crowding and squalor: rows of rooms no longer easily distinguishable from one another in function, disposed along facades or lightwells, and often reached by long interior corridors. In any event, nothing in the Ostian remains contradicts the picture of lower-class housing given by literary sources.[9] The great majority of the free Ostian population, perhaps some 90-95 percent, occupied these dismal buildings.

What was truly surprising about Ostia, however, was the discovery of a form of housing intermediate between these two extremes. The ruins have yielded up numerous well-built apartment houses that have an astonishingly modern look and "feel," especially in their standardized oblong apartment plan. This plan is also described in a *Digest* text (D. 9.3.5.2) from the jurist Ulpian (d. A.D. 223), which gives to the apartment its familiar name *cenaculum*.[10] The plan consists of two large dayrooms (*exedrae*) disposed at either end of a long axis running through a corridor-like central room (the *medianum*). All three rooms take light

[7] Built ca. A.D. 117-134 (Packer pp. 192-195, plan: p. 110).

[8] Built ca. A.D. 150 (Packer pp. 127-134, plan: p. 94). This famous and much described building is taken by B. W. Frier, (cited n. 2) 30-34, as an archetypal example of lower-class housing; G. Calza, *Not. Scav.* (1917) 322, thought that its first floor was a *piano nobile*, for reasons which in retrospect are unconvincing.

[9] Compare the classic pages of J. Carcopino, *Daily Life in Ancient Rome* (trans. E. O. Lorimer, 1940) 22-51; cf. also Packer pp. 72-79. Still worth reading is R. Pöhlmann, *Die Uebervölkerung der Antiken Grossstädte* (1884).

[10] See B. W. Frier (cited n. 2) 27-29, based partly on G. Hermansen, *Phoenix* 24 (1970) 342-347; cf. *idem, Historia* 27 (1978) 129-168, at 131. This form of apartment corresponds to Packer's types II C and D (Packer pp. 8-11). Most legal texts cited without extensive bibliography in this chapter are discussed at length in Chapter IV.

from large windows on the facade, and the *exedrae* are not infrequently two-storied with two ranges of windows. Across the *medianum* from the facade, therefore on the inner side of the *cenaculum*, are a row of from two to five bedrooms (*cubicula*), which are directly lighted only on the rare occasions when the back wall is free to the air (e.g. III, ix, 3-4 and 10). The apartment's entrance is almost without exception directly into, or through a vestibule-corridor into, the *medianum*, which provides access to all the other rooms. Many *cenacula* have internal mezzanines that cover the entire lower-floor area except for one or both of the two-storied *exedrae*. Their total floor area is normally 150-300 sq. m., thus very large.

There can be little doubt, especially in view of the Ulpian text, that the *cenaculum* form originated at Rome.[11] It first appears at Ostia in the reign of Trajan (98-117), obviously as an aftereffect of Ostia's greatly increased prosperity when Trajan's harbor opened. The earliest *cenaculum* form is the so-called Casette-Tipo (III, xii, 1-2; xiii, 1-2).[12] A small rectangular lot was developed as two very long rectangular apartment houses. From them survives, to just below windowsill height, the rather crudely constructed walls of four ground-floor apartments without mezzanines; in both buildings, steps to an upper story indicate that a second floor of apartments once stood above. The Casette-Tipo apartments are unusual in their provision of latrines, probably for the ground floor only.

In the reign of Hadrian (117-134) the *cenaculum* form proliferated at Ostia. It is most easily discussed in relation to the apartments associated with two tract-developments of these years. The first is a very large complex (III, iii-vi and

[11] At Rome, apartment living for the upper classes is first attested from the second century B.C.: Plut. *Sulla* 1.2, 6; cf. Livy 39.14.2; Diod. 31.18.2; and Val. Max. 5.1.1f.

[12] Built ca. A.D. 100-110 (Packer p. 185, plan: p. 108); cf. M. E. Blake and D. T. Bishop, *Roman Construction in Italy from Nerva Through the Antonines* (1973) 155.

xi-xii) built ca. 124-134 in the northeast of the city, between the river Tiber and the Via Ostiensis leading from the center of Ostia to Rome;[13] the complex (not fully excavated and partially reburied) includes the Baths of Neptune, the Barracks of the Vigiles, at least two *horrea* for grain storage, large industrial premises, and numerous small shops. Set into this predominantly commercial development are four *cenacula* that throw considerable light on the origin of the *cenaculum* form. The Insula dell' Ercole Bambino (II, vi, 3) best illustrates the point,[14] which is, however, also true of the Insula del Soffitto Dipinto (II, vi, 6) and of two other unnamed *cenacula* (II, iii, 3 and 4). The Insula dell' Ercole Bambino is part of a long block divided lengthwise; on the east side of this division are four virtually identical shops whose walls continue in plan through the central dividing wall. The *cenaculum* on the west side thus consisted originally of four approximately equal rooms (the northernmost shortened by the inclusion of an entrance hall and a staircase); these four rooms were linked by a "corridor" of doorways aligned just inside the west facade. The middle two rooms were later (but perhaps already at the apartment's first leasing) each divided from the "corridor" by brick partitions. The result was the creation of a *cenaculum* form, with *cubicula* at the rear of the central rooms and a long narrow *medianum* linking the *exedrae* at either end of the

[13] Archaeological evidence now suggests that this project was largely a reconstruction of an earlier Domitianic one: R. Meiggs (cited n. 5) 582-583, citing F. Zevi, *FA* 18/19 (1963-1964) 7429; *Not. Scav.* 24 (1970) 7.

[14] The complex II, 6 was published by D. Vaglieri, *Not. Scav.* (1913) 120-128. The door into the large *exedra* of II, vi, 3 was cut after the building's construction, as an inspection of the bricks shows. Both II, vi, 3 and 6 originally communicated with shops behind them, and were presumably occupied by wealthy merchants. On them, see also R. Meiggs (cited n. 5) 247; M. E. Blake and D. T. Bishop (cited n. 12) 193-194. II, iii, 3 and 4 are very interesting, though less known; on them, see G. Calza, *MAAL* 23 (1915) 602, with a plan at p. 582 and an exterior restoration at p. 594.

plan. The same thing happened in each of the development's other three apartments: a line of rooms was in effect converted into a *cenaculum*-form apartment.

The meaning of these conversions is obvious; the *cenaculum* form was created out of and evolved from "strip" apartments consisting of long files of rooms arranged behind a facade.[15]

The second Hadrianic project is the Garden House complex (III, ix), built ca. A.D. 128 in the extreme west of Ostia.[16] This primarily residential complex was developed in a large rectangular tract (ca. 100 m. x 130 m., with the northwest corner slightly truncated); a continuous line of exterior buildings surrounds a central park that contains the two rectangular units known as the Case a Giardino (III, ix, 13-20), each with four ground-floor *cenaculum*-form apartments. (In the Garden House complex, the *cenaculum* form was the original plan.) The northeast corner of the surround was given over to a splendid private house about an internal courtyard, the Casa delle Muse (III, ix, 2); as has been happily suggested,[17] this house may have been the developer's. Along the four sides of the great park are arranged, roughly alternating, groups of shops (III, ix, 2, 5, 7, 9, and 11) and *cenaculum*-form apartments (III, ix, 1, 3, 4, 6, 8, 10, 12, and 21), some of which were later substantially altered. The complex's ground floor thus contained sixteen *cenaculum*-form apartments. Further, many staircases go up to now vanished upper stories; it is reasonable to suppose that the whole complex averaged three or four stories in height. If the ground-floor plan repeated in upper stories (as is not

[15] See below at nn. 41-44.

[16] Excavations beneath the complex have revealed earlier efforts at systematic development: F. Zevi and I. Pohl, *Not. Scav.* 24 Suppl. 1 (1971) 43-234, esp. 74 (at p. 43, reference is made to further, as yet unpublished excavations by G. Ricci). On the complex, see R. Meiggs (cited n. 5) 139-140; J. E. Packer, in *The Muses at Work* (ed. C. Roebuck, 1969) 47-51; M. E. Blake and D. T. Bishop (cited n. 12) 188-191.

[17] Packer p. 176; on this house, see also at n. 3 above.

unlikely in a development of this sort), the entire complex may have contained fifty to sixty *cenacula*. The Garden House complex can be described as an upper-class housing project.

On the east a monumental triple archway gave entry to the central park; smaller passages led in from the other cardinals. The impressive triple arch, reached by the wide Via delle Volte Dipinte from a major thoroughfare, lay between the Domus dei Dioscuri (III, ix, 1; later extensively modified) on the left, and the Insula delle Pareti Gialle (III, ix, 12) and the Insula del Graffito (III, ix, 21) standing back-to-back on the right.

The Insula delle Pareti Gialle is not only a typical *cenaculum*, it is also extremely well preserved, and so warrants a closer examination.[18] It and its companion, the Insula del Graffito, are contained in a very slightly rhomboid plot about 21 m. on a side. The architect's intention may have been to divide this approximate square into two rectangular apartments, each having on the south a vestibule with a staircase to upper floors. However, the positioning of the triple archway required the displacement of the two doorways about 1.5 m. to the east; as a consequence, the Insula delle Pareti Gialle gained floor room and the Insula del Graffito lost it. Each apartment has two ground-floor *cubicula*; in plan these four rooms comprise a square that lies approximately in the center of the plot's north-south axis, but displaced on the east-west axis by the same 1.5 m. to the east. The vestibule, *medianum*, and smaller *exedra* of the Insula delle Pareti Gialle became thereby correspondingly larger; indeed, the *medianum* is virtually a square, and the smaller *exedra* is both broader and deeper by 2 m. than that of the Insula del Graffito. Only in the rear (west) portion of the plot were the larger *exedrae* of the two *cenacula* approximately equal in size—the large *exedra* of the Insula

[18] Besides the bibliography cited below, see G. Calza (cited n. 1) 136-137, 236. The following pages should be read together with the plan and plates.

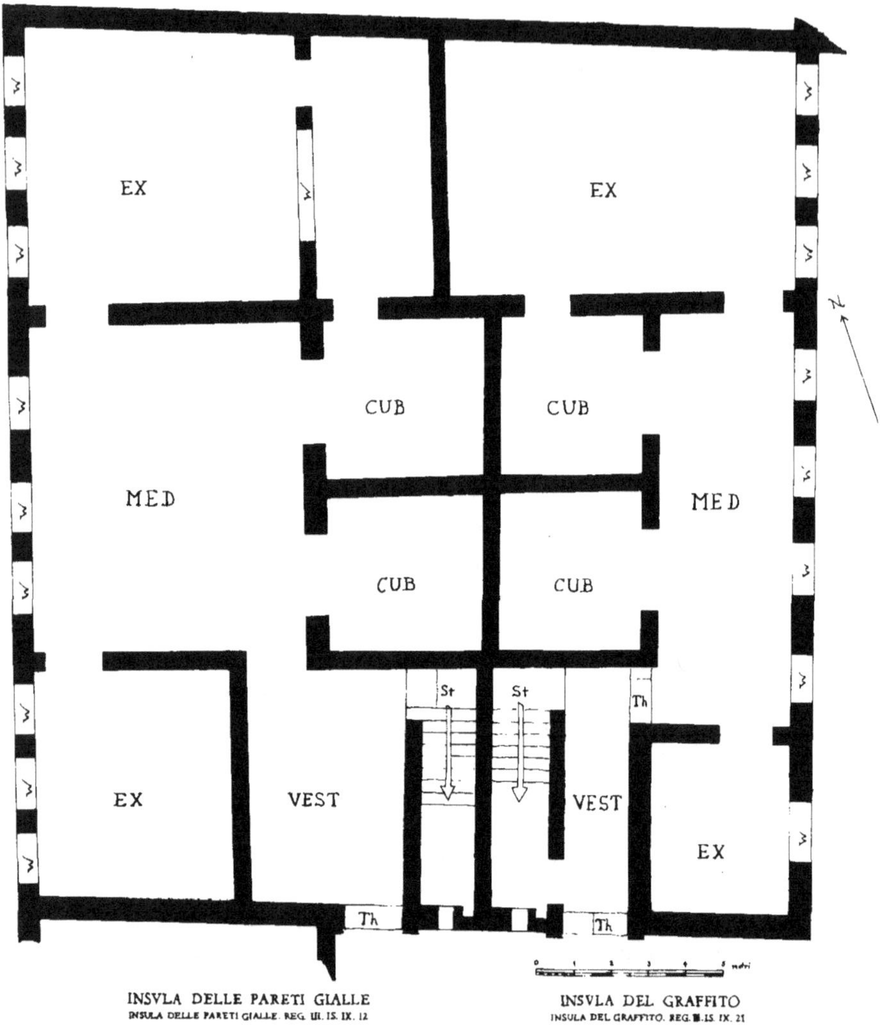

PLAN. Original plan of the Insula delle Pareti Gialle (III, ix, 12) and the Insula del Graffito (III, ix, 21), before the addition of internal buttresses in the former. The principal ground-floor rooms (*vestibulum*, *medianum*, *exedra*, *cubiculum*) are labeled; thresholds for lockable doors are also indicated. Ground-floor rooms except for the larger *exedra* of the Insula delle Pareti Gialle were all one story high (2.8 m.); all these rooms were originally covered with rafters, except for the vestibules which were barrel-vaulted. The better mosaics are confined to the *exedrae*. (This plan was drawn by Mr. Robert Bailey, after G. Beccati's plan in *Scavi di Ostia* vol. IV, 1961, tav. CCXXIV. North is up.)

delle Pareti Gialle being, however, divided by a partition with a door and a huge arched opening.[19]

The result of these adjustments in plan was the creation of two apartments, one of rather grandiose ground-floor dimensions (about 200 sq. m. excluding vestibule), the other somewhat cramped (about 145 sq. m.). The Insula delle Pareti Gialle, furthermore, had a mezzanine reached by the staircase from the vestibule. All rooms in the south two-thirds of the *cenaculum* (except for the vestibule, which was barrel-vaulted) had wooden rafters, the cornices and footings for which can still be seen in the *medianum*; in the small *exedra* and the two *cubicula* the rafters have been restored. The large *exedra*, however, lacks these emplacements and must have risen two stories with a double range of windows (like those in the *exedrae* of I, iv, 3 and 4).[20] The mezzanine was therefore confined to the apartment's southern two-thirds. By contrast, the Insula del Graffito has emplacements for rafters also in its large *exedra*. Furthermore, unlike the Insula delle Pareti Gialle whose vestibule gave access also to the mezzanine, the interior of the Insula del Graffito is divided from its vestibule by a threshhold block with sockets for a hinged door. It is therefore likely that this ground-floor *cenaculum* lacked a mezzanine, and that two or more independent apartments were constructed directly above it.[21]

Within the Insula delle Pareti Gialle space was given a deliberate hierarchy. The *cenaculum* takes afternoon sun

[19] Similarly divided *exedrae* occur also in I, iv, 3-4; II, iii, 3-4; and II, vi, 3 and 6. The reasons for this fashion are unclear.

[20] This is also shown by the arch in the large *exedra*; its crown is 4 m. above floor level, while the cornices in the remainder of the apartment begin at 2.8 m.

[21] The upper-story apartments above the Insula delle Pareti Gialle were presumably reached by the external staircase at the northwest corner of the Casa delle Muse (Packer p. 105, "rooms" 1-2). It is not clear why Packer (p. 89) limits this *insula* to two stories; the buttressing which it later required should indicate that it was substantially higher.

through a range of windows on its long western flank; they are divided into three groups of three each, corresponding to the two *exedrae* and the *medianum*. In the two *exedrae*, the sunlight streams down upon richly patterned mosaic floors; the *medianum*, *cubicula*, and vestibule have much simpler mosaics. All the mosaics date from the building's construction.[22] The walls were repeatedly decorated with elaborately painted plaster, the earliest surviving of which dates from the mid-second century, and the lastest perhaps from the fourth century—some measure of the apartment's very long life.[23] The fine yellow and scarlet wall paintings in the large *exedra*, its alcove, and one *cubiculum* (they date from ca. A.D. 175-185) gave the *cenaculum* its name: on a yellow field, broad vertical stripes of scarlet, out of which there develops a delicate and fantastic architecture of thin white columns and lintels.

The esthetics of this handsome imperial *cenaculum* deserve special mention. From the exterior doorway an uninterrupted line of sight extended from the vestibule (which lay in permanent gloom) through the drab *medianum* to the door of the large *exedra*, often brilliant with sunlight by virtue of its great size and fenestration (its windows are 0.25 m. higher than the others on the facade). The doorway of this room was also the focus of a secondary axis running into the elegant small *exedra*. The plan is simple and clear, yet very dramatic. The large *exedra* contains the only surprise: an enormous arch (2.90 m. high) opening on a shallow alcove that communicates with the master bedroom. The two *cubicula* are naturally given no special emphasis, but the corresponding windows on the facade are slightly asymmetrical so as to provide them the maximum light.

The architectural emphasis within this *cenaculum* was on light, privacy, security, and the orderly flow of spacious

[22] G. Becatti (cited n. 18) 123-125.

[23] On the painting, see B. M. Felletti Maj, *Monumenti della Pittura Antica Scoperti in Italia* vol. III (Ostia), fasc. 1-2 (1961) 41-54, with earlier bibliography.

volumes. Plainly, a well-to-do family might have dwelt here in more than moderate comfort; the mezzanine presumably housed their slaves. The source of the wealth sustaining this style of life is hinted at by the four heads of Oceanus (one now destroyed) that were placed at the cardinals in the lunettes of the large *exedra*'s mosaic. The apartment appears to have been continuously occupied, without structural alteration except for some buttressing soon after its construction, over more than two centuries.

The Hadrianic era saw even more lavish variants of the basic *cenaculum* form (such as I, iv, 3-4;[24] III, ix, 6 and 9), but also much humbler variants (I, xiv, 9; III, vii, 5;[25] V, iii, 3-4; V, xi, 2).[26] There are a total of more than thirty such ground-floor *cenacula* from Hadrian's reign, to which may perhaps be added some plans very hard to discern on the ground (such as III, vi, 2). The Hadrianic building programs permanently filled the need for this popular apartment form. Thereafter, the only possible instance of the *cenaculum* form (IV, iv, 6: built ca. A.D. 222-235) is not easy to understand.

Before discussing the social character of the tenants of these *cenacula*, it is best to shift the scene briefly to Rome. However, the housing patterns of Rome cannot without further comment be reconstructed on the basis of Ostia. To be sure, the link is obvious in one respect: the Ostians deliberately oriented their city toward a crowded, vertical housing pattern, rather than toward a horizontal spread. The Ostian pattern must recall, though perhaps in a somewhat relaxed fashion, the housing pattern of the capital—a

[24] These are the Insula dei Dipinti and the Insula di Bacco Fanciullo, respectively; their plans are virtually identical. On the former, see Packer pp. 139-141 (plan: p. 96); on both, M. E. Blake and D. T. Bishop (cited n. 12) 173.

[25] The Casa Vicina alla Domus Fulminata, built under Hadrian (Packer pp. 171-172, plan: p. 104).

[26] The Caseggiato del Temistocle, built under Hadrian (Packer pp. 193-195, plan: p. 110). One wing houses four extended *cenacula* which were directly lighted, if at all, through skylights.

mode of living, in short, which the Ostians intended as a mirror to Rome's urbanity. Still, what is known of the ground-floor plans of Roman *insulae* (whether from archaeological remains[27] or from the Severan Marble Plan)[28] does not clearly confront us with the Ostian *cenaculum* form. It is true that the preserved remains are in any event too scanty to allow a systematic view of Roman housing; and much the same criticism can be brought against the Marble Plan, which is also very difficult to read as regards housing. What remains of the Marble Plan may simply miss large isolated complexes similar to the Garden House development.

The most completely surviving Roman *insula*, and the only one with intelligible upper-story plans, is the Casa di Via Giulio Romano, constructed around A.D. 100.[29] What remains (from a much larger building) is principally the west wing backed up against the steep slope of the Capitoline Hill. The ground floor contains a row of shops behind a (later-constructed) arcade which runs along the facade of the wing. Above these shops a mezzanine floor was set on wooden raftering; the mezzanine rooms intercommunicated, with the likely consequence that a ground-floor shopkeeper could lease, as he desired, one or more mezzanine rooms in addition. The first floor (a sort of *piano nobile*) contained one or two large apartments. The major file of

[27] See the fundamental surveys in M. E. Blake, *Roman Construction in Italy from Tiberius Through the Flavians* (1959) 54-58, 125-131; M. E. Blake and D. T. Bishop (cited n. 12) 73-98; further, Packer pp. 74-79; all with further bibliography. On the area around the Piazza Colonna, see G. Gatti, *Saggi—V. Fasolo* (1961) 49-66.

[28] On house plans in the Marble Plan, see P. Ziçans, in *Opusc. Arch.* 2 (1941) 183-194; at p. 191 Ziçans claims to recognize a *cenaculum* form. The fragments of the early third-century A.D. Marble Plan were published by G. Carettoni *et al.*, *La Pianta Marmorea di Roma Antica* vol. 1 (1960).

[29] The *insula* is described in detail by J. E. Packer, *Bull. Comm.* 81 (1968-1969) 127-148, with reference to earlier literature; see also M. E. Blake and D. T. Bishop (cited n. 12) 81-83 (the date is discussed on p. 82).

rooms, at the southern end of the wing, begins with a well-lighted trapezoidal room on the extreme south, and then continues with three larger rooms of nearly identical size, and concludes in a still larger, somewhat irregularly shaped room. These five rooms are linked by a "corridor" of doorways just inside the facade. The apartment's total floor area is about 200 sq. m. Like the *cenacula* in the Baths of Neptune complex at Ostia, this apartment at some point in its life was apparently converted to the *cenaculum* form, as the remains of a partition dividing one of the middle rooms shows.[30]

By contrast, the second floor (and what survives of the third) develops as a warren of tiny, squalid rooms, most of them not directly lighted and served by long interior corridors. Most rooms are very small (about 10 sq. m.), but it is still entirely probable that a small family could have occupied such humble quarters.[31] The building obviously became more crowded and more lower-class in its upper stories.

The Casa di Via Giulio Romano indicates that, because of the extreme demand for ground-floor space at Rome, many apartments (including *cenaculum*-form ones) may have been located on upper floors. As for Ostia, the consequence is that we cannot automatically assume continuance of ground-floor plans in upper stories.[32] Still, in this matter we probably have at least three controls. First, it is plausible that buildings in general tended to become more lower-class in their upper stories, beyond the "*piano nobile*"—a sort of "vertical zoning."[33] Second, at least one floor of

[30] This partition is indicated in I. Gismondi's plan, which is reproduced by J. E. Packer (cited n. 29) 140; my discussion of the plan varies somewhat from Packer's (at pp. 138-139).

[31] So thinks J. E. Packer (cited n. 29), 146. Compare R. Pöhlmann (cited n. 9) 97-98, 104. Note P. A. Brunt, *Italian Manpower* (1971) 385-388, on the decay of lower-class family life in Rome; compare Pöhlmann, pp. 105-106.

[32] *Contra* Packer p. 70; cf. R. Meiggs (cited n. 5) 585.

[33] Compare R. Meiggs (cited n. 5) 250-251. However, some literary

cenaculum-form apartments should probably be restored above many of the ground-floor rows of shops that are widely found in Ostian and Roman *insulae*. Third, it is somewhat less likely that *cenaculum*-form apartments were located in the upper stories of the highly commercial Baths of Neptune complex, but somewhat more likely in the largely residential Garden House complex. At any rate, one's impression is that the classes were "horizontally zoned" to a considerable degree at Ostia; the fortress-like exclusivity of the Garden House complex significantly reinforces this impression. At Rome, "horizontal zoning" would presumably be less prominent, at least in the city's center.

Some 40 ground-floor *cenaculum*-form apartments are preserved in Ostia. Since one-third of Ostia is still unexcavated, we may suppose that there were about 60 in all. Upper-story *cenacula* probably multiplied this number by a factor of at least three or four: 180-240 in all. The average number of inhabitants per *cenaculum* is naturally harder to estimate: with slaves, perhaps 6 to 8.[34] These figures give a minimum of 1,080 residents, a maximum of 1,920: between 1,000 and 2,000, let us say. By contrast, the number of residents (including slaves) of Ostian private houses has been estimated at 660;[35] even if we add to this number the residents of luxury apartments, it is likely that the total was less than that for *cenaculum*-form apartments. But since the incidence of domestic slaveholding undoubtedly declined as one went lower on the housing scale (from houses to luxury

---

evidence suggests upper-class *cenacula* at the top of their buildings: Martial's third-story *cenaculum* had a view (1.108.3-4, 117.6-7), Augustus could watch horse racing from the *cenacula* of his friends and freedmen (Suet. *Aug.* 45.1), and the roof in Gabba's leaked (Quint. 6.3.64).

[34] Packer (p. 70) estimates that the "population of each flat was roughly equal to the number of bedrooms"; this assumption, which seems to me gratuitous (so also R. Meiggs, cited n. 5, 585-586), yields a population for Type II C and D apartment buildings of 763 (Packer p. 91; but he misses some examples). Cf. R. Meiggs, pp. 597-598.

[35] Cf. G. Girri (cited n. 5) 42 (using Calza's figures); Packer p. 70.

apartments to ordinary *cenacula*), it is extremely likely that the numerical majority of the Ostian upper classes, though not its most influential sectors, lived in *cenacula*.[36] The tenants of these *cenacula* would constitute the lower ranges of the upper classes: the shippers and merchants, wealthier freedmen, successful practitioners of the liberal arts, and so on. It is perhaps not entirely amiss to designate this group "the commercial class." (In the next chapter I will try to locate the equivalent group at Rome.)

A number of final comments on the *cenaculum* form need to be made. First, as to the amenities, most preserved *cenacula* had no running water, no latrines or bathing facilities,[37] and no clearly identifiable kitchens. There are some exceptions: the two-storied *cenacula* II, ii, 3-4 both had latrines, perhaps supplied with water from the Baths of Neptune across the street. More usually, only single-storied *cenacula* had latrines; for instance, the Trajanic Cassette-Tipo had latrines reached usually by corridors, clearly in order to keep resultant odors at a remove from the central dwelling area. So, too, in the variant forms V, iii, 3-4, where the corridors are even longer and dog-legged. In two-storied *cenacula*, both latrines and kitchens were for the same reason perhaps normally confined to the mezzanines where slaves slept. The reverse arrangement is perhaps found in the peculiar variant III, vii, 5,[38] which, since it had only one "*cubiculum*" on the ground floor, presumably had sleeping quarters for tenants also on the mezzanine; hence the latrine was on the ground floor, but divided from the rest by a long corridor. In any

[36] On the composition of Ostia's upper classes in the High Empire, see R. Meiggs (cited n. 5) 196-208; on freedmen, *ibid.* 217-224. My colleague John D'Arms has carried these studies still further.

[37] Cf. Frontin. *Aq.* 2.76, who complains that water from Roman aqueducts had been misdirected "even into *cenacula*"; the Roman authorities discouraged this practice. Martial's flat had no running water (8.67.7-8), and a tenant mentioned by Martial (12.32.13) obviously had no latrine. R. Meiggs (cited n. 5) 586, calls for more study of the subject.

[38] Cf. note 25 above.

event, the absence of running water meant that usually all water had to be toted in; the Garden House complex had six large fountains in the central park, obviously for the use of residents.

Second, since stone and brickwork are generally all that survive from these *insulae*, the amount of wood originally used in them can be underestimated. Still, it appears that most rooms in *cenacula* were ceiled with wooden raftering, and that the use of concrete vaulting was less than common; the Casa di Via Giulio Romano in Rome uses vaulting throughout (except for the shop mezzanines), but other Roman *insulae* plainly employed wooden rafters.[39] Wood was also used in window and door fittings, in partition walls, and in furniture, sometimes also for staircases. *Cenacula* were therefore not immune to fires. Despite the generally high standard of upper-class construction, there are also signs of shoddy building in other structures besides the Insula delle Pareti Gialle.[40]

Third, something must be said about the critical role of natural light. The conservative *cenaculum* form exploited a single, long, well-lighted facade. Its plan was dictated by a conscious architectural choice: granted the inadequacy of artificial lighting, a file of rooms behind a single facade could all be evenly lighted only at the cost either of diminished privacy (if all rooms interconnected) or of great inconvenience (if they interconnected via an unlighted rear corridor). In the *cenaculum* form, the Roman architect brought the corridor to the front of the structure, so that it joined the two rooms (the *exedrae*) at either end of the file; while the middle rooms (the *cubicula*) were partitioned off and left with little or no direct lighting, for use in hours of retirement. The deliberateness of this choice is clearly witnessed in the conversion of the apartments in the Baths of Neptune complex, or of the apartment in the Casa di

[39] Cf. M. E. Blake and D. T. Bishop (cited n. 12) 98, on the *insula* incorporated into the Aurelian wall.

[40] See R. Meiggs (cited n. 5) 250-251.

Via Giulio Romano, from a file of rooms to the *cenaculum* form. Elsewhere in Ostia, rows of interconnecting rooms seldom exceeded three rooms in length (e.g. those in the first floor of the Caseggiato del Triofore, III, iii, 1).[41]

Such practical considerations suffice to describe the generation of the *cenaculum* form.[42] From there, its evolution tended to follow the normal lines of Roman architecture. The principal axis was distinguished by the creation of spacious—even luxurious and two-storied—*exedrae* at either end; a widened *medianum* gave a convincing spatial link between the two principal dayrooms; while the intermediate rooms diminished to the dimension of *cubicula*.

This theory of the *cenaculum* form's development is to some extent confirmed by the more lavish variants at Ostia. In these variants, not one but two parallel facades were available to the architect. More conservative examples are the Insula di Bacco Fanciullo (I, iv, 3) and the Insula dei Dipinti (I, iv, 4);[43] here the architect made as much as possible of the superb view of the garden on one flank, and simply set a relatively bland corridor inside the street facade.

Far more startling is the recently excavated Insula delle Ierodule (III, ix, 6; 8 is presumably identical) on the west side of the Garden House complex.[44] Taking advantage of its two facades, the architect dramatically modified the standard plan: the two *exedrae* become smaller, balanced

[41] Built under Antoninus Pius (Packer pp. 164-166, plan: p. 102); the division of rooms on the first floor is restored at p. 166 n. 2.

[42] By contrast, some scholars see a relationship between the Pompeian *domus* and the *cenaculum* form: e.g. R. Meiggs (cited n. 5) 247; Packer p. 9; B. M. Boyle, *Journ. Soc. Archit. Hist.* 31 (1972) 257-258. While the *medianum* resembles the *atrium* in being a central room, its radical spatial deemphasis and the alteration in its source of light are sufficient to distinguish it entirely; in this respect, reliance on plans is misleading.

[43] At least in the former, the partitions date from the original construction, as is shown by the placement of floor mosaics, which are also original (G. Becatti cited n. 18, 16-17).

[44] See M. L. Veloccia Rinaldi, *RPAA* 43 (1970) 165-180 (plan: p. 167).

rooms on either end of the *medianum*; two *cubicula* are set back-to-back at one side; and the majority of the space along the *medianum* is given over to a large and handsome salon divided from the *medianum* by two columns. (The plaster ceiling of this salon survived nearly intact and is being restored.) This plan indicates a willingness to depart drastically from the standard *cenaculum* form when light was available from more than one facade. However, in other apartments (e.g. III, IV, 3 and 10) the same architect used the second facade only for direct lighting of the *cubicula*, otherwise preserving the standard plan.

This evidence strongly suggests that the *cenaculum* form derived primarily from the architectural necessity of handling light within a "strip" apartment.

Finally, the social significance of the standardized *cenaculum* form deserves stress. In Ostia's imitation of the dense Roman housing pattern, apartment tenancy in multiple-story *insulae* had obviously become a way of life also for most of the upper classes. The result was the emergence of "modern" apartments and apartment-house complexes. These apartments were erected by speculating landowners and then put at the disposition of a tenant class possessed of the means and position to defend itself, both socially and at law. Such were the architectural and social preconditions for the creation of classical Roman lease law.

II

The Social Institutions of the Roman Rental Market

The Owners

Wealthy Romans tended to invest their surplus wealth in land, and especially in farmland; they did so in the hope of a regular return on investment of somewhere around 5-6 percent a year.[1] While there is no doubt that agricultural land made up the bulk, nonetheless sufficient evidence survives to suggest that urban properties were also a part of the normal well-balanced portfolio.[2]

The economics of urban investment are brought home in a famous anecdote told by Aulus Gellius (*NA* 15.1.1-3) in the mid-second century A.D. A group of friends were accompanying the *rhetor* Antonius Julianus up the Cispian hill when they noticed a huge urban *insula* on fire; the conflagration threatened to engulf the whole neighborhood. One of the party observed that while the returns (*reditus*) from urban properties were high, the risks (*pericula*) were extremely high also;[3] were it not for the continual fires at

[1] See R. Duncan-Jones, *The Economy of the Roman Empire* (1974) 33 ff. (but on viticulture see p. 59); in general, M. I. Finley, *The Ancient Economy* (1973) 95-122, for the absence of "systematic, calculated policy" (p. 117) in these investments.

[2] This point was recently emphasized by P. Garnsey, in *Studies in Roman Property* (ed. M. I. Finley, 1976) 123-132; see also H. Schneider, *Wirtschaft und Politik* (1974) 81-86. (Both authors may exaggerate the significance of urban investment.)

[3] These risks included also the danger of collapse, much discussed

Rome, he would sell his farms and buy up urban properties. The group then discussed methods of fireproofing.

High profits and high risks. It is not easy for us to determine what Gellius meant with these categories. No information from Rome survives on the relation between the value of developed property and the yearly return from rent; 8.6 percent per year, a figure found in a Greek oration of the fourth century B.C. (Isaeus 11.42; two houses), has the ring of possible truth but is too isolated. This rate, which is at least 43 percent higher than the probably usual return for farmland, would at constant rates return initial investment in about eleven-and-a-half years, or five years sooner than that for agricultural land.[4] The crowded conditions at Rome may well have driven rents so high that the return was even greater.

But more underlay the calculation in Gellius than appears at first sight. Above all, Roman investors sought secure return, not just high return;[5] indeed, urban properties might well have been thought of as a hedge against the catastrophes that periodically rolled across the countryside.[6] But there

---

in legal texts. Gellius' fire may be compared with a fire under Antoninus Pius which destroyed 340 *insulae et domus*: SHA, *Ant. Pius* 9.1; for other sources on collapses and fires, see R. Pöhlmann, *Die Uebervölkerung der Antiken Grossstädte* (1884) 110-112; L. Friedländer, *Darstellungen aus der Sittengeschichte Roms* (10th ed. 1922) 23-26; and L. Homo, *Rome Impériale et l'Urbanisme* (1951) 589-591; Z. Yavetz, *Latomus* 17 (1958) 500-517. An assessment of relative risk lies behind Cicero's remark on urban investment in *Parod. Stoic.* 51; cf. *Off.* 2.88.

[4] To put this in modern terms: if the purchase price of a new building (including land) was completely amortized over 30 years (scarcely an unreasonable estimate in view of Vitruv. 2.8.8-9), and if upkeep in this initial period was negligible (which is likely), a gross return of 8.6% of initial value would *still* have a higher net yield than the rent from a farm of equivalent worth that was *not* amortized.

[5] On this characteristic of the ancient economy, see H. G. Kippenberg, in *Seminar: Die Entstehung der Antiken Klassengesellschaft* (ed. Kippenberg, 1977) 15-16, with earlier literature (esp. Weber).

[6] Farm disasters are neatly catalogued in the juristic sources on

PLATE 1. The Garden House complex (III, ix) lies in the middle distance; one of the subsidiary entrances to its central courtyard is partially visible on the right, with its elaborate and striking brickwork. The facade of the Insula delle Pareti Gialle, with three sets of triple windows, is visible within the courtyard on the left. The courtyard's main gateway lies beyond this Insula.

PLATE 2. The main gateway *into* the Garden *House* complex. *The* central passage originally had an arch over a flat brick lintel; the two side passages were later walled up. To the right of this gateway is the door of the Insula delle Pareti Gialle (III, ix, 12).

Plate 3. The exterior facade of the Insula delle Pareti Gialle, facing onto the central courtyard. Note the subtle variations in the size and placement of its windows. The sills are about 1.5 m. above ground level. The door directly to the left of the facade had a staircase which probably went up to apartments above the ground-floor *cenaculum*.

PLATE 4. A corner of the master bedroom of the Insula delle Pareti Gialle; the elaborate wall painting probably dates from ca. A.D. 180. The bright yellow field of this painted plaster gave the apartment its name. The plaster has been detached from the wall and remounted in order to protect it.

PLATE 5. A view from the vestibule through the *medianum* to the doorway of the larger *exedra*. Note the remains of the barrel vault which originally covered the vestibule; the use of reticulate instead of brick in walls of lesser structural significance; and, to the left of the *exedra* doorway, the remains of a wall buttress. All interior walls were originally plastered. Sand protects the original floor-mosaics of these rooms.

PLATE 6. The huge arched opening at one end of the larger *exedra*, with a small doorway into the alcove partially visible on the left. Before the alcove, a portion of the intricate mosaic pavement in the larger *exedra*; on the walls of the alcove, the yellow-field wall painting characteristic of this *cenaculum*. The slanted roof over the alcove is for protection and does not imitate the original roofing.

PLATE 7. The Insula dell' Ercole Bambino (II, vi, 3); a view through the door of the larger *exedra* into the *medianum*, with the door to the smaller *exedra* in the background. The masonry used to carve two bedrooms out of the *medianum* is clearly visible on the right of the *medianum*, and the line of plaster shows these walls rising above their preserved height. This *cenaculum* also has an internal staircase to a mezzanine floor.

PLATE 8. The "window wall" in the larger *exedra* of the Insula dei Dipinti (I, iv, 4). This wall had two tiers with three windows in each tier; the right windows are not visible. On the left, the doorway into the (one-storied) *medianum* is visible, and beyond it a doorway into the central garden. The Insula delle Pareti Gialle probably had a similar "window wall" in its larger *exedra*.

was a difference. A farm might remain unproductive for a year or two because of pestilence or plague; the farm *villa* might burn down; poor management might result in the necessity of considerable reinvestment for farm equipment and slaves (Plin. *Ep.* 9.37). But this was still minor beside the expense of entirely replacing an *insula* that unexpectedly collapsed or was gutted by fire. For urban properties, construction would probably constitute at least as heavy an investment as the cost of the land itself.[7] A vacant, unimproved urban lot normally earned its owner nothing.

The possibility of a sudden, massive expenditure was probably sufficient to deter some from urban investment, no matter what the long-term economics. Thus, Pliny the Younger, about whose finances we are relatively well informed, is not known to have held any urban property except his own house.[8]

But by no means all were so cautious. Much of our information comes from the late Republic, and it reveals that urban investment attracted a broad spectrum of the aristocracy. The urban properties at one time or another controlled by Cicero were perhaps typical: one-eighth ownership of an *insula* near the temple of Strenia; *insulae* on the Argiletum and Aventine, a part of Hortensia's dowry retained after divorce for the maintenance of their son; and a number of urban lodging houses in Puteoli, inherited in 45 from the

---

remissio mercedis (Ulp. D. 19.2.15.2-5, 7). Legal sources on rental are treated more fully in Chapter IV; I apologize in advance for unavoidable duplication.

[7] There is no real way to estimate Roman land prices; still the best study is R. Pöhlmann (cited n. 3) 86-88; cf. also R. Duncan-Jones, *PBSR* 33 (1965) 224-225; E. J. Philipps, *Latomus* 32 (1973) 86-95; H. Schneider (cited n. 2) 85. The land on which Cicero's house stood was apparently worth 43% of its total value (compare *Fam.* 5.6.2 and *Att.* 4.2.5). A study is needed of the construction industry in Rome; a large number of legal texts attest its importance. On the brick-making industry see now T. Helen, *Organization of Roman Brick Production* (1975).

[8] R. Duncan-Jones (cited n. 1) 22.

banker Cluvius.[9] Elsewhere we hear of urban properties held as investments by Cicero's brother Quintus (Cic. *Att.* 1.14.7; *Q. Fr.* 2.3.7); his close friends Atticus (Nepos, *Att.* 14.3), L. Lucceius, and M. Caelius Rufus (Cic. *Att.* 7.3.6, 9); his bitter enemy Clodius (Cic. *Cael.* 17); and some acquaintances in the lower nobility (Cic. *Off.* 3.66).[10] To M. Crassus, perhaps the largest holder of all (Plut. *Crassus* 2.5), we shall return below. Other casual references in Cicero (2 *Verr.* 3.199; *Fin.* 2.83; *Off.* 2.88) suggest that urban investment was entirely normal.[11]

The situation probably did not change in the Empire, though our information becomes spottier. The *columbaria* of the great Julio-Claudian families have yielded the names of many *insularii*, servile building attendants;[12] one inscription even names an *exactor ad insulas* (*CIL* 6.9383), whose duty was to collect rents (Ulp. D. 13.7.11.5). Two inscriptions (*CIL* 6.65, 67) refer to a Transtiburtine *insula* owned by M. Vettius Bolanus, probably the suffect consul of A.D. 66. Urban investment is considered normal for the upper classes by Martial in the late first century A.D. (3.31.2; 4.37.4) and by Lucian in the mid-second (*Merc. Cond.* 21). In the early third century, Ulpian drew the legal consequences (D. 5.3.27.1): the rents of urban properties are counted part of the fruits even when they result from houses of prostitution; "for houses of prostitution are operated in buildings owned by many respectable men."

No doubt it was the case throughout the early Empire that most urban property was controlled by the aristocracy.

[9] For sources and an analysis, see my article, "Cicero's Management of his Urban Properties," *CJ* 74 (1978) 1-6.

[10] Compare Hortensius' holding in Puteoli: Cic. *Att.* 7.3.9; J. H. D'Arms, *Romans on the Bay of Naples* (1970) 182.

[11] Outright speculation in urban land (e.g. Cic. *Att.* 13.33.1), whether for development or for subdivision, is something different: E. Rawson, in *Studies* (cited n. 2) 100-102; P. Garnsey, *ibid.* 124-125.

[12] See the long list (18 inscriptions) in B. W. Frier, *JRS* 67 (1977) 28 n. 8. Add *CIL* 6.5857. Examples come from virtually every dynastic family of the era.

Inevitably, however, some of it devolved to others. A speaker in the *Satyricon* (95.3) implies that women frequently owned urban property, presumably through inheritance in most cases, though urban property was also included in dowries (e.g. Cic. *Att.* 15.20.4; Ulp. D. 24.3.7.11). Two inscriptions (*CIL* 6.10248, 29791) and a legal text (Scaev. D. 33.7.7) show freedmen inheriting *insulae*. Perhaps Trimalchio had acquired his *insula* (Petron. *Sat.* 71.2) in this way; he proposes to legate it to a slave of his own. A funerary inscription tells us of a freedwoman who acted as priestess (*popa*) in an *insula* owned by her patron, also a freedman.[13]

Some urban property fell, by forfeit or escheat, to the imperial *Fiscus*. Servile *insularii* are recorded in the *familia Caesaris* (*CIL* 6.8856; 14.2769), and there is also a record of a freedman who acted as *praepositus insulariorum* (*CIL* 6.8855).[14] Seutonius (*Claud.* 38.2) records that Claudius relegated a Senator who, as Aedile, had fined the *inquilini* of imperial properties for selling food against a prohibition; the unfortunate Aedile had struck an imperial *vilicus* who tried to intervene. Most of the references to imperial ownership are early in date, and there is little sign of imperial involvement in urban housing on any massive scale; perhaps this was policy.[15]

It may be unwise to overestimate the amount of wealth concentrated in urban properties; compared with that in agricultural land, urban investment was no doubt relatively small, and much of it may have involved only that well-attested portion of the Italian aristocracy who also lived in

[13] *CIL* 6.9824. For other evidence of *insula*-related cults, see R. MacMullen, *Roman Social Relations* (1974) 86 and 182 n. 105. A *popa* may, however, be a cook.

[14] Cf. G. Boulvert, *Esclaves et Affranchis Impériaux* (1970) 37, 189. Alimentary funds were also reluctant to invest in urban properties; for an isolated example, see R. Duncan-Jones (cited n. 1) 296 n. 3.

[15] J. Vogt, *Das Erbbaurecht* (1950) 5-19, though he exaggerates, is still interesting on the management of public property through *superficies*.

Rome. Still, these holdings were not negligible. Herodian (7.12.5-7), commenting on a fire that broke out at Rome during civil disorder in A.D. 238, notes that the fire soon spread to catastrophic proportions among the densely crowded wood tenements; as a result, many wealthy men were impoverished through loss both of their own lavish dwellings and of their extensive income-producing properties.[16] At least in the early Empire, such losses were often made good out of imperial funds—a form of fire insurance that was, however, dependent on the emperor's generosity.[17] Some reports on imperial fire relief (esp. Vell. 2.130.2; Tac. *Ann.* 15.43.2) suggest that the owners of urban properties came from diverse classes.

Exploitation of Urban Property

The requirements for investing in urban properties are clearly listed by Cicero (*Off.* 2.83): the investor had to purchase,[18] construct, watch over, and repair his property. In this section we are mainly concerned with the methods an owner might use for exploiting property through lease to urban tenants. Presumably his choice among these methods might influence either the type of previously developed property which he purchased or the sort of building he constructed on a vacant or razed lot. He would also take into consideration such market factors as the location and character of available property, the current demand for specific types of rental housing, the amount of capital he had on hand, his access to staff in the form of slaves or free employees, and so on.

[16] Herodian may well exaggerate; C. R. Whittaker, in his Loeb translation, vol. II (1970) 245 n. 2, refers the reader to 7.3.5.

[17] These instances are catalogued by R. F. Newbold, *Latomus* 33 (1974) 861-863; cf. B. W. Frier (cited n. 12) 36.

[18] Or otherwise acquire. On land acquisition through purchase, see J. Crook, in *Studies* (cited n. 2) 80-82; on its frequency at Rome, Strabo 5.3.7.

Exploitation of Urban Property

Ancient sources suggest two principal types of rental housing and two principal modes of managing them.

A legal source clearly divides rental housing into two broad categories. Ulpian, 18 *ad Sab.* (D. 7.1.13.8):

> Item si domus usus fructus legatus sit, meritoria illic facere fructuarius non debet nec per cenacula dividere domum: atquin locare potest, sed oportebit quasi domum locare. nec balineum ibi faciendum est. quod autem dicit (*scil.* Nerva) meritoria non facturum, ita accipe quae volgo deversoria vel fullonica appellant. . . .[a]

The text describes two forms of urban exploitation (both forbidden to the fructuary of an urban residence).[19] The first was to create *meritoria*, by which is meant "spaces for rent" in the broadest sense; as the text goes on to say, this category would include lodging houses (*deversoria*) and commercial premises such as a fullery (*fullonica*). A companion text (Papin. D. 32.91.4) refers to a *domus* in portions of which there were a public bath and *meritoria*, rent-earning rooms. Quite often these rent-earning spaces were used to house lower-class tenants who could afford only a room or two; in cities, the lodging houses of the poor were known under a wide variety of more or less synonymous names (*meritorium*, *deversorium*, *stabulum*, *taberna*, *hospitium*, *synoecium*, *caupona*), and they appear to have formed the preponderance of lower-class housing.[20]

What is to be stressed about these lodging houses, as the remains of Ostia also make clear, is the absence of architectural planning in terms of discrete multiple-room units (*cenacula*). The first floor of the Casa di Diana (I, iii, 3-4) instead seems to develop as a series of small one- or two-

[19] Already considered in B. W. Frier (cited n. 12) 31. The first part of the text is apparently not interpolated. The two forms of organization mentioned here are vividly distinguished by the amount of rent tenants paid: *ibid.* 34-35.

[20] *Ibid.* 30-34. I omit discussion of the widespread use of small shops as dwellings; see Chapter I n. 5.

room units (*cellae*) interspersed with larger rooms that are relatively open to light and air—common rooms, probably, where the lodgers could gather for meals and social purposes. A closely similar disposition can be detected on the ground, mezzanine, and first floors of the Caseggiato degli Aurighi (III, X, I). All of this is fully consistent with the pattern of life in an urban *deversorium* as Petronius describes it.[21]

Lodging houses would necessarily demand a considerable amount of close supervision by the landlord of the *insula*; such supervision would normally involve a staff (*familia*). The lodging house in Petronius' *Satyricon* was run by the owner's procurator (96.4), and its staff included a concierge (90.7, 92.1; cf. 79.6), cooks or scullions (95.8), building attendants (95.8), and assorted slaves (96.8). The tenants were fed from a common kitchen (cf. esp. 82.1, 94f.).

The second method described in D. 7.1.13.8 was to organize an *insula* into apartments (*cenacula* or *aediculae*); if this was pursued in the Ostian manner, it involved a quite different set of problems. The Ostian apartment block was a series of independent *cenacula* joined mainly by a staircase, with no common rooms included in the plan; each apartment had its own bedrooms and dayrooms, and presumably also its own kitchen and toilet facilities, plus (usually) quarters for slaves. In its domestic autarchy it resembled the Pompeiian *domus*, though it forfeited much of the aesthetic subtlety of the *domus*. Since the tenants attracted into a *cenaculum* were relatively upper-class, it had to be appropriately outfitted, decorated, and maintained. A block of *cenacula* did not, on the other hand, require the close day-to-day supervision characteristic of a *deversorium*.

At Rome, due to the intense population pressure, the two principal forms of exploitation through leased housing may have been often combined, though only the Casa di Via

[21] B. W. Frier (cited n. 12) 31-32. On the Casa di Diana, see Chapter I n. 8; on the Caseggiato degli Aurighi, Chapter I n. 6.

Giulio Romano survives to confirm this inference.[22] Such combinations, especially when they resulted in "vertical zoning," complicated the pattern of leasing; but with a moderate amount of supervision the levels could remain distinct. Toward the edges of the capital, as in Ostia, a degree of "horizontal zoning" may also have occurred.[23]

The second choice faced by the owner was whether to manage the property directly or through a contractual middleman.[24] Self-management was presumably, in the great majority of cases, accomplished through representatives. The lodging house in the *Satyricon* was run, it will be recalled, by a procurator (96.4). This may have been common; a procurator is mentioned in the *Digest* (Ulp. D. 13.7.11.5), and a spurious procurator as well (Ulp. D. 19.2.15.8).

On the other hand, a slave could take up this role.[25] As with a free manager, the transactions of a servile *insularius* would then bind the one who put him in charge of the building (Ulp./Serv. D. 14.3.5.1). But the word *insularius* had other meanings. In one text (Pomp. D. 7.8.16.1) an *insularius* guards an urban property for the owner and against the fructuary; in Petronius (95.8) the *insularii* seem to be simply building attendants under the procurator.[26] Therefore it is not easy to define the function of the numerous *insularii* who appear in early imperial epitaphs,[27] though their owners must have managed urban properties directly.

[22] Cf. Chapter I at n. 30. An example of such "mixed use" is the *Insula Sertoriana* (*CIL* 6.29791): 6 *cenacula* and 11 *tabernae*.

[23] At least, this is my impression. Contrast R. MacMullen (cited n. 13) 67. A definitive study is needed.

[24] I leave to one side the institution of *superficies*, whereby the owner of land could lease the site on an extremely long term; for its (early imperial) extension to private citizens, see A. Palladini, in *Novissimo Digesto Italiano* s.v. "superficie" (1971) 941-944; F. Pastori, in *St. Donatuti* vol. II (1973) 871-896.

[25] A slave acted as the owner's rental agent in Pompeii: *CIL* 4.138.

[26] This is disputed; H. Rowell, *CPh* 52 (1957) 223-224, thought they were tenants, but see E. Paratore, in *Studi G. Funaioli* (1955) 343-344.

[27] Cf. n. 12.

Common parlance referred to the manager of a building as the bailiff (*vilicus*: Suet. *Claud.* 38.2; Mart. 12.32.23; Juv. 3.195), apparently without distinction of status; although this usage was deprecated by the jurist (Pomp. D. 50.16.166), it nonetheless found its way into a postclassical constitution (*Cod. Theod.* 16.5.1: A.D. 399). The manager's duties, as the sources show, were to supervise the renting of the premises and, in the case of *deversoria*, to preserve order. As we have seen, his staff might be very large. Further, the government did not hesitate to hold the owner or his manager responsible for the maintenance of public security; in a decree associated with the secular games of A.D. 224, owners are apparently required to keep their tenants under control (*CIL* 6. 32327 line 21), and an edict of Septimius Severus (*apud* Ulp. D. 1.15.5) gives the Praefectus Vigilum power to discipline *insularii*[28] and "those who keep fires negligently in their homes" (cf. Paul. D. 1.15.3.4-5). In a census the owner could be held to answer for his tenants (Suet. *Jul.* 41.3; cf. Ulp. D. 50.15.4.8).

Alternatively, the owner of urban property could lease it *en bloc* to a single lessee (a middleman), who would then sublease it to the actual tenants. This practice is so frequently mentioned in the *Digest*[29] that we can be certain it was extremely common; and in fact I have argued elsewhere[30] that Cicero utilized middlemen for the residential properties he controlled in Rome and Puteoli. Use of middlemen had two main advantages: first of all, it insulated the owner from the troublesome business of dealing with tenants on a day-to-day basis, and thus freed him from committing his own staff to managing the property; second, it had the advantage of

[28] Despite the difficulties, I think that *insularius* has its normal meaning here, and signifies that the *insularii* were required to keep a check on tenants' fires; the text may be abbreviated.

[29] Alfen. D. 19.2.30 pr.; Labeo D. 19.2.58 pr., 60 pr.; Labeo/Paul. D. 19.1.53 pr.; Afric./Serv. D. 19.2.35 pr.; Ulp. D. 13.7.11.5, 19.2.7; Tryph. D. 19.2.8. Cf. R. Pöhlmann (cited n. 3) 107-109.

[30] The advantages of using middlemen are fully explored in my article cited in n. 9.

passing to the middleman the entire risk of both incomplete occupancy and tenant's failure to pay, as well as part of the risk for catastrophic fires and the like. However, the owner also had to accept a reduction in his potential profit. One legal text (Alfen. D. 19.2.30 pr.) presents a hypothetical problem in which the principal lessor rents a whole *insula* for 30 (thousand sesterces) to a middleman who subleases the *cenacula* for a total of 40; this means in effect that the principal lessor received only about 75 percent of the potential rent.[31] (And the use of middlemen had other risks, which we will explore in the next section.) Nevertheless, this mode of management was doubtless attractive, especially to owners of smaller properties and most especially for lower-class housing.[32]

Varying estimates have been given as to the degree of economic organization in the Roman rental market. Some have not hesitated to discover here "Roman capitalists" who "found out as well as Mr. Sartorius that slums are particularly profitable."[33] Such remarks seem to imply a very high degree of economic organization; and plainly, in any case, Rome's rental market exhibits the threshhold level of capitalism, in which "property is an object of trade and is utilized by individuals for profit-making enterprise in a market economy."[34]

[31] If his potential return equalled 8.6% of value, he would be settling for a return of 6.45%, which would normally be paid in advance; the middleman's management costs must also be figured in, however. With this text, compare Ulp. D. 19.2.7.

[32] Legal texts seem to confirm this inference; when a tenant (which usually means an upper-class tenant) is one party to a suit on lease, the owner is most often the other party.

[33] F. Schulz, *Classical Roman Law* (1951) 544-546 (at 545). (Schulz apparently refers to the economic historian August Sartorius von Waltershausen; modern studies tend not to support this observation.) On capitalism in the Roman rental market, compare R. Pöhlmann (cited n. 3) 106-109; G. Salvioli, *Le Capitalisme dans le Monde Antique* (1906) 54-56. Many modern works stop just short of using the actual word.

[34] M. Weber, *The Agrarian Sociology of Ancient Civilizations*

Still, classical sources on urban lease cannot easily be construed to yield any of the *modern* forms of capitalism,[35] and seem rather to suggest a much less systematically organized enterprise that was frequently governed more by casual attitudes or by inherited traditions and values than by rational calculation of profitability. For example, the typical upper-class lease, which featured a very long term of lease, long payment periods, and payment after use, was not (unlike the modern lease) shaped primarily by economic considerations.[36] Also, the widespread use of middlemen shows a tendency by property owners to consider their property more in terms of steady "rent" than of "profit."[37] With one possible exception, notions of capital concentration, systematic accounting, or competitive advantage are largely missing, as are the expressions of consumer resentment which such activities usually provoke. In truth, even the acquisition of urban properties was often an accident,[38] sometimes perhaps the simple consequence of having to do *something* with excess wealth.

The one possible exception is M. Licinius Crassus, the vastly wealthy late-Republican politician. A famous story is told about him just once, by Plutarch (*Crassus* 2.5, cf. 34.1). Crassus observed the frequent fires and collapses occurring at Rome as a consequence of overcrowding. He thereupon bought 500 servile architects and builders; and then he proceeded to purchase, at a low price from their confused and frightened owners, buildings either actually

(trans. R. I. Frank, 1976) 51; compare closely Weber's discussion at pp. 48-77, still probably the best general treatment of these matters.

[35] Cf. M. I. Finley (cited n. 1) 121 (and *passim*); compare M. Weber, *The Theory of Social and Economic Organizations* (trans. A. M. Henderson and T. Parsons, 1947) 278-280.

[36] Cf. B. W. Frier (cited n. 12) 35-36, with further examples.

[37] Compare M. Weber (cited n. 34) 57, on the lease of skilled slaves.

[38] Thus, Cicero's Argiletum and Aventine *insulae* were dowry property (Cic. *Att.* 15.20.4), his Puteoli *tabernae* an inheritance (*Att.* 14.9.1).

on fire or adjacent to those on fire. In this way he allegedly acquired "most of Rome."[39] Thus Plutarch, whose version is not entirely coherent, on the face of it. Oddly, this passage is the sole definite reference to Crassus' income-producing property at Rome.[40]

Perhaps it is wise to disentangle the threads of the story. First, Crassus is the only Roman ever alleged to have bought up large tracts of urban property on a systematic basis; however, in view of the absence of other testimonies, it is improbable that he in fact owned "most of Rome." Second, his large staff of architects and builders plainly indicates that Crassus intended to develop his land,[41] and Plutarch makes clear (2.6) that this was not for his personal use; an imperial inscription (*CIL* 6.33893) also refers to a master-workman (*officinator*) on the staff of a Roman *insula*. Third, the "fire sale" should probably be treated as anecdotal,[42]

[39] This oft-told tale has been frequently rewritten to make it more rational; e.g. H. Gummerus, *Klio* 16 (1920) 190-192; T. Frank, *An Economic Survey of Ancient Rome* vol. 1 (1933) 395; F. Adcock, *Marcus Crassus Millionaire* (1966) 16-17. Contrast R. Pöhlmann (cited n. 3) 89; M. Gelzer, *RE* s.v. "Licinius" (1926) 299. E. Rawson (cited n. 11) 187-188 (n. 64), observes that the story may be "too good to be true"; but most scholars accept it.

[40] The other references collected by I. Shatzman, *Senatorial Wealth and Roman Politics* (1975) 377, refer to farm property; on Cic. *Att.* 1.4.3, see D.R.S. Bailey's commentary *ad loc.*

[41] *Contra*: R. Pöhlmann (cited n. 3) 89 and n. 3, who misconstrues Plut. *Crassus* 2.6. On architects, compare Cic. *Att.* 14.9.1.

[42] But Plutarch (2.4) opposes this view: the "majority" of his holdings were acquired through public catastrophes, namely fire and war (the latter a reference to Crassus' purchasing the property of the proscribed). Supposing the story to be an anecdote, we might explain it this way: a building endangered by fire loses much of its economic value as soon as the fire takes hold, even though most of it is still undamaged; Crassus thus saw two desirable alternatives: either the fire would in fact be contained (in which case he would profit immediately from the remaining building); or it would destroy the building (in which case he would lose relatively little and could rebuild). On the use of *fabri* for firefighting, see E. Kornemann, *RE* s.v. "Fabri" (1909) 1905-1918, with literature.

rather than as an essential part of Crassus' scheme; his offer of purchase makes sense only if he believed he could put out the fire, but there is no real likelihood that he kept teams of firemen waiting throughout Rome for fires to break out, nor, had he done so, would five hundred men have sufficed. Fourth, it is unclear *why* Crassus developed his property: whether he intended to rent it out himself or to resell it to others for a profit; the former is usually assumed, but the latter is not at all improbable.[43] Finally, his motives are not clear; Plutarch ascribes his conduct to "avarice" (*philoploutía*),[44] but we need to know precisely where and how he expected to turn his profit. Plutarch gives no sign that this profit lay in urban rental itself.

In any event, Crassus stands out as an exceptional figure. We know too little about his activities to designate him a prototype of the modern slumlord. Within Plutarch's text Crassus does not assume that role; there is no reference to his relations with tenants. In short, the story told by Plutarch is insufficient to confirm the existence of an advanced capitalism within the Roman rental market.

The Roman Rental Year

The date July 1 had critical importance for owners, middlemen, and upper-class tenants; this day marked the start of the rental year, the day on which long-term urban leases were normally taken up.[45]

Preparations for this day began long in advance. On March 28, 45 B.C., Cicero [46] wrote to his friend Atticus, who

[43] So R. Pöhlmann (cited n. 3) 89.

[44] But why? Plutarch apparently resented Crassus' conducting business with distraught owners.

[45] Cic. *Fam.* 13.2; *Q. Fr.* 2.3.7; Petron. *Sat.* 39.10; Martial, 12.32.1; Suet. *Tib.* 35.2; Labeo D. 19.2.60 pr.; *CIL* 4.136; see L. Homo (cited n. 3) 581-582. July 1 to June 30 is a sort of "fiscal year" which recurs in commercial contracts: e.g. Afric. D. 20.4.9 pr.; Bruns[7], no. 112 (*Lex Metalli Vipascensis*); below, n. 56.

[46] The sources on Cicero's urban properties are analyzed by B. W. Frier (cited n. 9).

was supervising the lease to middlemen of Cicero's dotal *insulae* on the Argiletum and Aventine (both lower-class districts); in his interviews with these potential lessees, Atticus should take careful note of their character and number, and be sure they were the sort who paid promptly (*Att.* 12.32.2). Quite likely Atticus' interviews were scheduled to start on April 1, exactly three months before the rental year began; and in mid-April, 44 B.C., Cicero concluded his own lease with middlemen for some tenements he had inherited at Puteoli (*Att.* 14.9.1, 10.3, 11.2).

Cicero's concern about the good character of middlemen was probably justified.[47] A hypothetical legal case (D. 19.2.7-8) describes a situation in which *A* leases to *B* an entire *insula*, for 50 (thousand sesterces); *B* then subleases the same *insula* to Titius for 60. It appears that Titius was to have been the actual landlord for the premises, and that *B* was a speculator seeking a quick 20 percent profit. As it turned out, however, *A* lacked the right to lease, and the true owner forbade Titius to dwell in the building; the legal complications were decidedly unpleasant. *B*'s anticipated profit in this case corresponds broadly to that in another legal text (D. 19.2.30 pr.), considered in the previous section.

Middlemen, who leased out parts of buildings without claiming to own them, no doubt produced considerable insecurity in the rental market.[48] But insecurity was inevitable in a rental market as loosely organized as Rome's. Deceit had many faces; one could also pretend to be the owner, or else the owner's procurator (Ulp. D. 19.2.15.8). A legal text (Papin. D. 12.6.55) describes two types of fraud. In one type a *praedo* seizes urban property (usually after the owner's death) and then in bad faith rents it out to unsuspecting tenants; in the other, the *praedo* seizes the property and

[47] Nothing is known of these middlemen at Rome; but at Athens (where they used a similar system), one middleman was a freedwoman renting from her former master (Isaeus 6.19).

[48] Cf. R. Pöhlmann (cited n. 3) 109-110.

collects rent from tenants who have previously contracted with the owner. A famous text from Ulpian (D. 13.7.11.5), although its exact meaning is obscure, apparently presupposes an acute conflict between owner and middleman, with the tenant caught between.

Middlemen were essentially businessmen; two legal texts indicate clearly that they paid their entire annual rent in advance (Ulp. D. 19.2.7, 30 pr.)—an arrangement that accorded well not only with the nature of their contracts but perhaps also with their somewhat unsavory reputation. A series of letters from Cicero to Atticus, in 44 B.C., show the former becoming increasingly alarmed that by the middle of June his middlemen had not paid their next year's rent on the Argiletum and Aventine *insulae* (*Att.* 15.17.1, 20.4, cf. 15.4); but on July 8 Cicero seems to count on the money (*Att.* 16.1.5).

It appears that in May most upper-class tenants concluded *their* leases, either with middlemen or with the owners themselves (often through representatives). Occasionally tenants would band together and lease a *cenaculum* as a group (D. 9.3.1.10-4, 5 pr.). An important text from Labeo (D. 19.2.60 pr.) is exceptionally informative as to the normal date of leasing. A *domus* had been leased for a term of many years to a tenant, who had the intention of living there himself but also subleasing portions; due to repairs the house had been closed for a portion of the term, beginning on January 1. The lessor was obliged not only to provide the house as of each July 1, but also during the term of lease to give the lessee a fair opportunity for sublease. But the house remained closed for repair on June 1, so that the lessee was unable to show it to prospective subtenants. Labeo's ruling is that the lessee can break the lease. Obviously underlying this text is a calculation that it would be difficult to find tenants so late as just one month before the start of the rental year.

As this text suggests, it was normal for upper-class tenants to inspect their leaseholds before moving in. A poem of

Martial (12.32.23-24) describes a frantic and almost penniless man asking unsympathetic building managers for shelter as late as July 1. As several inscriptions[49] and two passages in Petronius (6-8, 38.10) show, tenants of all classes usually learned of available housing through crude advertising or oral report.

We know little about the sorts of contracts obtained by upper-class tenants.[50] The term of lease no doubt varied: one year (Ulp. D. 19.2.19.6; 43.32.1.4), several years (Ulp. D. 19.2.60 pr.; 43.32.1.4; Paul. D. 20.4.13), five years (Ulp. D. 19.2.24.2). What may seem surprising is the number of references to multiple-year lease of dwellings; but there is little reason to doubt that this was as common at Rome as in Egyptian house leases.[51] Rent arrangements usually appear to involve single annual payments,[52] though six-monthly payments are also mentioned (Ulp. D. 43.32.1.4); this, too, parallels the situation in Egypt.[53] (Monthly or quarterly payments for dwellings were not witnessed at Rome.) Finally, it appears to have been the norm in both Rome and Egypt that rent was to be paid at the end of the payment period,[54] and the one legal text which mentions payment in advance (Ulp. D. 19.2.19.6) describes the practice in such detail as to argue for its rarity. Middlemen who subleased upper-class *cenacula* must therefore normally rave anticipated making up what they had paid at the start of the rental year by collecting rents at its conclusion—a risky business.

49 *CIL* 4.138, 1136 (cf. 807).

50 Contracts seem to have been predominantly oral; only in the late Empire do legal sources talk of written contracts (Diocl. C. 4.65.9, 24; Justin. C. 2.55.5.3). See Chapter IV n. 10. The form of the urban lease is discussed in *ibid.*, at nn. 11-14; other special clauses in leases, at nn. 16-21.

51 See the sources cited in B. W. Frier (cited n. 12) 29 n. 17, esp. A. Berger, *Zeitschr. f. Vergl. Rechtswiss.* 29 (1913) 369-373.

52 Suet. *Nero* 44.2; Ulp. D. 36.2.12.5, 43.32.1.4.

53 A. Berger (cited n. 51) 387; B. W. Frier (cited n. 12) 29 n. 17.

54 For Rome, cf. Alfen. D. 19.2.27 pr., 1; Ulp. D. 19.2.9.6; 43.32.1.4; B. W. Frier (cited n. 12) 29 n. 16. For Egypt, A. Berger (cited n. 51) 387-389.

On July 1, at the height of summer, came "moving day": large numbers of upper-class tenants removing their belongings from former dwellings and placing them in new ones. To compound the confusion, July 1 was also the normal date for ending and beginning yearly contracts in the warehouses where many Romans stored valuables.[55] The scene must have been tumultuous; Martial (12.32) has left an unforgettable description of a tenant and his family, ousted on July 1 for nonpayment of rent, with most of their possessions forfeit, wandering the streets in search of new housing.

About the furnishings of upper-class *cenacula* we learn little. The legal sources mention a strongbox (Ulp. D. 19.2.19.5), also various foodstuffs (*penus*: Scaev. D. 33.9.7) that were presumably kept in a pantry. For the rest, the landlord's tacit lien on the tenant's furnishings (cf. Chapter IV, fourth section) presupposed for its effectiveness that the upper-class tenant normally furnished his *cenaculum* himself, and at some considerable cost.[56] By contrast, the landlord provided the fittings of the dwelling. A legal text pertaining to legacy (Ulp. D. 33.7.12.16-26) distinguishes things intrinsic to a house, *portio domus*, from the *instrumentum* and *ornamentum*; in the former category are included artwork in place (e.g. painted wall plaster), water pipes and receptacles, door bolts, and keys. Such things presumably accompanied the leasehold. So also did the windows and doors, which the *locator* had a duty to maintain (Gaius D. 19.2.25.2). But some tenants must have been tempted by the long term of their leases to install their own fixtures, es-

[55] G. Rickman, *Roman Granaries* (1971) 198-199.

[56] Cf. Chapter IV at n. 180. It is interesting to compare the household of four persons (the tenant, his wife, mother, and sister) described by Martial 12.32; stripped of most furnishings, they still keep pieces of domestic furniture (a bed, a table), a lamp, some kitchen utensils, assorted food and cosmetics, and a chamberpot. This is property "essential to life," which was probably excepted from the landlord's lien (Chapter IV at n. 137) in Martial's time, still doubtless by custom.

pecially windows and doors; two legal texts (Jul. D. 6.1.59; Ulp. D. 19.2.19.4) deal with the problems that arose when they later sought to remove them.

After July 1, upper-class rents dropped sharply as landlords filled remaining vacancies at sacrifice figures. Suetonius (*Tib.* 35.2) tells of a senator who tried to take advantage of this fact by remaining on his suburban estates until after July 1, and only then entering a lease; the emperor stripped him of his rank. The rental market appears to have remained largely dormant, except for a small amount of leasing at its halfway mark on the New Year,[57] until with the coming of Spring the cycle began once more.

Upper-Class Tenants

Historians of Roman law often convey the impression that the law of urban lease was designed primarily for the hordes of depressed lower-class tenants who constituted the vast majority of the Roman tenantry.[58] However, the legal sources themselves do not bear out this view; they describe details of lease and leasehold that have nothing to do with low tenant status.[59] It was surely not the poor who rented houses or apartments for multiples of years, or who paid rent in lump sums at yearly or six-monthly intervals; it was not the poor who would have been allowed delayed pay-

[57] Cf. Ulp. D. 19.2.60 pr. A Pompeian dipinto offers an *insula ex I.* (= *Idibus*?) *Iuliis*: *CIL* 4.138.

[58] See the authors cited in Chapter III n. 20 (F. Schulz, B. Nicholas); Chapter IV n. 25 (A. Pernice, F. Schulz, A. Beck), n. 84 (M. Marrone), n. 180 (M. Kaser).

[59] Of course, as Prof. Watson reminds me, some rules of urban lease law might have strengthened the slumlord's hand (e.g. the rules on preclusion); but this is true only of the grossest rules, and in general it seems unlikely that the bulk of urban lease law was designed with the lower classes specifically in mind. Did the lower-class landlord in fact require any legal support? Ulp. D. 20.2.3 indicates that the extension of preclusion to lower-class housing was still controversial in the late classical period.

ment. Indeed, there is (I think) no credible evidence that lower-class tenants are ever referred to at all in the legal sources on urban lease.

I may seem to overstate this point; however, the argument in this book rests on my belief that when the Roman jurists wrote of *inquilini,* they did *not* typically intend lower-class tenants. My belief thus runs counter to that of most previous legal scholarship, which is in my opinion deeply flawed in two respects. First, modern scholarship has rarely paid attention to the law of urban lease as such, but has instead made only passing references to it in the context of broader discussions.[60] Second, modern legal scholarship has often been characterized by an imperfect methodology, both as to the evidence on the Roman rental market and as to the ties between law and society.[61] My argument, therefore, is that this scholarship is *prima facie* wrong in regarding urban lease law as being primarily directed toward lower-class tenants; and that, if this *prima facie* judgment is not in fact correct, the burden of proof is with those who would deny it.

Who, then, are the *inquilini* of the jurists?

Ancient literary and legal sources, when examined closely, show that there were a considerable number of upper-class tenants, surely enough to have constituted a body of litigants for whom urban lease law *could* have been designed.[62]

[60] Only thus is it possible to understand M. Kaser, *Römisches Privatrecht* (Studienbuch 9th ed. 1976) 176: "Die Bezeichnung des Landpächters als *colonus*, des Wohnungmieters als *inquilinus* hat keine juristisch-technische Bedeutung." (Contrast Chapter VI at n. 19.) A major exception is A. Pernice, *SZ* 19 (1898) 89-97. But (apart from a few short articles) urban lease law is not treated as a separate category in any modern work on Roman lease.

[61] An egregious example is M. Marrone, *La Legittimazione Passiva alla "Rei Vindicatio"* (1970) 126-130; see my criticism in Chapter IV n. 84.

[62] This was the real starting point, and also (I think) the absolute prerequisite, for the creation of an area of Roman private law. See in general Chapter III below.

Senators, to be sure, may always have preferred to own their own houses;[63] for them, lease would be at most a temporary matter, as when in 56 B.C. Q. Cicero's family rented a house on short notice following the destruction of their Palatine home by Clodius (Cic. *Q. Fr.* 2.3.7), or when in 55 the proconsul L. Calpurnius Piso hastily rented a house after his ignominious return from his province (Cic. *Pis.* 61).

Nonetheless, even some senators were attracted by the advantages of rental. In 125 B.C. the augur M. Lepidus Porcina acquired for himself a censorial *nota* by renting a house at more than HS 6,000 a year—a rent which Velleius Paterculus (2.10.1) considered ridiculously low for senators in the reign of Tiberius.[64] The Triumvirs in 43 B.C. anticipated raising money by placing a "roof-tile tax" on senators living in rented houses (Dio 46.31.3).

In the reign of Nero, especially after the Great Fire of 64, which drastically reduced available housing,[65] we even hear of senators living in rented *cenacula*. In A.D. 68 the future Emperor Vitellius, hard-pressed financially, leased his house and moved his family into a *cenaculum meritorium* (Suet. *Vit.* 7.2). An interesting letter of Seneca, written during his retirement, describes the noisiness of his dwelling upstairs from a bath near the Meta Sudans (*Ep.* 56.1, 4); Seneca bears stoically the continual racket from passing chariots, from a blacksmith who was his neighboring tenant, and from the flautists at the Meta. Finally he humorously announces his imminent *migratio* (56.15); that word is the usual one for tenants who abandon their leaseholds.[66]

[63] So E. Rawson (cited n. 11) 87; cf. H. Schneider, (cited n. 2) 178-184, based esp. on Cic. *Off.* 1.138-140. The fourth-century regionary catalogues list about 1,800 private homes in Rome, most no doubt owner occupied.

[64] Cf. Suet. *Tib.* 35.2, on a senator under Tiberius who sought to evade high house rents.

[65] On the effects of the fire, see R. F. Newbold (cited n. 17) 863-865.

[66] Cf. Chapter IV at n. 89.

We can justifiably anticipate that, below the senatorial level among the lower ranks of the upper classes, renting was much more common, and that apartments tended to be more attractive than whole houses. The offspring of aristocratic families found it desirable to take up residences away from their parents. In the late second century B.C. young Sulla lived in a lodging house, for HS 3,000 per year (Plut. *Sulla* 1.2, 6); the globe-trotting Aelii Lamiae rented a house on the Carinae from Q. Cicero in 56 (Cic. *Q. Fr.* 2.3.7); and the escapades of M. Caelius Rufus in his Palatine *cenaculum*, for which he allegedly paid his landlord Clodius HS 10,000 per year in 56 B.C. (Cic. *Cael.* 17), became notorious—his enemies claimed that the figure was 30,000. Cicero (18) defends Caelius' decision to leave his father's house; and in 45 B.C. we learn that Cicero's own son had considered renting a house (Cic. *Att.* 12.32.2), while in 44 Cicero's nephew proposed the same thing (12.38.1). The endurance of the custom into the Empire is confirmed by several references in legal sources (Gaius D. 44.7.5.5; Ulp. D. 9.3.1.7; Paul. D. 39.2.21), as well as by, for instance, a mention in Pliny (*Ep.* 4.13.5).

Below the level of these young aristocrats, Rome's urban elite[67] would have included, for instance, the two apocryphal advocates mentioned by Martial (3.38.6); their fees did not even cover one entire rent payment. This urban elite was probably the principal intended victim of Nero's desperate

[67] I must mention P. A. Brunt, *Italian Manpower* (1971) 383, who estimates the Roman upper classes in the 50's B.C. at "some 600 senators and (at a venture) 2,000 *equites*"; he comments: "There is no evidence for a middle class in the city, intervening between them and the poor, except for some rich freedmen." I think that Prof. Brunt has missed a good deal of evidence, especially in Cicero's speeches and letters (and, for a later era, in Martial); but the total numbers would no doubt still be small. Compare C. Nicolet, *Les Structures de l'Italie Romaine* (1977) 202-204; and, for the Empire, P. Huttunen, *The Social Strata in the Imperial City of Rome* (1974) 189-191.

scheme in 68 to divert annual rent payments from landlords to the Fiscus (Suet. *Nero* 44.2).[68]

Wealthy freedmen naturally gravitated to *cenacula*. Upstairs from Sulla lived a freedman who paid HS 2,000 a year in rent (Plut. *Sulla* 1.2). A letter from Cicero (*Fam.* 13.2) discusses the plight of a freedman, the distinguished sculptor C. Avianius Evander; he had been expelled from his dwelling in the family shrine of the Memmii as of July 1, 52 B.C. The Emperor Augustus liked to watch horse races from the upper-story *cenacula* of his friends and freedmen (Suet. *Aug.* 45.1; cf. Dio 57.11.4-5), and on occasion even slept over in a servant's *cenaculum* when he had business in the vicinity the next morning (Suet. *Aug.* 78.2). Augustus' court jester, Aulus Gabba, complained of a leaky roof in his *cenaculum* (Quint. 6.3.64).[69] Indeed, a wealthy family might even put up their slave in a *cenaculum* (Ulp. D. 9.3.1.8).

Long-term visitors to Rome also sought out *cenacula*. In 164/163 B.C. the dethroned king of Egypt, Ptolemy VI, together with a eunuch and three slaves, were received into a shabby apartment by the landscape painter Demetrius of Alexandria (Diod. 31.18.2; Val. Max. 5.1.1f.); Ptolemy had been deterred from living elsewhere by the enormously high rents at Rome. Still earlier, the Senate had used a *cenaculum* above a house for a witness in the Bacchanalian conspiracy (Livy 39.14.2). The Apostle Paul, awaiting trial under Nero, lived for two years together with a soldier in a rented dwelling, where he had room enough to receive and preach to the Jewish community of Rome (*Acts* 28.16-31);[70] his rent was presumably paid by the wealthy Christians at Rome, such as the traveling military provisioner Aquila and his wife Priscilla from Pontus (*Rom.* 16.3; *Acts* 18.2-3).

[68] Cf. R. F. Newbold (cited n. 17) 866-869; B. W. Frier (cited n. 12) 36.

[69] Unless I am mistaken, all these sources are ignored in G. Boulvert, *Domestique et Fonctionnaire sous le Haut-Empire Romaine* (1974).

[70] On the passage, Mommsen, *Strafrecht* 317.

Lease of dwellings is occasionally mentioned in the upper-class context of estate settlement.[71] Ulpian (D. 36.4.5.22) refers to a rented *habitatio* used as a storeroom for the property of a dead man. Paul (D. 37.9.4 pr.) states that a curator appointed to protect an unborn heir might arrange, as a legitimate expense, a rented *habitatio* for the widow.

Perhaps the most typical of all upper-class tenants, certainly the best known, is the poet Martial in the years before he won lasting fame. Before then he had been a longtime tenant in a *cenaculum* on the west edge of the Quirinal (1.108.3), up three flights of steep stairs (1.117.6-7).[72] He felt that he had grown old in this city-district; his apartment looked out over the laurels in the Plane of Agrippa (1.108.3-4), and, perhaps because of its exposed position, it was uncomfortably drafty in Winter (8.14.5-8). Martial had a kitchen fire, but no running water (8.67.7-8). He writes of the problems of getting his rent together (7.92.5-6). In one playful poem (1.86) he talks of "Novius" who lived in the adjacent apartment; by stretching out from the windows they could touch hands, but never saw or spoke to one another, presumably because they used separate entryways. Elsewhere, Martial complains of the noise associated with the crowded urban environment (12.27; *et al.*). Yet despite all the trials of getting ahead at Rome, Martial displays none of the bitterness toward city life that characterizes his younger contemporary Juvenal; for in the end Martial did get ahead, and probably in A.D. 94 he obtained, as a token of success, a house on the Quirinal (9.18.2, 97.8; 10.58.10). His success story, which undoubtedly typified the aspirations of

[71] Cf. D. Daube, *Roman Law* (1969) 71-75, on the upper-class character of the law of succession.

[72] In addition to the sources cited below, see Mart. 5.22.3-4; 6.27.1-2; L. Friedländer's commentary (esp. pp. 4-11); R. Helm, *RE* s.v. "Valerius" (1955) 55-58. Some references may be topical. Even before he began writing epigrams, Martial was an honorary Roman knight (3.95 *et al.*) and, though unmarried, had the *ius trium liberorum* (9.97.5); he owned several slaves (1.101; 5.34 *et al.*).

Rome's urban elite, is thus vividly reflected in his choice of housing. Compare, in this regard, a wealthy freedman described by Petronius (38.10).

The gods did not allow that everyone succeed. The other side is also well-represented in verse by the "Tenant's Lament" which Ancarenus Nothus, a freedman dead at age 43, had inscribed on his gravestone (*CIL* 6.7193a). Ancarenus counted it among the blessings of death that now his body knew no hunger or gout, that now it was not a deposit on his rent but enjoyed for free an eternal lodging. These elegaic distichs were doggerel, really, but they doubtless struck in readers a responsive chord, for they were repeated on another stone (*CIL* 6.33241); they are the only surviving evidence of any kind of "class-consciousness" among Roman tenants. Significantly, this consciousness reflects only on the common woes of tenants and is not directed, in the modern fashion, toward their landlords as a group. I might observe, finally, that Roman landlords were required to pay an indigent tenant's burial costs out of the possessions left behind in his dwelling (Ulp. D. 11.7.14.1).

The upper-class tenants of Rome moved their dependents into their spacious dwellings. The legal sources suggest that their households were often large, sometimes very large. The dependents can be divided into classes: wives and family members (e.g. Ulp. D. 9.3.5.4; 19.2.11 pr.; 39.2.13.5), guests (Ulp. D. 9.3.1.9, 5.1 and 4; 19.2.11 pr.; 39.2.13.5; Marci. D. 20.2.5 pr.), even freedmen and clients (Ulp. D. 9.3.5.1). Perhaps the largest group of dependents were the tenant's slaves (Paul. D. 20.2.9; Ulp. D. 9.2.27.11; 19.2.11 pr. and 4; 20.2.6).[73] Some tenants gave over unwanted space to subtenants (Ulp. D. 9.3.5.1-2, 4). In this respect, too, the legal sources are apparently concerned primarily with upper-class tenants.

Finally, it is worth noting that the references to urban

[73] On accommodations for slaves, cf. R. Meiggs, *Ostia* (2d ed. 1973) 585-586 (partially reversing p. 226).

tenancy in legal sources seem to correspond broadly with the distribution of upper-class tenants that in Chapter I was inferred from the Ostian remains. There are only 15 references to the lease of houses or urban villas.[74] By contrast, some 6 sources refer to the lease of apartments within houses,[75] and some 22 further sources to rented apartments;[76] most of this last group was probably located in apartment blocks. About 65 percent of the references are thus to tenants of apartments. The distribution of these sources strongly suggests that the preponderance of Rome's upper-class tenants resided in apartments rather than in houses.

It is true that, when all is said, our knowledge of the upper-class Roman rental market is more one of contour than of reliable statistical detail. Here, as often elsewhere in ancient society, the numbers elude us. For purposes of the present study, however, we need not feel in any sense helpless as a result.[77] It is probable that our knowledge of the Roman rental market is qualitatively similar to that which the Roman jurists had: few statistics, but rather a composite of general impressions and direct (often personal) experience. This sort of knowledge would have sufficed, in my opinion, to permit the jurists to make an accurate although "commonsensical" prediction (an "educated guess") as to the effect their rules would have on the upper-class

[74] *Domus*: D. 19.2.9. pr. and 6, 24.2, 28.2, 45 pr., 60 pr.; *Cod. Theod.* 11.20.3.4 (A.D. 400); C. 4.65.5 (A.D. 223). *Aedes*: D. 19.2.19.4-5, 25.1; 29.2.20.1; 31.88.15; 39.2.13.6; 41.2.37. *Villa urbana*: D. 19.2.11.4-12. Compare the *inquilini privatarum aedium* in Suet. *Nero* 44.2.

[75] D. 7.8.2.1, 4; 8.2.41 pr. (next to house); 19.2.28 pr.-1, 60 pr.; 43.17.3.7. Note the *cenacula* carved out of a house in Ulp. D. 7.1.13.8; and also Apul. *Mag.* 57-58.

[76] *Cenaculum*: D. 1.15.3.4; 9.2.27.11; 9.3.1.7 and 10, 5 pr. and 2 and 4 and 9; 13.7.11.5; 19.2.25.2, 27 pr., 30 pr.; 33.9.7; 39.2.43.1; 44.7.5.5; *Cod. Theod.* 11.20.3.4 (A.D. 400). Places in an *insula*: D. 19.1.53.2. *Hospitium*: D. 9.3.5.1; 19.2.13.7; 39.2.29. *Habitatio*: D. 19.2.19.6. *Diaeta*: C. 4.65.3 (A.D. 223). These are the *inquilini insularum* in Suet. *Nero* 44.2 (cf. D. 9.2.27.11).

[77] In general, compare M. Frederiksen, *JRS* 65 (1975) 164-171.

rental market. By contrast, to be sure, their knowledge would not have sufficed for any modern variety of scientific policymaking.[78]

[78] The distinction here is drawn from B. A. Ackerman, *Private Property and the Constitution* (1977). The Roman jurist was, in Ackerman's terms (p. 15), an "Ordinary Observer" who "elaborates the concepts of nonlegal conversation so as to illuminate . . . the relationship between disputed legal rules and the structure of social expectations he understands to prevail in dominant institutional practice"; but he was not thereby incapacitated from recognizing social problems and dealing with them on a case-by-case basis. The jurist, however, was *not* (could not be) a "Scientific Policymaker," who "manipulates technical legal concepts so as to illuminate . . . the relationship between disputed legal rules and the Comprehensive View he understands to govern the legal system." Ackerman's framework of ideal types helps to distinguish the Roman jurist from modern Continental jurists (cf. Ackerman pp. 185-189); it gets at the very essence of a "case law," which is still widely misunderstood in Europe. On the modern social disutility of "case law," see below, Chapter VI n. 19.

III

Introduction to the Jurists' Treatment of Urban Leasehold

WITHIN a system of private law, the law of procedure has the primary purpose of providing individuals with a mechanism whereby they may realize their legitimate claims against one another. Nonetheless, it is extremely probable (in the ancient world no less than in the modern) that many claims, and perhaps the great majority, never come to the attention of a court of law. A potential plaintiff may have a variety of reasons for not pressing a claim:

(1) he may not realize that he has a claim;[1]

(2) he may lack access to skilled authority who can help him to formulate and pursue his claim, or who will represent or help him before a court of law;[2]

(3) he may be deterred from litigation by the initial outlay involved;[3]

[1] On "legal insecurity" in Rome, see F. Schulz, *Principles* 243-247. Rather too trusting is C. A. Maschi, in *St. Betti* III 411-449.

[2] These problems were briefly treated by J. M. Kelly, *Roman Litigation* (1966) 44-45, cf. generally 31-68; P. Garnsey, *Social Status and Legal Privilege* (1970) 218, questions the access to jurists; and P. A. Brunt, *JRS* 62 (1972) 169-170 (reviewing Garnsey), to orators.

[3] See P. A. Brunt (cited n. 2) 169; also E. Parks, *Roman Rhetorical Schools* (1945) 56ff., on fees to orators (and there were other costs); but also J. M. Kelly (cited n. 2) 84 n. 1. Note that the condemned defendant did not normally recompense the plaintiff's procedural costs: M. Kaser, *RZ* 288.

(4) he may be unable (or may fear that he is unable) to carry through a summons of the defendant;[4]

(5) he may believe that pursuit of his claim would be in itself degrading to him personally, or an offense against social convention;[5]

(6) he may fear that pursuit of his claim would expose him to public humiliation of an unacceptable magnitude;[6]

(7) he may believe, with or without justification, that his claim would not be given a fair hearing due to the bias or corruption of the court system;[7]

(8) he may be indifferent or apathetic about courts in general;[8]

(9) he may have alternative methods of settling the claim, as for instance through self-help or private settlement;[9]

[4] Cf. J. M. Kelly (cited n. 2) 7-12; substantially modified in P. Garnsey (cited n. 2) 187-194; and cf. A. S. Hartkamp, *Der Zwang im Römischen Privatrecht* (1971) 279-284. Critics of Kelly should read with care Apul. *Met.* 9.35-38.

[5] Cf. J. M. Kelly, *Studies in the Civil Judicature* (1976) 95-111. Typical of classical views is Martial 10.47.5.

[6] Cf. J. M. Kelly, *Studies* (cited n. 5) 98-102 (rhetorical vituperation). While private *iudicia* could take place in the homes of *iudices* (esp. Vitruv. 6.5.2), we should not follow Kelly in thinking of them as therefore closed to the public; Vitruvius specifies the need of spacious halls, obviously to accommodate crowds. By ca. 70 A.D. most *iudicia* were held in auditoriums and registry offices, still not without orators though audiences dwindled: Tac. *Dial.* 39, with W. Kunkel, *Kleine Schriften* (1974) 249 n. 164.

[7] In the work cited in n. 2, J. M. Kelly conducted a preliminary study of this problem, and his conclusions were extended by P. Garnsey. There is, however, much more work still to be done on the social patterns of Roman litigation.

[8] J. M. Kelly, *Studies* (cited n. 5) 97-98, on this attitude in the late Republic.

[9] On the frequency of resort to self-help, see above all G. Wesener, in *Fs. Steinwenter* 100-120; T. Mayer-Maly, *RE* s.v. "vis" (1960) 315-323; A. W. Lintott, *Violence in Republican Rome* (1968) 6-34. A major study is needed. On arbitration: K. H. Ziegler, *Das Private Schiedsgericht* (1971). On settlement (esp. "out of court"): bibliography in M. Kaser, *RPR*² I 642-643; *II* 606-607; add J. M. Kelly, *Litigation* (cited n. 2) 132-152; P. Garnsey (cited n. 2) 195-197. The

(10) or, finally, he may believe that the reward he would be likely to obtain through a suit simply does not suffice to warrant his investment of the time, expense, or trouble required.[10]

Many considerations act to discourage litigation, today as in antiquity. Of these factors, the last one, namely the ratio of "reward" to "investment," is perhaps crucial. As this ratio increases, the other factors predictably dwindle in importance: the plaintiff is likelier to know of his claim and likelier to overcome, if at all possible, the obstacles to realizing it. However, realization of a claim is not simply a matter of court judgment; the plaintiff must also be able to collect his reward,[11] and, as Gaius dryly remarked (D. 4.3.6), a valid claim is the same as no claim at all when the defendant is insolvent. Such a defendant is, in the modern idiom, "judgment-proof."

In Rome, most of the factors listed above acted to deter members of the lower classes from bringing suits;[12] they were probably ignorant of the law, and they were also the

---

consequences of such arbitration are not always socially beneficial; cf. R. MacMullen, *Roman Social Relations* (1974) 39-40 (observing the need for further study).

[10] I intend this calculation in a large sense; it should not be forgotten that the factors mentioned above often had a larger psychological weight in Rome than in the modern world. But there are countervailing factors: a plaintiff may pursue an unrewarding claim to "set an example," or because of a high sense of "justice," or from personal animus against the defendant, or the like.

[11] On the defendant's personal power to prevent execution, see J. M. Kelly, *Litigation* (cited n. 2) 12-14 (exaggerated). Personal execution against the insolvent debtor obviously became very rare in the Empire; cf. M. Kaser, *RZ* 300, against F. Schulz, *CRL* 26-27.

[12] Cf. D. Black, *The Behavior of Law* (1976) 21-30. That is the most which can be deduced from the factors cited above; the sweeping conclusions about differences between Roman and modern law in J. M. Kelly, *Litigation* (cited n. 2) 173-174, are not warranted. Compare N. Luhmann, *Rechtssoziologie* (1972) 166-190, whose view of the social achievements of "premodern law" seems to me in general confirmed by D. Nörr, *Rechtskritik in der Römischen Antike* (1974).

victims of a social structure that was not only exaggeratedly pyramidal in its distribution of wealth and influence, but also bound by stark social conventions that sometimes had overt legal support.[13] Simultaneously, however, their poverty effectively protected these same lower classes against private lawsuits by others. Much of Roman private law may therefore have remained confined for all practical purposes to the upper social tiers—an inference that seems confirmed in certain areas of substantive law.[14] In any event, beyond all doubt the incidence of litigation tended to increase dramatically as one moved higher in the social order.[15]

This "relative imbalance" in litigiousness is likely to have been still further accentuated in the area of urban lease by the Roman rental market itself. Here the poor, the vast majority of all tenants, were mostly housed in squalid tenement houses (*deversoria*) where they paid rent on an essentially short-term basis, perhaps most commonly daily. Such a system of rental is, as Pernice may already have seen, not productive of many suits on leases;[16] when landlords were dissatisfied with their lower-class lodgers, or when these lodgers were dissatisfied with their quarters and could find an affordable alternative, they simply moved on. The sums

[13] Many social distinctions are explored in R. MacMullen, (cited n. 9); the economic basis for these distinctions is treated in R. Duncan-Jones, *The Economy of the Roman Empire* (1974); the gradual incorporation of these distinctions into legal procedure is studied by P. Garnsey (cited n. 2); on method, see above all M. W. Frederiksen, *JRS* 65 (1975) 164-171, reviewing M. I. Finley, *The Ancient Economy* (1973). I do not deny offsetting tendencies, nor am I cynical about the "humanism" of the High Empire.

[14] Cf. D. Daube, *Rom. Law* 71-91. How else could Rome have tolerated so small a judicial apparatus?

[15] Cf. D. Black (cited n. 12) 16-21. At the top of the social pyramid, however, a certain number of persons and institutions were perhaps legally untouchable: E. Volterra, *Riv. It.*[3] 11 (1967) 239-271. In my opinion, Volterra's arguments do not meet the central issues raised above; further I find his inference about the "economic unimportance" of Roman private law (p. 269) entirely unfounded.

[16] Cf. A. Pernice, *SZ* 19 (1898) 92-93 (a short-term lessee is a "Zugvogel," a bird of passage).

involved were rarely large enough to warrant litigation. This is not to say that suits were never generated among lower-class tenants, only that suits were probably very uncommon.[17] Thus, the "relative imbalance" produced by factors inhibiting litigation was probably converted, in the area of urban lease, into a virtually "absolute imbalance."

The resulting imbalance is clearly reflected in the jurisprudence of urban leasehold. Wherever we can assess the content of the real or hypothetical cases discussed by the jurists, these cases reflect the upper classes—either upper-class tenants or the entrepreneurial middlemen who rented and then subleased *insulae*.[18] The *inquilini* of slum tenements find no place in juristic discussions on leasehold, despite their numerical preponderance among urban tenants.

This imbalance and the consequences that it had for Roman jurisprudence lie at the core of the thesis of this book. In the next three chapters, the Roman law of urban leasehold will be discussed on the assumption that the jurists limited themselves *de facto* to "legalizing" that portion of the rental market which private law could reach and influence; thereby the jurists created what can be described as a "law of upper-class leasehold," albeit with allowance (through generalized statement of rules) for occasional cases concerning lower-class tenants. Because the type of analysis here proposed is different from that usually accorded Roman legal sources, a few words of explanation are called for.

Rome's problems in housing a tenantry that numbered

[17] As the pages of Petronius suggest (cf. *Satyr.* 95ff.), absence of legal restraint does not mean that lower-class tenancy was therefore necessarily "lawless"; this absence was compensated for by social restraint, often in the form of "popular justice," such restraint being undermined, however, by demoralization among the urban plebs. Compare D. Black (cited n. 12) 107-111, 126-130.

[18] Reference back to the sources employed in Chapter II should make this point clear. The same rule prevails also for sources outside lease law proper. The only surviving description of a *cenaculum* is D. 9.3.5.2, a source on the *actio de effusis*: B. W. Frier, *JRS* 67 (1977) 27-29.

probably at least half a million persons (including dependents) were undoubtedly as great as or greater than those of any city before modern times. Here it is necessary no longer to speak merely of the imbalance in private law, but rather of the pure and simple inadequacy of *any* system of private law constructively to approach problems of such magnitude, particularly as they touch on the lower classes. Modern experience has clearly and repeatedly shown that the problems of urban housing not only are predominantly problems of public law but also are exceptionally difficult to handle even for a State armed with a mass of economic and sociological theory, an adequate tax structure, and a policing force able to carry out its legislation. By contrast, Rome not only lacked a comparable conceptual, financial, and bureaucratic capacity, it also lacked the will to master these problems; legislation on urban housing was indeed not negligible in quantity, but hardly sufficient to the task.[19]

Without a strong legislative tradition behind it, Roman private law necessarily lacked the breadth of vision even to contemplate urban housing in its entirety. No matter how much or how little concerned we suppose the jurists to have been with social and economic problems (and frankly I find it difficult to accept the icy conservatism occasionally thrust upon them by modern scholars),[20] in a trouble area like urban housing the extent of their difficulties should not be underestimated. The social range of the impulses that flowed into the law in the form of claims by plaintiffs and defend-

[19] There is no exhaustive compilation. On the "building codes," see L. Homo, *Rome Impériale et l'Urbanisme* (1951) 597-637; on regulations for *tabernae*, T. Kleberg, *Hôtels, Restaurants et Cabarets* (1957) 98ff.; on the responsibilities of the Praefectus Vigilum, cf. A. dell'Oro, *I Libri de Officio* (1960) 250-254. On housing in the Welfare State, see T. H. Marshall, *Social Policy*[3] (1970) 153-167.

[20] See e.g. on *locatio conductio*, F. Schulz, *CRL* 544-546; B. Nicholas, *An Introduction to Roman Law* (1962) 184. The jurists are all "upper-class," but of diverse origins within this category; in general it is not easy (they do not make it easy) to evaluate their opinions on nonlegal matters. See also n. 22 below.

ants was relatively small, could not adequately represent the entire spectrum of interests, and clearly did not constitute an adequate basis for generalized social planning.

It is, I think, entirely fair to observe that Roman jurists did not in general aim to "change society"[21]—but this needs qualifying. Obviously, they did not consciously aim at altering the social structure of Rome, or at "social engineering," in Roscoe Pound's phrase; on the contrary, they displayed a considerable loyalty to existing social structures.[22] However, "legalization" itself—by which is meant the relentless propagation of law, the patient exposure of hitherto nonlegal or quasi-legal relationships to public scrutiny and legal analysis, with the consequent transformation of such relationships into rule-guided activities—involves a "change" in society that should not be labeled obvious or trivial because the step seems to have been so easy in retrospect. Nor, as I hope to show, can a line be clearly drawn between such legalization on the one hand and the use of law as an instrument of social control on the other.[23] The transition from one to the other can be virtually indetectable.

Rome's housing problems involved not only an immense throng of lower-class tenants, but also (apparently for the

[21] See e.g. N. Luhmann (cited n. 12) 182 (of "premodern" law in general): no intention "auf planmässige Veränderung der sozialen Wirklichkeit mit Hilfe des Rechts." On p. 183 it is clear that he means not only change in swift response to stimuli, but also what B. A. Ackerman, *Private Property and the Constitution* (1977) 10-20, calls Scientific Policymaking.

[22] See on this problem D. Nörr, *SZ* 88 (1971) 413-417, reviewing Garnsey. Where this loyalty involved them in choices, their decisions are not easy to predict: cf. D. Nörr (cited n. 12) 54-56.

[23] I mean here something similar to N. Luhmann's contrast between jurisprudence at the "input boundary" (the standardization and classification of cases or case elements subjected to decision making; law as regulation of conflict) and jurisprudence at the "output boundary" (law directed toward the attainment of desired social consequences): *Rechtssystem und Rechtsdogmatik* (1974) 25-30. A similar cybernetic analysis (input/output/feedback) is adopted in L. M. Friedman, *The Legal System* (1975), and underlies Chapter VI below.

first time in history) a relatively large number of well-off ones. No matter the size of the latter group, they obviously cannot be compared with the poor in any framework defined by social conscience; nor do I see any sign of the jurists having made such a comparison. That is not the question. Rather, the question is and was: what can a system of private law realistically be expected to accomplish?

IV

The Roman Law of Urban Leasehold

Locatio Conductio Rei and Urban Leasehold

The law of urban leasehold was for the most part established in relation to two fundamental contractual actions, reciprocal in character: the *actio locati* and the *actio conducti.* The procedural formula for the *actio locati* was reconstructed by Otto Lenel:[1]

> Quod Aulus Agerius Numerio Negidio fundum (opus faciendum, operas) quo (quibus) de agitur locavit, qua de re agitur, quidquid ob eam rem Numerium Negidium Aulo Agerio dare facere oportet ex fide bona, eius iudex Numerium Negidium Aulo Agerio condemnato; si non paret, absolvito.

With the substitution of one word (*conduxit* for *locavit*), the formula for the *actio conducti* was identical. The praetor simply orders the *iudex* to decide the case and then if the plaintiff wins, to award the plaintiff the monetary value of what the defendant was obliged to do or give in accordance with good faith under the contract of *locatio conductio.* Though the two formulas are mostly reconstruction,[2] their

[1] O. Lenel, *EP* 299-300. A standard account of the contract is in M. Kaser, *RPR*[2] 1 562-572; in English: W. W. Buckland, *A Textbook of Roman Law*[3] (1966) 498-506. In my opening section, legal sources are mainly cited without extended commentary or bibliography.

[2] The Edict may not have listed all three forms of contract, cf. M.

basic correctness is not in doubt. For urban leasehold, the *actio locati* belongs to the landlord (*locator*); the *actio conducti*, to the tenant (*conductor*).

Since the procedural formulas are so brief, and since no legislation influences the development of urban leasehold, most of the law on the subject had to stem from juristic interpretation of the words *dare facere ex fide bona*. It would perhaps be fair to regard this interpretation as an attempt to objectify the originally uncircumscribed domain of *bona fides*; what had at first been left entirely to the socially formed consciousness of the *iudex* ("how do you think the defendant should have behaved?") became more and more a matter of positive law ("does the defendant's conduct correspond to this specific norm or standard of behavior?"). As we shall see, the development of the law on urban leasehold was sometimes a more or less straightforwardly cumulative process, but at times also marked by ideas tried out and then discarded. It is probable, furthermore, that the law as it is presented by Justinian's *Digest* is considerably simplified, especially as to the suppression of classical controversies.[3]

The contract *locatio conductio* is vast and heterogeneous.[4] Common elements are few. Like all consensual contracts it requires only the agreement of both parties for its existence. It almost always involves the passage from one party to the other of a fixed sum of money (usually called the *merces*, see Gaius 3.142; sometimes the *pretium*), and beyond that it involves a legal relationship that the Romans embraced

---

Kaser, *Iura* 11 (1960) 234; H. Kaufmann, 353-359 (at pp. 345-349, he supposes, probably wrongly, that the amount of rent was also included). The considerations in C. Alzon, *Location des Entrepôts* (1966) 221-225, are unconvincing; cf. C. A. Cannata, *Iura* 18 (1967) 273-275 (review).

[3] On postclassical developments, M. Kaser, *RPR*² II 400-407.

[4] *Locatio conductio* is unified only in the broadest sense; rights, duties, and liabilities are regularly distributed between the parties on the basis of economic sense, and not through doctrine.

with the verbs *locare* and *conducere*: the *locator* places his thing or a job or his services at the disposition of the *conductor*, and he either gives or receives the *merces* depending on the economic circumstances. While the broadness of this definition is not very helpful, the critical point is that all the numerous types of *locatio conductio* (lease of land and chattels, lease of dwellings and storage facilities, hire of services, hire of labor, carriage, and so on) shared many common and generalizable features in their formation, many recurring problems in their execution, and one single and simple action at law. Because of the polymorphous "unity" of this contract, the jurists could move easily from one type of *locatio* to another as it became necessary; but they could also zero-in on the particular problems of a single type of *locatio*.

Urban leasehold is one form of *locatio conductio*.[5] It was singled out as requiring special legal treatment in the later Roman Republic, probably by the jurist Ser. Sulpicius Rufus (cos. 51 B.C.).[6] We find in his writings and in those of his students not only the first juristic mentions of urban leasehold but also the first traces of many classical doctrines

[5] Urban leasehold was obviously recognized as a type of *locatio* very early: at least by the second century B.C., thinks H. Kaufmann, 54-57. The origin of urban leasehold should not be sought in clientship, but rather in the growth of a free urban economy; there is no sign that urban tenants were ever regarded as clients of their landlords, and such isolated testimonies as Milo's hire of quarters for his gangs (Cic. *Mil.* 64) or the custom of offering free quarters to clients and freedmen (e.g. D. 9.3.5.1) actually point in the opposite direction. Cf. A. Herdlitczka, *RE* Suppl. v. s.v. "Miete" (1935) 386; in general, H. Kaufmann, 118-131, and T. Mayer-Maly, *SZ* 82 (1965) 408 (reviewing Kaufmann); *contra*: M. Kaser, *RPR*² I 564-565 (himself doubtful), with bibliography.

[6] It should not be forgotten that Q. Mucius (cos. 94 B.C.) did not include a section on *locatio* in his influential *Ius Civile*. Other distinctive types of leasehold are farm lease and lease of storerooms in *horrea*; commercial lease (of stores and industrial premises) is witnessed in some sources but does not seem to be considered a special form.

specifically concerning it, such as justified expulsion (D. 19.2.30 pr., 35 pr.), justified abandonment (D. 19.2.27.1), and deduction from rent (D. 19.2.27 pr.); Servius also first mentions the *insularius* (D. 14.3.5.1). From the Augustan jurist M. Antistius Labeo comes the earliest evidence for the tenant's pledge of furnishings and the juristic interpretation of the interdict *de migrando* (D. 43.32.1.4), for the particularized *culpa*-liability of the urban tenant (D. 9.3.5.4; 19.2.11.4, 13.7), and perhaps for the possibility of ameliorating damages (see D. 19.2.60 pr.). The evidence for the isolation of urban leasehold as a special type of *locatio* is already clear in sources that speak not merely of property in general, but of places of habitation (*habitatio*, *domus*, *aedes*, *insula*, *cenaculum*, *diaeta*, and so on); nonetheless, at a very early date the jurists also hit on the idea of using the rather slangy word *inquilinus*[7] as a technical term for the urban tenant (probably first in Labeo: D. 19.2.58 pr.; 43.16.20).[8] Earlier, Alfenus may have preferred *habitator* (D. 19.2.27 pr., 30 pr.), which was less satisfactory because it did not imply rental. The emergence of *inquilinus* as a technical term is paralleled by the more readily foreseeable use of *colonus* for tenant farmer. The urban and rural landlords, by contrast, have no special names; nor do the contracts for lease of (urban and rural) immoveables.

The deliberate juristic isolation of urban leasehold presumably reflects the recognition that it required a body of specially designed law; in any event, this result was grad-

[7] This vulgar diminuitive from *incola* is apparently first attested in a rude remark from Catiline (compare App. *BC* 2.5 with Sall. *Cat.* 31.7), and was clearly still mirth-provoking in the 40's B.C. (Cic. *Att.* 14.9.1; *Phil.* 2.105). The word, never common in Latin, often has a low connotation. Cf. R. Leonhard, *RE* s.v. "inquilinus" (1916) 1559-1560.

[8] Ulpian's citation of Servius in D. 19.1.13.30 uses *inquilinus*, but the rule is general and the phrasing probably Ulpian's; at D. 19.2.35 pr., Alfenus, citing Servius, has *conductor* for the urban tenant. In legal sources, *inquilinus* never has a derogatory sense. The subtenant of an *inquilinus* was also an *inquilinus* (D. 43.16.20).

ually achieved.[9] The new body of law did not, however, involve all aspects of urban leasehold. Left to one side, it seems, were all problems regarding the formation of the urban lease; we should understand that such problems as arose were solved in court through application of the generalized rules on the formation of a consensual contract, or by analogy from specialized rules in other areas of *locatio*. The jurists do not seem, therefore, to have encountered particular problems in the formation of an urban lease.

Not only do the sources presuppose the existence of a lease reached by the agreement of the two parties,[10] they also presuppose, in all cases where we have evidence, that this lease had a number of specific clauses. These clauses include:

(1) a fixed *merces*. This was a legal requirement for *locatio* (Gai. 3.142; D. 19.2.2 pr.; *Inst.* 3.24 pr.). Nugatory rents did not meet the requirement (D. 19.2.20.1, 46; 41.2.10.2). While there may have been doubt among classical jurists as to whether rent had to be in money,[11] we do not know of any urban leases where this was not the case;

(2) a term of lease, during which, in the expectation of the parties, the lessee will hold the dwelling. Such a term of lease was not required; nonetheless, no authenticated examples of the lease of an immoveable without such a term are known from our sources.[12] To have been meaningful, a

[9] Naturally, this law has points of similarity with other distinctive bodies of lease law (especially farm lease).

[10] But not necessarily (indeed, normally not) a written lease: T. Mayer-Maly, *LC* 86-88, with literature. Where the lease fails for want of *consensus*, the "landlord" has a *condictio* for the subjective value to the tenant of any service rendered: D. 12.6.65.7.

[11] Cf. Gaius 3.144; and literature in M. Kaser, *RPR*² 1 566 n. 29. (Leasehold in return for services is common today.) Within wide limits the equivalence of the *merces* with the value of the service rendered made no difference: D. 19.2.22.3-23. In some circumstances, difference of opinion on the amount of rent could be judicially resolved: D. 19.2.52 (farm lease).

[12] On D. 43.32.1.4 (first sentence), which has been so interpreted, see below at nn. 251-253. Sources combining leasehold and a *pre-*

lease must of course have had at least a date of commencement;

(3) agreement on the dwelling to be leased. The lease of an unspecified immoveable (e.g. the lease of one unspecified apartment from among many similar apartments in an *insula*, the landlord to pick the apartment before the start of the term of lease) was probably possible but is not attested.[13] All sources presume agreement between the parties as to the rented dwelling;

(4) agreement on payment periods and conditions of payment. Again, these provisions seem to be taken for granted. For instance, no source discusses whether, when no agreement on the matter had been reached, the tenant had to pay in advance or at the end of the payment period.[14]

The Roman law of urban leasehold thus begins with the assumption of a rather detailed but nonetheless sufficiently unambiguous contract. Clearly, this assumption cannot always have been true, and in the event that it was false, the Roman *iudex* had available an arsenal of doctrines whereby the process of the contract's formation and the details of the contract could be examined and, if need be, interpreted.[15] For the jurists, however, the special difficulties with urban lease evidently began after this point, when the full lease was already in existence (usually, in fact, the tenant was already in residence) and something had gone wrong. We have no choice but to follow them in their orientation.

Onto the main body of the rental contract were frequently grafted additional clauses, which are referred to in

---

carium without possession (e.g. D. 19.2.4) are not germane, see below at nn. 86-87.

[13] Probably because the lessor's liability for defects would thereby be increased: P. Stein, *Fault in the Formation of Contract* (1958) 107 (all sources discuss moveables).

[14] Cf. T. Mayer-Maly, *LC* 138-140, with literature. Damage deposits by the tenant are not witnessed.

[15] Interpretation is discussed by M. Kaser, *RPR*² I 234-237, with bibliography.

the sources as *pacta* or *leges locationis*. Such clauses could include:

(1) elimination of the right to sublease.[16] This right was presumed in the absence of contractual provision to the contrary (C. 4.65.6: Alex., A.D. 224). It should be remembered that sublease was not only very frequent in Rome, it also often constituted the primary reason for making a lease;

(2) alteration of the normal contractual liability of the parties. This was possible within very wide limits. Julian, cited by Ulpian (D. 19.2.9.2), approved a term whereby a *colonus* assumed liability even for *vis maior*; in D. 19.2.30.4, Alfenus cites a term interpreted as establishing (in principle) a *colonus*' vicarious liability for his slaves. No such clauses are known for urban lease, but similar clauses probably do occur in the *leges horreorum*,[17] and D. 19.2.11 pr. (Ulp.) indicates that a contract provision might establish a tenant's vicarious liability for those persons received by him into the leasehold;

(3) alteration of the normal liability for interest on late payment of rent: D. 22.1.17.4 (here the liability is increased);

(4) provision that the tenant's furnishings serve as a pledge for the rent.[18] This clause was later implied in all

[16] An example of such a clause: *CIL* 6.33747 (= *FIRA* 3.145a), from a *lex horreorum*: "Quisque in his horreis conductum habet, elocandi et / [substituendi ius non habebit.]"[b] In the reconstruction, assignment of contractual rights is also forbidden. The tacit right to sublease is denied for lessees of *habitationes* by L. Amirante, *St. Biondi* 1 464-465, wrongly; see also D. 19.2.60 pr. (Labeo).

[17] Cf. the clauses in the *lex horreorum* cited n. 16: "[Invectorum in haec horrea cu]stodia non praestabitur. . . . [Quisque habens conductu]m horreum su[a ibi] reliquer(it) et custodi non adsignaver(it), horrearius sine culpa erit."[c] The former clause has also been more narrowly reconstructed.

[18] So in the *lex horreorum* (cited n. 16): "Quae in his horreis invecta illata / [erunt, pignori erunt horreario, si quis pro pensionib]us satis ei [non fece]rit."[d] A similar clause has been restored in another *lex*: *CIL* 6.37795 (= *FIRA* 3.145c).

urban leases (D. 2.14.4 pr.; 20.2.4 pr.—1, 6), save apparently for leases where the opposite had been expressly provided;

(5) a provision eliminating the tenant's contractual right to remove his fixtures (the so-called *ius tollendi*).[19] This right was apparently presumed in the absence of explicit provision, though the landlord could exact a stipulation against damage arising from removal (D. 19.2.19.4);

(6) provisions regulating the tenant's conduct within the dwelling, and especially his right to have a fire (D. 19.2.11.1, cf. 9.3, 30.4 on farm lease). One provision forbids a haystack in a *villa urbana* (D. 19.2.11.4, 12), perhaps from fear of fire.

As can readily be seen, these provisions stem from the side of the landlord and impose restrictions on the tenant.[20] The *leges horreorum* show that such clauses were often presented to the tenant in a more or less standardized form: "the rules of the house." Nonetheless there seems to be little doubt about their legal validity,[21] and by and large they do not appear to have been particularly onerous—nothing so complex and imposing as in modern contracts. Such clauses also required consent, so that the tenant had to know of their content when the contract was concluded.

As a consequence of this contract, the landlord was obliged to make available the dwelling for the term of lease, or, when there was no term, for so long as neither party renounced the lease. The landlord's duty is referred to as *frui licere* or *habitare licere*, the latter being naturally

[19] In the *lex* cited n. 18, such a clause is restored: "S[i quid in his / horreis conductor in]aedificaverit, [tollendi ius / non habebit, nisi dat]a ei po [testas fue/rit.]"[e] A similar clause has been restored in the *lex* cited n. 16.

[20] An exception (for farm lease) is D. 19.2.54.1, discussed below.

[21] See recently R. Knütel, *Contrarius Consensus* (1968) 61-70, with bibliography. The problem of "form contracts" (contracts of adhesion) is not faced in the Roman sources. On the social significance of the *lex locationis*, see T. Mayer-Maly, *LC* 106-112, who perhaps exaggerates. There is no evidence that a stipulation was ever substituted for a consensual contract in urban lease.

more frequent in the case of urban lease.[22] The expression means that the landlord will furnish the tenant with the dwelling; it does not mean, of course, that the dwelling was the landlord's property (this was often not the case), but it does seem to imply that the landlord had the right to lease.

After the landlord had carried out his duty, the tenant is said by modern authors to have taken detention (*detinere* or *tenere*). The verbs are not used of an urban tenant in our sources,[23] and detention itself is basically a modern conceptualization from the word often used to express the relation of a lessee (or of some other holder) to another's property held under a contract. The modern concept expresses basically the *absence* of property rights; a detaining tenant enjoys during the term of lease no protection through *in rem* actions or possessory interdicts, and thus if he is (for instance) expelled from his dwelling no matter by whom, his only remedy lies through the contract.[24]

The failure of Roman law to accord some degree of possessory protection to tenants is often said to "reflect" the preponderant social and economic weight of Roman property owners, and also by contrast the relative weakness of tenants.[25] In general terms there is no doubt much truth in

[22] *Frui*: D. 19.2.9 pr., 15.8; *habitare*: D. 19.1.13.30; 19.2.7, 25.1, 60 pr. On *locare habitationem*, cf. L. Amirante, *St. Biondi* 1 455-465.

[23] *Tenere* is used of a *colonus* at D. 43.16.1.22 (and only there). At Gaius 4.153, the *colonus* and *inquilinus* are said to be "nostro nomine . . . in possessione," which is the same thing. Absence of a tenant's possession is clearly stated in (e.g.) D. 41.2.25.1; 43.26.6.2; also C. 7.30.1 (A.D. 226).

[24] On detention, cf. M. Kaser, *RPR*² 1 389-390, with literature, and compare p. 563.

[25] Classic statements to this effect in A. Pernice, *SZ* 19 (1898) 89-97; F. Schulz, *CRL* 544-546; A. Beck, in *Fs. Lewald* 9-11. (The verb "reflect," or *widerspiegeln*, is a frequent feature of such accounts, which should not, I think, be labeled sociological.) The weakness of these statements in the light of the Ostian remains was seen already by H. Stoll, *SZ* 47 (1927) 528. K. Genius, *Der Bestandsschutz des Mietverhältnisses* (1972) 39-42, has a balanced discussion. In the state of the sources, it can hardly be maintained that the rule

this view; however, when we get down to particulars, the view becomes decidedly less enticing. To limit ourselves strictly to urban tenancy: taken as a whole, the Roman tenantry ranged from senators at the top down to the lowest elements of the *plebs* at the bottom. While the lower classes obviously made up the huge majority of this tenantry, the upper classes are, because of their greater capacity and propensity for litigation, far better attested in the juristic sources on urban leasehold.

A legal rule such as that according the tenant no access to possessory interdicts has a varying significance depending on which portion of the tenantry one observes. For the impoverished majority (those depicted, let us say, in Juvenal's third satire), the rule represented one more misery; but it is doubtful that it materially worsened their already very weak position. Thus, the right of the urban landlord to expel, which seems to us undeniably objectionable, is complained of neither in Juvenal's very full list of complaints nor in any other source from the Roman Empire.

The matter is quite otherwise with the upper classes, those capable of defending themselves both socially and legally. Obviously, from their standpoint the absence of possessory protection was not a "reflection" of social weakness, but was rather purely and simply a nuisance—one which should be neither underestimated nor overestimated. The nuisance lay in the absence of legal protection against third-party intruders,[26] but far more significantly in the elimination of

---

on possession was deliberately propagated to oppress the poor; so already A. Pernice, 89, against (e.g.) F. Schulz.

[26] In this area, the tenant has the *actio iniuriarum* against intruders (D. 47.10.5.2), plus delictual claims with regard to theft or damage of personal property; and since he is also contractually obliged to "defend" the dwelling from damage by outsiders (D. 19.2.13.7, discussed at nn. 96-98 and 190), he resorted, perhaps not infrequently, to self-help; cf. D. 43.16.12, 18 pr. (farm leases), with J.A.C. Thomas, *TR* 41 (1973) 35-44. Otherwise, his legal defenses against disruption of his detention (through e.g. squatters, or immissions from outside)

legal defense against expulsion by the landlords or owners of their dwellings; tenants were particularly vulnerable in relation to the owner, who almost always figures as the expeller in legal sources.[27] With the exception of expulsion, there is no indication in these sources that landlords were *legally* in an especially strong position against tenants; in one source (D. 43.17.3.3), the landlord has to resort to an interdict *uti possidetis* in order to gain admittance for the purpose of making necessary repairs. Certainly the assertion that a landlord could "enter the *habitatio* at will" does not correspond to our legal sources, as far as they go;[28] nor has it support in literary sources.

There remains the nuisance value of expulsion, and also the seemingly firm conviction of the juristic sources that the irresponsible use of expulsion could be adequately curbed through the contractual suit alone; as we shall see in the next section, round about this apparently archaic aspect of Roman law the jurists wove the sophisticated doctrine of justified expulsion, details of which have been taken over into some modern legal systems despite their rejection of possessionless leasehold.[29] In the absence of further evidence

---

were limited to an action on the contract; if his detention was disturbed by a third party, only the possessor had the interdicts (D. 43.16.20; 43.24.17). The landlord's liabilities in such cases are discussed below (under "Justified Abandonment" and "*Deductio ex Mercede*"). To be sure, the contractual action might be meaningless if the landlord was bankrupt.

[27] So far as I know, D. 13.7.11.5 (discussed below at nn. 154ff.) is the only source where, as it seems, a tenant is expelled by a landlord who is not also the owner or possessor. On expulsion by the owner, see below n. 44.

[28] *Contra*: M. Marrone, *La Legittimazione Passiva alla "Rei Vindicatio"* (1970) 126-130 (at 128), whose demonstration is not a model of source criticism; see below n. 84.

[29] The grounds for justified expulsion in C. 4.65.3 (see below, nn. 45-46) have great influence in later European law, cf. M. Battaglini, in *St. Betti* IV 523-542; in general, Genius (cited n. 25); e.g. they constitute four of the first five grounds for justified expulsion in the Austrian *Mietengesetz* (1922).

(and the absence deserves stressing), we may suppose, first, that the jurists were probably right in assuming that the contractual action had a deterrent effect on heedless expulsions (a discussion like that in D. 19.1.53.2 is otherwise senseless); second, that this contractual deterrent was probably supplemented among the upper classes by a not inconsiderable social pressure;[30] and third, that in any case the nuisance value of possessionless leasehold was simply not sufficient in and of itself to bring about a rethinking of the interdicts and of the doctrine that had originally resulted in the nuisance.[31] A contractual device to discourage unjustified expulsion, namely an agreement on liquidated damages, is in fact recorded in the *Digest* (19.2.54.1, Paul), but, perhaps significantly, only for farm lease.

Typical of the problems caused by the tenant's absence of possessory protection are those in D. 19.2.25.1 (Gai. 10 *ad Ed. Prov.*):

> Qui fundum fruendum vel habitationem alicui locavit, si aliqua ex causa fundum vel aedes vendat, curare debet, ut apud emptorem quoque eadem pactione et colono frui et inquilino habitare liceat: alioquin prohibitus is aget cum eo ex conducto.[f]

[30] So, as it seems, A. Pernice (cited n. 25) 92 n. 3, on Mart. 12.32; and thus, explicitly, Seneca, *Ben.* 7.5.2-3. Cf. Cic. *ad Quint.* 2.3.7: Quintus' Palatine house had burned, his Carinae house was already let; with no thought of expelling the tenants (cf. C. 4.65.3), Quintus' family rented another house for themselves. I would suggest that later legal systems required possession for tenants because they could not rely on the social stability evident in the Roman upper classes; I am in any event skeptical of the view that before modern times the granting of possession was intended to benefit the *lower* classes.

[31] This last factor needs emphasis; possessory protection of tenants is usually reached in modern European law only with the aid of more or less fictional constructions that would not have appealed to the Roman jurists. A line of distinguished scholars has attacked the "reflection" theory, without ever being refuted: e.g. W. Kunkel, 112 n. 10; E. Rabel, *Grdz.* 62 (citing Jhering). In any case, the doctrine of possession took form long before the law of urban leasehold.

There are perhaps some light revisions in this text.[32] The owner-landlord sells the property during the term of lease; he should take care that included in the sale is a pact whereby the buyer will allow the tenant to remain for the term; otherwise, the tenant, if expelled, can sue on the contract. This is a so-called spurious contract to the benefit of a third party; it is clear from C. 4.65.9 (Alex. Sev., A.D. 234; farm lease) that unless a term protecting the tenant was included, the buyer could expel the sitting tenant without becoming liable to a suit *by the seller* (cf. D. 19.1.13.30). The tenant, however, could in any case still sue the landlord *ex conducto* for damages resulting from his premature and unjustified expulsion; the right to this suit remained unaltered by the sale. In practical terms, therefore, the pact shifted to the buyer the final liability for an unjustified expulsion by him, nevertheless without making him into the tenant's landlord.[33]

As between landlord and tenant, a suit on a single contract could in principle be brought only once; thereafter the claim (and, as later classical sources put it, also the obligation) was extinguished.[34] Because of this extinction, a suit on the contract could not be brought in the midst of a term of lease without, in effect, bringing the contract itself to an end, insofar as the future contractual duties of the other party were concerned. In order to avoid this unpleasant consequence, the plaintiff was allowed to insert into the *formula* a *praescriptio* (*pro actore*), whereby only the reciprocal relationship up to the time of the suit was taken into account

[32] The problems center mostly on the vague phrase "aliqua ex causa"; see the good discussion in T. Mayer-Maly, *LC* 42-46, with literature; but on his conclusions cf. K. Genius (cited n. 25) 28-30 and 35-37; M. Kaser, in *Festschrift E. Seidl* (1975) 79-80.

[33] Thus, the seller continued to collect rent (D. 19.2.58 pr.; cf. 18.1.68 pr., farm lease), and the tenant was still liable to the seller for negligent damage (D. 19.1.13.30).

[34] Cf. M. Kaser, *RZ* 227-228; *RPR*² 1 658-659; on *praescriptio*, *RZ* 192; and W. Selb, *Formeln mit Unbestimmter Intentio Iuris* (1974) 19-28; K. Hackl, *Praejudicium* (1976) 48-50; M. Kaser, *Labeo* 22 (1976) 21-26.

and future obligations were severed for procedural purposes (Gaius 4.131-131a). Whether or not the *praescriptio* was made use of, the extinction of claim that occurred with the admission of the suit meant that the Roman law of urban leasehold typically tended to look back on the contract after it (or a portion of it) had ended. Because, however, the plaintiff's claim was for as much as should be paid or done *ex fide bona*, the counterclaims of the defendant were also given weight in assessing the amount (if any) that the defendant owed. The suit on the contract therefore had the quality of a "settling up," either final or intermediate.

The following sections are in two respects ordered so as to take account of this procedural consideration. First, they follow the juristic evidence in not laying great weight on the content of the reciprocal rights and duties of the two parties under the contract. The jurists are more frequently concerned with what one party can or cannot claim in a court, and therefore with the liabilities of the parties. Rights and duties usually emerge through these liabilities. Nonetheless, the jurists tend to blend together liabilities arising from a party's conduct (typically, the violation of a duty) with liabilities arising otherwise (e.g. from *vis maior*); they even reason back and forth from one to another. The analysis below preserves this form of reasoning.

Second, the sections below are ordered principally in terms of liability-producing circumstances.[35] The first two begin from the most drastic circumstances: a total breach of contract, where one party or the other has not continued

[35] Thus, we are not concerned with e.g. a mutual agreement by the parties to end the contract, on which cf. R. Knütel (cited n. 21) 122-123; nor with termination of the lease if the tenant through some circumstance became owner of the leasehold (D. 19.2.9.6, 10), cf. J.A.C. Thomas, *Index* 2 (1971) 283-290. The death of the tenant may or may not have resulted in continued contractual liability of his heirs: no (?): Labeo in D. 19.2.60.1; yes: all later sources, including D. 19.2.15.9, 19.8; C. 4.65.10; *Inst.* 3.24.6; the sources are all either for farm lease or generalized, cf. T. Mayer-Maly, *LC* 222-223. On the death of the landlord, see *ibid.* 46-48.

fulfilling his side of the contract. In the case of landlords, this failure is named "expulsion" (which includes original failure to place a tenant in occupancy, the legal consequences being identical); in the case of tenants, this failure is "abandonment" (including initial failure to take up residence). The third section discusses the wind-up of the lease and the problems arising from the tenant's pledge of furnishings. The fourth and fifth sections treat the circumstances in which the tenant could become liable to the landlord (or vice versa) other than through breach of contract. Finally, in the last two, the somewhat exceptional problems of holding over, lease without term, and mitigation of damages are discussed.

Expulsion and Procedures for Expulsion

The general rule for expulsion and abandonment appears to have been, first, that the owner or the landlord could, with legal irreversibility, expel a sitting tenant at any time,[36] neither notice nor specification of grounds being required; and, second, that the tenant could similarly leave the premises at any time.[37] The capabilities had no relationship to the term of lease. The effects of expulsion were that the tenant was allowed to consider the lease terminated (D. 19.2.60 pr., considered below), and that he could proceed forthwith *ex conducto* against his landlord;[38] the effect of the tenant's

[36] *Expello*, which, like other *pello* cognates, is used in juristic writings for *coloni* (e.g. D. 7.1.59.1; 19.2.54.1; 39.4.10.1), is applied also to *inquilini* in C. 4.65.3, discussed below. No "expulsion after a period of notice" is known from classical sources: T. Mayer-Maly, *SZ* kan. 72 (1955) 412-415; *LC* 215. An Egyptian "eviction notice" is discussed in Appendix A below.

[37] His pledges, however, could be held by the *locator* pending payment of outstanding debts from the contract. See the section below on "Tenant's Pledges."

[38] Compare D. 19.2.24.4 (Paul), where however (in the present text) the expeller of a *colonus* is given a few days' grace in which to change his mind; on farm lease, also C. 4.65.15 (Valer., A.D. 259). The

abandonment was to allow the landlord to cease holding open the premises and to proceed immediately *ex locato* against the tenant (D. 19.2.24.2).[39] Expulsion or abandonment therefore allowed the aggrieved party to consider the contract irrevocably broken. In either event, the two parties could then settle between themselves, if necessary by adjudication, the balance of any outstanding debts stemming from the contract.[40]

On the other hand, the situation might arise where the aggrieved party was willing to continue the contract, even after an interval of time. Such a situation is envisaged in D. 19.2.60 pr. (Labeo, *Post.* 5 *a Jav. Epit.*):

> Cum in plures annos domus locata est, praestare locator debet, ut non solum habitare conductor ex calendis Iuliis cuiusque anni, sed etiam locare habitatori si velit suo tempore possit. itaque si ea domus ex kalendis Ianuariis fulta in kalendis Iuniis permansisset, ita ut nec habitare quisquam nec ostendere alicui posset, nihil locatori conductorem praestaturum, adeo ut nec cogi quidem posset ex kalendis Iuliis refecta domu habitare, nisi si paratus fuisset locator commodam domum ei ad habitandum dare.[g]

---

tenant's success in a suit depended on whether the expulsion was justified, see below.

[39] Compare D. 43.32.1.4; and for farm lease, D. 19.2.55.2 (= Paul. *Sent.* 2.18.5), where a *lex locationis* is involved. The landlord's success in a suit depended on whether the abandonment was justified, see below on "Justified Abandonment."

[40] It seems to me that the issues here were somewhat confused by F. Gallo, in *Synt. Arangio Ruiz* II 1198-1211, at 1198-1201. Clearly the *liabilities* of the active party did not terminate because of expulsion or abandonment, nor do I think that S. Perozzi, II 294-295, cited by Gallo, maintained anything different. (Gallo, p. 1198, has also misunderstood T. Mayer-Maly, *LC* 215.) Three different questions must be asked: (1) Can either party at any time cease performing under the contract? (2) If so, is the other party still obliged to continue performance? (3) What recompense can the other party then obtain?

The final *nisi* clause is a postclassical addition, which, however, may reflect classical law in garbled form.[41] The rest of the text is probably genuine, though "*adeo ut . . . habitare*" has sometimes been held suspect.[42] The long-term tenant of a *domus* both dwells in it himself and, as a middleman, subleases parts of the structure to others. Not only must the *domus* be available to him at the start of each rental year (on July 1); during the term of the lease it must also be available in advance, so that he can show it to a prospective sublessee. But the principal tenant has been unable to occupy the dwelling for five months (January 1 to June 1), while repairs are being made. The sense of the final sentence is that if the building is still unfit for occupancy and showing on June 1, just one month before the start of the rental year, the tenant is entitled to determine that he will be unable to find subtenants and so does not wish to resume the lease; in that event, he owes nothing to the *locator*, so much so that he cannot himself be compelled (through the lease) to dwell in the *domus* when it becomes available on July 1. It seems obvious that had the building been ready on June 1, and had the tenant therefore been willing to take up the lease again,

[41] This text is discussed below, at nn. 259-260.

[42] "adeo" to the end is excised by S. Perozzi, II 292 n. 4, followed by, e.g. F. Schulz, *Principles* 227; T. Mayer-Maly, *LC* 147-148, who comments that the passage is "verfehlt formuliert: Der Mieter ist . . . keinesfalls einem Aufenthaltszwang unterworfen." But that seems to be just what the passage says. In the first sentence, I have followed a suggestion of Prof. Kaser in emending the meaningless *ex calendis illis* to *ex calendis Iuliis*. In the second sentence, Mommsen (against the *Basilica*) altered *in kalendis Juniis* to *in kalendas Julias*; but the *conductor* is primarily afraid that he will find no subtenants so soon before the rental year, so that Labeo's ruling is clearer with the original text. On the decision, see F. Horak, 103; it cannot be used to support a theory of lease as a real contract, *contra*: S. Perozzi, II 289 n. 2. It should be noted that the doctrine in this passage does not involve the lessee's *anticipation* that the lessor will be unable to fulfill his side of the contract; the lessor has *in fact* not fulfilled it. Anticipatory breach of contract does not exist in Roman lease law; *contra*: H.-P. Benöhr, *Das Sogennante Synallagma* (1965) 101-103.

then the reciprocal obligations of the parties under the lease would simply have resumed—though of course the tenant would owe nothing for the lost interval.

There is no hint in classical sources that the urban tenant was in any way directly prevented from abandoning his dwelling at any time (although, to be sure, he could thereby become subject to an *actio locati*).[43] On the other hand, that not only the landlord but also the owner (where the two were not identical) could at will expel the *inquilinus* seems clear from those passages in which the *dominus* is said simply to forbid (*prohibere*, *vetare*) further habitation by the *inquilinus*, or not to allow it (*non pati*).[44] These texts imply that no legal obstacle to expulsion could be raised by the tenant, even where the expulsion was not justified. (In this regard, unlike in modern law, the term of lease was irrelevant.) The tenant's remedy, if any, lay elsewhere, above all in a suit *ex conducto* against the landlord.

Nonetheless, classical law distinguished between justified and unjustified expulsion. This is clear from a rescript of Caracalla of A.D. 214 (C. 4.65.3):

> Diaetae, quam te conductam habere dicis, si pensionem domino insulae solvis, invitum te expelli non oportet, nisi propriis usibus dominus esse necessariam eam probaverit aut corrigere domum maluerit aut tu male in re locata versatus es.[h]

The rescript[45] lists the proper causes for expulsion: the

[43] The situation is different as regards his pledges. Broadly similar to the rules on justified expulsion are those on justified abandonment, discussed below under that heading.

[44] Forbid: D. 19.1.53.2; 19.2.7-8, 25.1; 43.17.3.3; not to allow: D. 19.2.15.8.

[45] The text was attacked by F. Eisele, *SZ* 11 (1890) 29-30, followed by M. Battaglini, in *St. Betti* IV 523-542, at 523-532 (with literature); see G. Longo, *Ric.* 539. Eisele raised three objections: (1) *corrigere* is not otherwise used of buildings (but since the usage is singular, this argument miscarries); (2) *malo* is used for *volo* (but this usage,

owner's desire to use the premises himself; the necessity of repairing the premises; and the tenant's gross abuse of the property. One further cause is listed, apart from these: the tenant's failure to pay rent.[46]

These justifications for expulsion are found in part in earlier juristic literature, in part not. The need to demolish a crumbling building was accepted as a valid reason for expulsion only in the case of farm lease (D. 19.2.54.1; suit *ex conducto* an expelled tenant could recover only a prorated portion of any rent prepaid.[48] Similarly, payment of rent was obviously a fundamental duty of the tenant, and although failure to pay rent is given as a justification for expulsion only in the case of farm lease (D. 19.2.54.1; 39.4.10.1),[49] nonetheless, especially on the basis of Martial

---

favored by the linguistic development of *malo*, is found already in the second century A.D., compare Gran. Lic. p. 26 line 6 F, with Plut. *Sulla* 23.9); (3) the true condition for expulsion is that the owner needs the land, not that he should prove his need (this seems a quibble). The text is usually accepted without comment, e.g. by T. Mayer-Maly, *LC* 215-216; M. Kaser, *RPR*² I 568.

[46] Presumably the tenant had written to complain that he was being expelled despite his payment of rent; the construction of the rescript reflects the letter.

[47] Probably the owner must not himself be responsible for the deteriorating condition of the building: M. Kaser, *SZ* 74 (1957) 157-158, *arg. ex* D. 19.2.35 pr. (*propter vetustatem*).

[48] D. 19.2.30 pr. (Alf.), 35 pr. (Afr./Serv.). The possibility of expulsion in order to repair is also raised by D. 43.17.3.3 (Ulpian); and D. 19.2.60 pr., discussed above.

[49] But cf. D. 19.2.56, where the text as preserved suggests that an urban tenant's nonpayment of rent was justification for the owner's inventorying goods held in pledge. On expulsion for failure to pay rent, note also D. 19.2.61 pr.; 33.4.1.15 (farm leases). In Ulp. *Inst.* (*Frag. Vindob.* 1.2), the lessee's duty to pay rent was traced to the *ius gentium*. There was perhaps a custom of allowing a maximum of two years' rent in arrears (Mart. 12.32; D. 19.2.56, cf. 54.1 on farm lease); but no clear legal rule can be made out, cf. M. Kaser, *RPR*² II 406 n. 42, with literature, and below at nn. 178-179. Interest is collectable on overdue rent: D. 19.2.54 pr.; 22.1.17.4 (Paul; partially interp.); C. 4.65.17 (Diocl., A.D. 290); on these texts, see G. Cervenca, *Contributo allo Studio delle "Usurae"* (1969) 54-55, with bibliography.

12.32, this justification can be confidently extended to housing as well.

The other two reasons are more problematic, however. The phrase *versari male in* occurs in juristic literature only in Ulpian (D. 1.12.1.7; 3.2.6.6; 26.10.3.8), always in situations where someone is holding or protecting the property of another as the result of a legal relationship with strong fiduciary overtones (tutelage and curatorship; deposit and mandate); these words imply, as regards that property, virtually criminal misconduct, which was sometimes even subject to criminal prosecution.[50] In land leases it appears that the *colonus* could be justifiably evicted for failure to cultivate the land (D. 19.2.54.1, cf. 24.2, 3), which was regarded by the jurists as a basic duty under the lease (D. 19.2.24.3, 25.3; Paul. *Sent.* 2.18.2)—so basic in fact, that this duty was normally written into leases.[51] No similar "basic duty" is known to have existed in the case of urban tenancy. But the urban tenant had a (publicly imposed) duty to exercise extreme care in the handling of fire (cf. D. 1.15.3.4, 5), and this duty as well was often provided for, or further enforced by a clause in the lease (D. 19.2.11.1; cf. 19.2.9.3, farm lease).[52] Perhaps criminally negligent mishandling of fire should be regarded as a typical instance where subsequent expulsion is justified. In any event, the rescript does not suggest that the tenant's violation of some

[50] Cf. esp. D. 1.12.1.7, where the text seems never to have been suspected.

[51] T. Mayer-Maly, *LC* 180-181; cf. D. 19.2.15.3, 51 pr., 55.2 (= Paul, *Sent.* 2.18.5). Immediate *actio locati* for failure to cultivate: D. 19.2.24.3. This is not just a matter of the *colonus* being unable to pay rent when he does not cultivate; the land itself deteriorates when not cultivated. Failure to cultivate is also *culpa*: Paul. *Sent.* 2.18.2. Note the public duty to cultivate one's land in Gell. *NA* 4.12; and the requirement of work from *coloni* in Colum. 1.7.1.

[52] D. 19.2.11.4 (cf. below at nn. 198-199) refers to a contract provision against hay in a *villa urbana*, the danger of fire being envisaged. Cf. G. MacCormack, *Index* 3 (1972) 382-396, at 390-391. Presumably violation of such a contract clause would, if serious, be itself a valid ground for expulsion.

lesser contract duty would be a justification for expulsion; and far less (for example) the tenant's "immoral" conduct in the dwelling.

The fourth ground for expulsion, namely the owner's need of the premises for his own use, is the most difficult to understand. Stress lies on the words *propriis usibus* (that is, the owner must need the premises for his own personal use)[53] and on *necessariam* (that is, his need must be vital). We may deduce that the owner's interest may not lie, for instance, merely in a more profitable disposition of the property,[54] nor in some peripheral use. The bounds of this reason for justified expulsion are (and perhaps were) hard to make out. Nevertheless, as a reason for expulsion it is perhaps not incomprehensible or unreasonable.

The list of reasons for justified expulsion in C. 4.65.3 probably derives, therefore, from the body of case law and jurisprudence surrounding the *actio conducti*; here the major question was: what recompense should the tenant receive if he was expelled? Broadly put, the answer was: if the expulsion was justified, then (as the case might be) the tenant could obtain either the return of a prorated portion of prepaid rent or the elimination of the duty to pay further rent; if it was not justified, then he could also obtain *id quod interest* damages.[55] We may assume rather confidently that the list of grounds for justified eviction in C. 4.65.3 was a compilation from such sources; but the crisp legislative format of this constitution should not make us forget the slow process of case-by-case assemblage that had preceded it.

[53] Compare above all D. 34.2.10 (Pomp.). The need could have been foreseen by the landlord.

[54] This seems clear from D. 19.2.30 pr. (Alf. 3 *Dig. a Paulo Epit.*), on demolition: the owner must pay *id quod interest* when he demolishes the building, "sin autem non fuisset necesse demoliri, sed quia melius aedificare vellet"—i.e. mere building improvements did not suffice.

[55] See M. Kaser, *RPR*² I 566, with bibliography. Most of the texts concern the owner's recompense to middlemen; cf. esp. D. 19.2.7-8, 30 pr., 35 pr.

Expulsion

Only one source illustrates the standard methods of calculating the *id quod interest* of an urban tenant. D. 19.2.28.2 (Labeo 4 *Post. Epit. a Jav.*):

> . . . sed si locator conductori potestatem conducendae domus non fecisset et is in qua habitaret conduxisset, tantum ei praestandum putat, quantum sine dolo malo praestitisset. ceterum si gratuitam habitationem habuisset, pro portione temporis ex locatione domus deducendum esse.[j]

If the landlord does not present to the tenant the opportunity of taking the house in leasehold, and the tenant is thereby obliged to rent a dwelling elsewhere, the landlord must furnish to the tenant the cost of equivalent housing (*scil.*, for the remainder of the term of lease). The text is relevant both to expulsion and to initial failure to install the tenant in the premises. The final sentence is interesting: it seems to recognize that the landlord's financial obligations were related to the actual expenses of the tenant for alternative housing; if he paid nothing, then the landlord owed nothing.[56] This passage does not speak of other possible costs to the tenant, such as moving costs or his lost time.

In D. 19.2.28.2, as in other passages (e.g. C. 4.65.15: Valer., A.D. 259; farm lease), it seems to be assumed that an expulsion was unjustified unless the landlord could prove otherwise. This is the meaning of the word *probaverit* in C. 4.65.3. Over time there evolved the list of standardized excuses which Caracalla presents.

However, the list is not quite complete. We may perhaps

[56] On the passage, cf. most recently H. Honsell, *Quod Interest* (1969) 121, with literature, including T. Mayer-Maly, *LC* 155-156; M. Kaser, *SZ* 74 (1957) 160-161; D. Medicus, 46-47. Most texts simply describe the landlord's obligation as "ut frui / habitare liceat" or the like; cf. above n. 22. What is envisaged is the difference between the originally contracted rent and the higher rent required for alternative housing of equivalent quality; the tenant sues after his expenses are incurred. The jurists seem to have left the difficulties in such calculations to the discretion of the *iudex*.

add a *vis maior* that rendered the dwelling uninhabitable, as where the *insula*, through no fault of the landlord, collapsed or was destroyed by fire; in this event, as with justified expulsion, the landlord was not obliged to provide further housing, nor the tenant to pay further rent.[57] This reason for justified "expulsion" is mainly interesting because it found analogous application in situations where the tenant was expelled from his dwelling by human forces outside the landlord's control, as through an illegal but irremediable act of a public official.[58] Naturally, such situations were not envisaged in C. 4.65.3.

There are, however, further and hitherto largely unrecognized extensions of the analogy to *vis maior*. A line of "trouble cases" discusses the situation where the putative owner of an *insula* leases to a middleman, who thereafter, whether for good reasons or for bad, is expelled from the *insula* before the term of lease ends; the middleman's tenants are simultaneously expelled. From these texts it is clear that the principal lessor's contractual duty to provide the lessee with the structure was absolute to the extent that the lessor warranted lack of right without regard to his fault. Therefore, if it emerged that the lessor had no right to let the structure, the expelled middleman could recover *id quod interest* damages.[59] This theme is addressed by D. 19.2.7 ([Paul.] ⟨Ulp.⟩ 32 *ad Ed.*)[60] and 8 (Tryph. 9 *Disp.*):

[57] See M. Kaser, *RPR*² I 566 and n. 37 (the point is uncontested). For urban housing see D. 19.2.9.1, 19.6 (destruction by fire). Rent was due up to the catastrophe (D. 19.2.9.1); if it had been prepaid, it could be recovered for the period thereafter (D. 19.2.19.6). Cf. also D. 19.2.30.1 (lease of a bath).

[58] T. Mayer-Maly, *SZ* 74 (1957) 363-373. There are no texts for urban housing; D. 19.2.13.7 (cf. Mayer-Maly pp. 370-373, and below nn. 99-100) involves justified abandonment.

[59] So M. Kaser, *SZ* 74 (1957) 166-169; *RPR*² I 566, rightly rejecting at n. 36 the views of N. Palazzolo, *Bull.* 68 (1965) 275-321, who saw the lessor's knowledge of his right as the determinant. Against this view, D. 19.2.9 pr., 15.8 (both from Ulpian) are conclusive.

[60] Ulpian, not Paul, handled *locatio* in 32 *ad Ed.*; cf. O. Lenel,

7. Si tibi alienam insulam locavero quinquaginta tuque eandem sexaginta Titio locaveris et Titius a domino prohibitus fuerit habitare, agentem te ex conducto sexaginta consequi debere placet, quia ipse Titio tenearis in sexaginta.[k]

8. Nos videamus, ne non sexaginta praestanda nec quinquaginta sint, sed quanti interest perfrui conductione, tantundemque consequatur medius, quantum praestare debeat ei, qui a se conduxit, quoniam emolumentum conductionis ad comparationem uberioris mercedis computatum maiorem efficit condemnationem. et tamen primus locator reputationem habebit quinquaginta, quae ab illo perciperet, si dominus insulae habitare novissimum conductorem non vetuisset: quo iure utimur.[l]

A leases an *insula*, which he does not own, to *B* for 50; *B* subleases it to Titius for 60; the true owner refuses to allow Titius to reside; what does *A* owe *B*? There is no suggestion that either party is in bad faith. It is presupposed that both *B* and Titius have paid in advance. According to D. 19.2.7, Ulpian determined that *A* owes 60 to *B*, *because B* owes 60 to Titius; that is, *A* is held to *B* for an *id quod interest* standard that is determined by the amount which Titius can recover from *B*. What is interesting here is that the sum

---

Paling. 1 1033 n. 4. On the text of the two fragments, see H. Kreller, *SZ* 66 (1948) 76-79; G. Beseler, *SZ* 66 (1948) 355; M. Kaser, *SZ* 74 (1957) 166-168; D. Medicus, 97-98; H. Honsell (cited n. 56) 132-133 (wrong text of D. 19.2.8). The Tryphoninus fragment was, at the least, badly confused by the compilers; cf. below n. 61. It translates: "Let us see whether neither 60 nor 50 is owed, but rather so much as it lay in his interest to enjoy the leasehold; and the middleman should obtain so much as he must provide to the one who rented from him, since the profit from the contract (which was concluded for the purpose of a higher rent) raises the sum adjudged. But nevertheless the chief lessor will have a counterclaim for the 50 which he would have received from him if the owner of the *insula* had not forbidden the subtenant to dwell; which law we use." As the text stands, D. 19.2.8 does not contradict, but only elucidates, D. 19.2.7.

owed by *A* to *B* is an *id quod interest* sum, while the sum owed by *B* to Titius is limited to the prepaid rent.[61] *A*, as the chief lessor, plainly warrants to his lessee the existence of his right to rent the building; but the warranty in this case seemingly extends no further down the contractual ladder, since *B* is liable to Titius only in the sum of Titius' rent. Yet surely it is impossible to believe that *B*'s contractual warranty was substantially different from *A*'s.[62] Therefore it seems better to interpret the warranty rather differently from the way we usually do today. *A*'s lack of right in this case is clear; *B*, on the other hand, was able at least to claim that his own right did not derive from *A*'s right, but rather was founded in the validity of the contract with *A*. The consequence of this argument would be that *A* owed to *B id quod interest* damages because of his lack of right, but *B* owed to Titius only return of the rent, since *B*'s warranty remained unviolated. That such an argument was acceptable seems to be the doctrine of D. 19.2.7.

If, however, we turn this analysis around and look at the situation from the viewpoint of the rules for expulsion, a

[61] As H. Honsell (cited n. 56) 132-134, observes, the *Basilica* (20.1.7-8, = Heimb. 2.336, Schelt. BT 983-984 and BS 1172) attribute to the author of D. 19.2.7 the view that *B* must pay *id quod interest* to Titius, and that *A* must pay *this* sum to *B*; perhaps due to confusion in assembling the *catena*, traces of this view may survive in D. 19.2.8 (but this is not certain, cf. n. 60). Honsell rightly conjectures (p. 134) that in Ulpian's original text a controversy was reported (cf. *placet*, and *quo iure utimur* at the end of D. 19.2.8); but (*contra*: Honsell) the preserved text is only explicable if the award of *id quod interest* was the *older* view, rejected by Ulpian and then revived by the compilers. (Honsell reverses the classical development; but why then would the compilers have tampered with Ulpian's text?) Only the last (and relatively trivial) sentence of D. 19.2.8 is reflected in the *Basilica*; the rest is probably Justinianic.

[62] This alternative is rightly rejected by M. Kaser (cited n. 60) 168, who, however, could only explain the 60 figure as a scholastic approximation. The alternative is acceptd by Medicus, 97-98, whose arguments are refuted by H. Honsell, (cited n. 56) 132. N. Palazzolo (cited n. 59) 316-318, wrongly attributed bad faith to *A*, thereby explaining the difference.

disquieting possibility arises. As a consequence of *A*'s lack of right, Titius has been expelled. Since *B* now owes to Titius only the return of the prepaid rent, Titius' expulsion is (in effect) justified. The justification must lie in the fact that the expulsion did not result from circumstances over which *B* had, or could be considered to have had, control. Suppose, however, that the expulsion of Titius had not been a matter of *A*'s lack of right, but had stemmed directly from the will of *A*, whether for justified reasons or not; the thrust of the argument given above would indicate that in this event also (so long as *B* acted in good faith), *A*'s reasons for the expulsion would be relevant only in a suit *ex conducto* between *A* and *B*, but not in a suit between *B* and Titius. *A*'s act (like that of the true owner in D. 19.2.7) would be a form of "higher force" which *B* could not resist. If this argument is correct, then we should assume that the possibility of *B*'s obtaining damages from *A* was considered by the jurists sufficient to prevent *A* from an ill-considered expulsion of Titius; and also, as between *B* and Titius, we should add another reason for justified expulsion to the list given in C. 4.65.3.

There was perhaps a general tendency toward the end of the classical period to release the landlord from *id quod interest* damages whenever the tenant was expelled by a third party not subject in some legal sense to the landlord's authority. D. 19.2.33 and 35 pr. (Afr. 2 *Quaest.*) preserves an interesting discussion in which Africanus for once rejects the opinion of his teacher Julian and argues that, when a farm is confiscated by the State, the owner owes his *colonus* only return of prepaid rent, not *id quod interest.* Africanus goes on to generalize this point, arguing that in the case of expulsion by one *quem prohibere non possit* (*scil. locator*; so D. 19.2.35 pr.) the tenant is entitled only to return or remission of rent. Africanus specifically compares this rule to the *vis maior* rule. Finally, he makes (as it seems) a specific exception for a *locator* who lacks the right to rent.[63]

[63] On the passage, H. Honsell (cited n. 56) 122-130; A. Wacke, in

This passage supports the interpretation given above of D. 19.2.7.

It constitutes no obstacle to this interpretation that, if an owner-landlord sold the *insula* during the term of lease and the new owner expelled the former owner's tenants, the tenant could probably obtain *id quod interest* damages from his landlord the former owner; the sale clearly endangered the tenant's undisturbed detention, and so (as these texts also make clear) the landlord was expected to provide against the tenant's expulsion in the terms of sale.[64] The distinction is between expulsions that may be considered (in one way or another) to originate in the *locator*'s conduct, and those that cannot be so considered.

C. 4.65.3 should therefore be understood as limited to the concrete case therein proposed, namely the direct confrontation between an owner-landlord and a tenant. Additional complications, mostly not in the tenant's favor, must be understood as arising whenever a third party is involved in the expulsion of a tenant.

Finally, it deserves careful attention that, whereas the earlier sources on justified expulsion seem without exception to regard the *actio conducti* after an expulsion, C. 4.65.3 is

---

ANRW II.15 (1976) 463-494; and of earlier literature: E. Seckel and E. Levy, *SZ* 47 (1927) 219-244, esp. 221-224; T. Mayer-Maly, *LC* 163-166; M. Kaser (cited n. 60) 177-182; K. H. Below, *Die Haftung für Lucrum Cessans* (1964) 109-115; N. Palazzolo (cited n. 59) 292-305. The last sentence of D. 19.2.35, while its meaning is not profound and its alternatives not exhaustive, need not be interpolated. D. 19.2.34 (Gaius 10 *ad Ed. Prov.*), a fragment *in catena*, also raises the comparison with external *vis* (*latronum incursus*). Where the landlord could prevent the expulsion, a *colonus* was entitled to damages: D. 19.2.24.4 (Paul), with D. Daube, *Iura* 11 (1960) 104-109.

[64] Cf. J.A.C. Thomas, *TR* 41 (1973) 44; the major text for urban lease is D. 19.2.25.1, examined above at nn. 32-33. The same rule was adopted by Julian for *publicatio*: D. 19.2.33 (farm lease), and above n. 63; and for legacy *per vindicationem*: D. 19.2.32; 30.120.2 (= *Frag. Vat.* 44; farm lease); and cf. n. 61 above. Cf. M. Kaser, *RPR*[2] I 567 and n. 44, with bibliography. A doctrine similar to that in the text is expressed in C. 4.65.15 (Valer., A.D. 259; farm lease).

differently framed: it is a norm (cf. *oportuit*) governing expulsion itself, without specific reference to the *actio conducti*. In part this is doubtless a matter of emphasis: as the rules on justified expulsion became fixed and well known, landlords were bound to begin interpreting their duties *ex fide bona* in terms of these concrete rules; so that it was natural for Caracalla to think of a duty imposed in advance on the lessor. However, that is only one aspect of the progressive legalization of this area of landlord-tenant relations. Especially in the later classical period the jurists began to realize the potential of their procedural system to assist the expeller. The following developments can be signaled:

Self-help

It is plain, first of all, that the normal method of expulsion throughout the classical period was self-help, and that the State not only was normally uninvolved in the actual process of expulsion, it even tacitly approved the use of self-help as the legitimate defense of a right. However, with such self-help the Romans felt a natural and growing unease, which is clearly reflected in Marcus Aurelius' famous *decretum* (D. 4.2.13; 48.7.7), even though that emperor fell far short of banning self-help altogether.[65] By the late classical period, a number of procedural alternatives to self-help had evolved.

The Actio Locati

As a mean of expulsion, this would have availed only the tenant's landlord. The use of the *actio locati* for expulsion is problematic; our assessment depends on the extent to which that action had restitutory functions. No classical source clearly indicates that it did; D. 19.2.11.3 (Ulp.) refers to *locatio operis*. Several texts provide that the lessee's "theft" of a leased moveable would subject him to concurrent suits

[65] G. Wesener, in *Fs. Steinwenter* 113-114 (on the decree, pp. 119-120); T. Mayer-Maly, *RE* s.v. "vis" (1960) 319. The most common form of self-help for expulsion is discussed below in the section on "Tenant's Pledges."

ex locato and *furti*;[66] the latter suit was not available in the case of immoveables. None of these texts come from contexts discussing the *actio locati* itself: D. 44.7.34.2 (Paul. *Lib. Sing. de Conc. Act.*) comes from a monograph on concurrence; D. 19.2.42 (Paul. 13 *ad Ed.*) from a comparative discussion of concurrence in relation to quite another theme;[67] and D. 17.2.46 (Paul. 6 *ad Sab.*) from a simple list of concurrences between contractual and *furtum* actions. All three texts are from the late classical jurist Paul, and none makes reference to earlier writers. Further, these texts do not specify the basis for the *actio locati* in such cases; they speak in delictual terms, of a *colonus* "making off with" (*subtraxerit*) an object from a *fundus* (D. 44.7.34.2),[68] or of a person "stealing away with" (*subripias*) a rented slave (D. 19.2.42). The restitutory function of the *actio locati* therefore remains, in the state of the sources, decidedly vague; perhaps it was limited to recovering damages resulting from the failure to restore. Since there would be no doctrinal reason to limit such recovery to moveables, a general contractual liability may be assumed for failure to restore a rented object.

There is no evidence that a *iusiurandum in litem* (a device whereby the plaintiff was allowed, in the late classical period, to set an abnormally high compensatory value on the object being sought, and thus to force its restitution)[69] was ever

[66] See before all D. Liebs, *Konk.* 90-91: the suits were cumulative. Of the texts referred to below, only D. 44.7.34.2 has been held suspect (cf. *Index Interp.*). Somewhat different are D. 12.1.4.1; 47.2.68.5, which do not speak of concurrence; both passages concern *furtum* when fruits are detached from a *fundus* detained by a *colonus* against the owner's will. "*Furtum usus*" is not known for immoveables.

[67] The context concerned the *actio de receptis nautarum* etc., so O. Lenel, *Paling.* 1 992, who notes D. 4.9.3.5 (Ulpian), also on concurrence.

[68] The equivalent in urban lease would be the tenant's removal and appropriation of a fixture, such as a window.

[69] See the views of E. Betti (below, n. 70), and above all S. Schipani, in *Studien M. Kaser* (1971) 194, who considers the legal develop-

used in suits *ex locato* for immoveables. The single source for the *actio locati*, D. 19.2.48.1 (Marcell. 8 *Dig.*), a source which is poor evidence anyway,[70] specifically limits the *iusiurandum* to moveables. The reasons for this limitation (if it existed) were perhaps practical.[71] In any event, it is clear from the absence of discussion that the *iusiurandum* was at the most very rarely used in the *actio locati*.

Two points may be made about the *actio locati* in relation to expulsion. First, the *actio locati* was probably not understood, even in the late classical period, as a direct means of expulsion from urban properties; rather, it acted as a subsidiary threat against a resisting tenant. If the tenant delayed in surrendering the premises, he would be subject to a suit for any damages thereby caused the landlord. Such damages were probably never conceived in relation to the (actual or pretended) value of the rented *res*; rather, they were most likely defined as *id quod interest*.[72] The texts from Paul

---

ment of the *iusiurandum* (though not in specific relation to this question).

[70] "Qui servum conductum vel aliam rem non immobilem non restituit, quanti in litem iuratum fuerit damnabitur."[m] The text is interpolated, at least as to "non immobilem," see *Index Interp.*; G. Broggini, *SZ* 76 (1959) 601, excises "vel aliam rem non immobilem," perhaps rightly, though the original content is probably preserved (the compilers would not have narrowed the classical rule). It is unclear which action is involved: either the *actio locati*, see esp. S. Solazzi, I 77; G. Provera, *Iusiurandum in Litem* (1953) 51-53; A. Watson, *TR* 34 (1966) 183-185; H. Honsell (cited n. 56) 144-146; or the *actio furti*, see esp. E. Levy, *SZ* 36 (1915) 67-68; G. Broggini, in *St. Betti* II 152-155; D. Medicus, 182-184. The question is very close, and E. Betti wavered: *Litis Aestimatio* vol. I (1915) 62-63; vol. III (1919) 17; *Ist.* I 297 n. 69. D. 12.3.5 pr.; 13.6.3.2, both interpolated, are usually considered no evidence for the *iusiurandum* in *bonae fidei iudicia*.

[71] According to Watson (cited n. 70) 184, the limitation to moveables looks toward *relocatio tacita* in the case of immoveables; according to Honsell (cited n. 56) 144, in practice the problem of restitution did not arise in the case of immoveables. Neither view is convincing.

[72] That is, they stood in some relation to the plaintiff's losses as a

apparently show, however, that at least to this extent the limited restitutory function of the *actio locati* was understood already in the classical period; perhaps it was also realized that, in the case of immoveables, the inapplicability of the *actio furti* reduced the effectiveness of the *actio locati* for this purpose.

Second, it is entirely possible that the jurists established a contractual duty to surrender without relation to the term of lease. At any rate, such is the burden of several post-classical constitutions,[73] and no reference to the term of lease is made in the sources on moveables we have just considered. If this view is right, then the resisting tenant would be *ipso facto* in violation of his contractual duty, nò matter under what circumstances he was ordered by his landlord to surrender; it would therefore always be against the tenant's financial interests to resist. Such considerations would help to explain why we find no case of controversy over whether expulsion should occur in classical sources on urban leasehold. Rather, these sources tend to focus on the landlord's reasons for expulsion, which became of crucial importance in an *actio conducti* after a successful expulsion. The tenant was encouraged by the law to evacuate first and sue later.[74]

The Interdicts de Vi and Uti Possidetis

These interdicts were available only to the legitimate possessor:[75] that is, normally to the building's owner, and not to

---

consequence of the defendant's failure to surrender. Such losses could be quite considerable.

[73] C. 8.4.10 (Zeno; A.D. 484), = 4.65.33; C. 4.65.25 (Diocl.; A.D. 293) orders the *colonus* to leave even if he has a property claim. In C. 4.65.32 (Zeno), the urban tenant is ordered to surrender to a new tenant coming *domini voluntate*; nothing is said of the term of lease. In C. 4.65.3, considered above, the term of lease had obviously not yet expired.

[74] Illustrative is D. 19.2.30 pr.: the tenant departs because the owner *says* the building is defective; the truth of this claim is explored later.

[75] See M. Kaser, *RPR*[2] I 396-397; on the possessory interdicts in general, *ibid.* 398-400.

a middleman who might be the tenant's actual landlord. The principal interdictal means for expulsion was the interdict *unde vi* (together with that *de vi armata*). The preserved sources concern only farm lease, but are unequivocal in their phraseology: the resisting tenant transformed himself into an illegitimate possessor and thereby became subject to the interdict *unde vi*, upon the application of which he was obliged to evacuate.[76]

The interdict *uti possidetis* had a supporting function, namely to assist the possessor in exercising the normal functions of possession. The only text concerning urban rental is D. 43.17.3.3 (Ulp. 69 *ad Ed.*):

> Cum inquilinus dominum aedes reficere volentem prohiberet, aeque competere interdictum uti possidetis placuit testarique dominum non prohibere inquilinum, ne habitaret, sed ne possideret.[n]

The landlord who wished to make a repair could use this interdict against a resisting tenant. The last portion of the sentence (especially *testarique* to the end) has been considered interpolated, above all by Beseler, who questioned the character and purpose of the *testatio*.[77] Beseler may be correct. In any event, the interdict *uti possidetis* was being used, here as occasionally elsewhere in classical sources, not as a prelude to vindication,[78] but rather as an instrument to

[76] D. 43.16.12 (Marcell. 19 *Dig.*), 18 pr. (Papin. 26 *Quaest.*): both passages mention in passing the rights of the *dominus*; on them, see before all J.A.C. Thomas, *TR* 41 (1973) 35-44, at 36-37; also, G. Nicosia, *Studi sulla Deiectio* (1965) 160-162; M. Marrone, in *Studi G. Scherillo* vol. 1 (1972) 341-376, at 362-364; *idem, La Legittimazione Passiva alla "Rei Vindicatio"* (1970) 123-125, cf. 133. Expulsion would occur when the tenant was obliged to surrender possession to the plaintiff. The interdict *de vi* also availed the possessor against third parties expelling either his tenants or subtenants: D. 43.16.20; likewise the interdict *quod vi aut clam*: D. 43.24.17.

[77] G. Beseler, *SZ* 43 (1922) 423, who also reversed the ruling in the main sentence; *contra*, as to this, S. Perozzi, 1 870 n. 2. The interpretation here proposed resembles that in A. Hägerström, 1 88 n. 2.

[78] The interdict could of course also be used for this purpose, e.g.

ensure quiet possession.[79] The *testatio*, if it was required, was not designed merely to allay the fears of the tenant that he would be expelled; it also prepared his position in an *actio conducti* should the owner then use the interdict in order to expel him. While parallels are unknown, surely it is not impossible that the praetor could have required such a *testatio* so as to avoid misuse of this interdict.

Rei Vindicatio

This action *in rem* avails the owner (or one exercising the rights of ownership) against a sitting tenant who has offered resistance and thereby taken possession of the premises. Under normal circumstances a vindication could not then be resisted by the tenant, provided that the owner could establish his title.[80] This was the classical view of vindication.

On the strength of the much disputed final sentence of D. 6.1.9 (Ulp. 16 *ad Ed.*),[81] whereby Ulpian, against the earlier classical view, allowed vindication from all those "qui tenent et habent restituendi facultatem," some modern scholars have come to believe that in the late classical period

---

against an upstairs tenant (or another) who was claiming ownership: D. 43.17.3.7 (Ulpian/Labeo), on which see now J. P. Meincke, *SZ* 88 (1971) 160-163.

79 See before all L. Labruna, *Vim Fieri Veto* (1971) 228-229. We know very little about this aspect of the classical interdict. The contractual right of the landlord to make repairs is also known from D. 19.2.27 pr. (on which, below at nn. 211-216). It may be that the landlord also had the right to inspect the premises for defects or damage done by the tenant.

80 There is no clear classical source for this view, though it seems obvious; see, e.g. M. Marrone, *La Legittimazione Passiva* (1970) 133; M. Kaser, *RPR*² I 433.

81 The text was forcefully attacked by H. Siber, *Die Passivlegitimation* (1907) 26-37; see also, e.g. E. Levy, *VL* 228-229; and a long list given by M. Marrone, in *Studi G. Scaduto* (1967) 5 n. 5 (of the extract). As is observed by M. Marrone (cited n. 80) 42-47, the structure of the passage points toward Ulpian's remarks, so that we would have to suppose considerable reworking. The text is defended in large measure by Marrone 54-57, 73-80, cf. 130-133.

a vindicator could have proceeded, at least sometimes, even against a nonpossessing tenant.[82] There are undoubtedly problems with such a position; and recently Matteo Marrone has attempted to limit the seeming sweep of Ulpian's *dictum.*[83] In particular, he seeks to disqualify the urban tenant as a defendant to a vindication, by interpreting the above conditions in a rather narrow sense. It appears to me, however, that even under Marrone's rather stringent rules the urban tenant might still have qualified as a defendant in a vindication[84]—and particularly in circumstances where vindication was an instrument of expulsion and not an assertion of a contested title of ownership. In such cases, Ulpian's legitimation of the tenant would merely amount to eliminating the requirement that the tenant take possession before a vindication could occur.

When a vindication was brought by an owner who was also the tenant's landlord, the nonpossessing tenant would

[82] See before all H. Siber, II 97-98; H. Kunkel, in *Symb. Lenel* 70 n. 6; M. Kaser, *RPR*² I 433. On F.B.J. Wubbe, *Res Aliena Pignori Data* (1960) 151-160, see M. Kaser, *SZ* 78 (1961) 215-216.

[83] Marrone believes that Ulpian requires "exclusive detention" and "the material and juridical possibility of restitution," by which is meant that "neither the defendant nor any third party extraneous to the suit can suffer, as a consequnce of restitution (or production), any prejudice worthy of juridical consideration"; Marrone refers to his own works: *APal* 28 (1961) 49-50, on detention (but n.b. p. 50 n. 11; *tenere* is used of a *colonus* at D. 43.16.1.22); and *Studi G. Scaduto* (1967) 3-12 (of extract), on *facultas restituendi*; see also *idem* in *St. Grosso* VI 175-192; and there also G. Provera, at pp. 209-231.

[84] Marrone starts from an erroneous view of the urban tenantry as socially dependent. But the proofs in Marrone (cited n. 80) 126-130, are mostly mistaken: e.g. the sources at p. 128 n. 212 are all irrelevant; D. 19.2.27 pr. and 43.17.3.3 (examined above) scarcely imply that the landlord could "enter the *habitatio* at will"; Marrone gives a flagrantly erroneous interpretation of D. 19.2.19.5, one at odds with his own *Actio ad Exhibendum* (1958) 318-323; Marrone's social inferences, mostly drawn from A. Pernice, *SZ* 19 (1898) 93-95, and J. Carcopino, *Daily Life* (1941) 22-51, also misconstrue the literary and archaeological evidence.

still probably have been able to avail himself of the *exceptio doli*.[85] Against a third party (including an owner above the tenant on a contractual ladder), this would apparently no longer have been the case.

Interdict de Precario

It appears that toward the end of the classical period leasehold and *precarium* were sometimes combined into a sort of termless "contract" whereby the lessor (abnormally) provided no more under the *precarium* than he did under the leasehold: namely the bare detention of the premises.[86] The main advantage of this new institution was that the grant could be revoked at any time by the grantor, and this right was reinforced by the interdict *de precario*. This interdict had one great advantage:[87] it was available to a landlord who wished to move swiftly in expelling the tenant, while reserving the outstanding contractual questions for a subsequent suit on the contract. This peculiar form of grant-leasehold would have removed from the tenant even the relatively small security of a fixed term of lease. As a legal institution, grant-leasehold was well suited for situations where the tenants were starkly dependent on the will of the

[85] This defense was hypothesized by B. Kübler, *SZ* 29 (1908) 483, reviewing Siber, *Passivlegitimation*; see M. Kaser, *RPR*² 1 433 n. 12. The *exceptio* would perhaps not have availed if the tenant's landlord was a middleman.

[86] M. Kaser, *SZ* 89 (1972) 94-148, at 103-111, using D. 19.2.4; 41.2.10 pr.-2; 41.3.33.6; 43.24.11.12. As regards the first three texts (all probably in postclassical form), the problem is well known, and Kaser cites a large bibliography; notable are G. Scherillo, *RIL* 62 (1929) 9-12 (of the extract), and S. Tondo, *Lab.* 5 (1959) 190-192, who both accepted the classical character of the institution; against are most scholars, including V. Silva, *SD* 6 (1940) 240-242; P. Zamorani, *Precario Habere* (1969) 132-150. The difficulty (as Silva notes, p. 241) is not so much to recognize the institution as to determine its juristic characteristics and function.

[87] M. Kaser (cited n. 86) 106-107. A more regular form of precarian grant, that of *habitatio* of *diaetae superiores*, is mentioned in D. 39.5.32 (Scaev.).

lessor; we should thus think of it in the context of lower-class tenants. However, while one text (D. 43.24.11.12, Ulp.) shows the combination as applied to farm lease, there is no evidence for urban dwellings.

The legal devices brought to bear against the tenant were undeniably impressive. The expeller was allowed to select the grounds that suited him best and were easiest to prove: ownership, possession, the contract, even in some cases the bare grant of detention. We have no definite proof that the tenant could resist any of these claims once it had been substantiated. Furthermore, there is perhaps a movement in these sources away from procedures depending upon the real or simulated use of violence (self-help; the interdict *de vi*; vindication in the "classical" view), and toward procedures that allow the expeller to act at once without such preliminaries (the *actio locati*; vindication in Ulpian's view; the precarian lease form).

It is difficult not to see this development as part of a gradual evolution whereby expulsion, once more or less exclusively a matter of self-help, was being gradually brought into the ambit of State-controlled legal institutions. Both the existence of procedural mechanisms for expulsion and the creation of a doctrine on justified expulsion were necessary in order to achieve this goal: namely, that the expeller must first present for examination his reasons for expulsion, and then, if expulsion were justified, the State accomplished it through appropriate legal pressures. Within the tentative, injury-remedying procedural system of classical Roman law, such a goal was never achieved. We should perhaps think, rather, of the gradually rising prominence of extraordinary cognition, a system that, theoretically at least, gave to the presiding magistrate both the authority to consider legal questions in a far more sweeping fashion and the power to implement his judgments.[88] There is no sign, how-

[88] One must consider, especially, the intervention of the Praefectus Vigilum in the process of *preclusio*; see below at nn. 176-179, and A. dell'Oro, *I Libri de Officio* (1960) 253-254.

ever, that the stunted jurisprudence of the late Empire led this evolution to its goal.

Justified Abandonment

The usual word for tenant abandonment is *migrare*, that is, to change residences.[89] Juristic sources occasionally employ, as apparent synonyms, words such as *relinquere* or *deserere*,[90] which signify the crucial aspect of *migratio*, namely that the tenant has left his former dwelling for good and intends not to live there again. It is perhaps typical of Roman jurisprudence that in surviving sources the concept of *migratio* was never precisely defined;[91] the noun *migratio*, though it is good classical Latin, was not used by the jurists.

The tenant could abandon his dwelling at any time; however, he could be prevented from removing his furnishings if he had not satisfied his landlord as to the rent (see following section). Also, whether the tenant owed rent for the period from the abandonment to the end of the term of the lease was a question of whether his abandonment was justified (in which case he did not owe rent) or unjustified (in which case he did). The structure of juristic thought for abandonment was thus broadly similar to that on expulsion, save that the tenant was required to pay all outstanding rent (instead of *id quod interest* damages) in the case of unjustified abandonment.

The principal source on unjustified abandonment is D. 19.2.24.2 (Paul. 34 *ad Ed.*):

Si domus vel fundus in quinquennium pensionibus locatus

[89] *Migrare* is first in Alfenus (D. 19.2.30 pr.) and Labeo (D. 32.30.5); *emigrare* in Alfenus (D. 19.2.27.1; 39.2.43.1; otherwise not found in the jurists); an excellent illustration of its meaning in Cic. 2 *Verr.* 2.89; *emigratio* occurs in D. 39.2.28 (Ulpian), though in no conceptualized usage.

[90] *Deserere*: D. 19.2.24.2; *relinquere*: D. 19.2.25.2, cf. 50.1.27.1.

[91] The concept of *domicilium* was, however, available for this purpose; cf. D. 9.3.1.9; 50.1.27.1 (both Ulpian).

sit, potest dominus, si deseruerit habitationem vel fundi culturam colonus vel inquilinus, cum eis statim agere.°

This fragment, despite its undeniable awkwardness, is probably not interpolated;[92] all the details of the text, including the multiple-year lease,[93] are just as applicable to dwellings as to farms. In either case, the landlord could sue *ex locato* (obviously, for unpaid *pensiones*) after abandonment had occurred. Further, we are also specifically told that the tenant must pay the rent if he had the power to take a property in leasehold and did not use that power (D. 19.2.28.2, Lab. 4 *Post. Epit. a Iav.*);[94] and also that the urban tenant's pledges could be retained until he satisfied the landlord on the account of all *pensiones* not yet paid (D. 43.32.1.4, Ulp. 73 *ad Ed.*, citing Labeo).

These texts seem at first to establish what we might call a "duty to reside"; the tenant, by unjustifiably abandoning the property, makes himself at once liable for all the outstanding rent, and hence he is strongly encouraged to remain in the dwelling for the entire term. In fact, however, the sources are ambiguous on this point, and allow the alternative explanation that the tenant continues to be liable for the rent only as it falls due (an alternative which I consider to be classical law). Gaius 4.131, which provides exactly that solution when a stipulation for a series of payments has been made, supports this: If the stipulator sues before some of the payments fall due, he must insert a *praescriptio* (cf. above,

[92] All the references to urban lease are interpolated, at least according to S. Solazzi, *Studi G.P. Chironi* vol. 1 (1915) 595 n. 2 (the citation in the *Ind.* is from an extract); G. Longo, *Ric.* 532 (article published 1953). Even more radical: G. Beseler, *SZ* 53 (1933) 53, who also involved D. 19.2.24.3. These views were then combined in T. Mayer-Maly, *LC* 139-140. But similarly awkward texts are met elsewhere, without arousing suspicion; e.g. D. 19.2.25.1. The core of the text is defended by E. Nardi, *Case "Infestate da Spiriti"* (1960) 63 n. 43. On these texts, see also D. Medicus, 182; H. Honsell, *Quod Interest* (1969) 182.

[93] See D. 19.2.60 pr.; 20.4.13; 43.32.1.4; *CIL* 4.1136 (= *FIRA* 3.143b).

[94] See above all M. Kaser, *SZ* 74 (1957) 160.

n. 34) in his *condictio incerti*, or else he will lose his claim to future payments. Gaius 4.131a implies that this logic prevailed also for *bona fide* contracts. By contrast, D. 19.2.55.2 (= Paul. *Sent.* 2.18.5) discusses a tenant's breaking of a lease clause through his abandonment of a farm *sine iusta ac probabili causa*;[95] in that event, the owner can obtain *ex locato* the *totius temporis pensiones*. This text should probably be explained through reference to the special lease clause.

As D. 19.2.55.2 suggests, it is *iusta causa* that forms the core of Roman thinking on justified abandonment, and this is also true for urban lease. The juristic sources seem to establish, though the evidence is fragmentary, a list of justifications for a tenant abandoning the premises and refusing to pay any further rent. Since nothing survives that is comparable to the list of grounds for justified expulsion in C. 4.65.3, our knowledge in this area is limited to the categories mentioned in scattered sources.

The earliest such source is D. 19.2.27.1 (Alf. 2 *Dig.*):

> Iterum interrogatus est, si quis timoris causa emigrasset, deberet mercedem necne. respondit, si causa fuisset, cur periculum timeret, quamvis periculum vere non fuisset, tamen non debere mercedem: sed si causa timoris iusta non fuisset, nihilo minus debere.[P]

The tenant has abandoned his dwelling because of fear; if there was *causa* for this fear, then whether or not there was a *periculum*, he owes no further rent; but if the *causa timoris*

[95] This phrase caught the critical eye of G. Beseler, 1 5-6; accepted by G. Longo, *Ric.* 532. The original probably had only *sine* (*iusta*?) *causa*: E. Nardi (cited n. 92) 64 n. 44, citing *Basilica* 20.1.54 (= Heimb. 2.363-364; Schelt. *BT* 995). The last clause of this text ("quatenus . . . servetur"), which limits the landlord's claim to *id quod interest*, is undoubtedly interpolated, cf. *Index Interp.*; and note the *Basilica*, which strike out the claim for rent altogether, as also in their version of D. 19.2.24.2 (*Bas.* 20.1.24.2, = Heimb. 2.349-350; Schelt. BT 989 and BS 1189 no. 5). On the question, see also below at nn. 261-264.

was not *iusta*, he does owe rent. The text, which has been only lightly criticized,[96] is specifically attributed by the *Basilica* to Ser. Sulpicius Rufus, the teacher of Alfenus.[97] The fragment has the sweeping and overstated quality of a breakthrough. The two crucial terms, *periculum* and *iusta causa timoris*, are left entirely undefined; must the danger be (at least in part) of physical character, or are purely psychological fears also embraced? Nor is it clear whether the tenant's fear is to be objectively or subjectively defined. The alternatives can be illustrated: an *insula* creaks in the wind, and the tenant, fearing its collapse, abandons the building. An analysis can begin with Servius' belief that it is unreasonable to require a tenant to remain in, and pay rent for, a dwelling which will probably collapse. But in evaluating whether a specific case meets the standard of Servius, we may on the one hand look to the reasons that justify abandonment by a particular man (and that would include an account of his personality: was he e.g. actually frightened at the time of the abandonment? is he exceptionally timorous?);[98] or on the other hand we may try to typify the situation, by asking whether a "reasonable" man would have concluded in this situation that the building was about to collapse and that he should therefore leave. The Roman

[96] F. B. Bremer, who was widely followed (e.g. by Krueger), excised *tamen* and the last sentence: *Iurisprudentia Antehadriana* vol. 1 (1896) 316; but left them alone at p. 205. However, *tamen* is required by *quamvis*, and I cannot regard the last clause as superfluous. G. Beseler, v 11, began the process of further whittling down the text; compare F. Schulz, *Principles* 227 n. 3; L. de Sarlo, *Alfeno Varo* (1940) 98-99; G. Longo, *Ric.* 533, 539; T. Mayer-Maly, *LC* 217. The text has recently been defended by A. Watson, *Obl.* 115-116; and, somewhat more prudently, by E. Nardi (cited n. 92) 66 n. 51. To my mind the entire passage is defensible. Nardi (pp. 63-71) discusses fear as a motive for abandoning a house.

[97] *Bas.* 20.1.27.1 (= Heimb. 2.354; Schelt. BT 990). Cf. F. Horak, 106 and n. 16.

[98] E. Nardi (cited n. 92) 66 n. 51 (at the end), and A. Guarino, *Lab.* 6 (1960) 424-427, argue (wrongly) for a subjective interpretation of *timor* in this passage.

jurists apparently limited *iusta causa timoris* to direct physical threats (especially to the tenant's life) that could be objectively determined.

The problem of *iusta causa timoris* can be approached from two different ways. To what extent is a tenant obliged to resist his subjective fears? D. 19.2.13.7 (Ulp. 32 *ad Ed.*):

> Exercitu veniente migravit conductor, dein de hospitio milites fenestras et cetera sustulerunt. si domino non denuntiavit et migravit, ex locato tenebitur: Labeo autem, si resistere potuit et non resistit, teneri ait, quae sententia vera est. sed et si denuntiare non potuit, non puto eum teneri.[q]

An army (probably not a hostile army)[99] approaches; the tenant abandons the premises; the soldiers quarter there and strip the dwelling. Must the tenant pay for the damage done by the soldiers?[100] Ulpian puts three propositions: if the tenant leaves without informing the *dominus*, he is liable for the damage; but if he was *able* to resist the soldiers and did not, he is liable, according to Labeo (whom Ulpian supports). By analogy, so Ulpian maintains, he is liable only if he was *able* to inform the *dominus*. The text is probably not interpolated.[101] It is the second rule that interests us; Ulpian sets it in no hierarchical relation to the first and third.

What was it that Labeo required of the tenant? His rule is not so crudely mechanical as it first seems; much hinges on the ambiguity of *potuit*, since the rule (at least, in Ulpian's

[99] T. Mayer-Maly, *SZ* 74 (1957) 363-373, at 368-373.

[100] That is clear from the context, where the liability of the lessee for damages to the lessor's property is being discussed: D. 19.2.13 pr.-8.

[101] Some have claimed to detect interpolations: e.g. F. Haymann, *SZ* 40 (1919) 235-236; H. H. Pflüger, *SZ* 65 (1947) 202-203: in Labeo's rule, *resistit* is used instead of *restiterit*, *potuit* and not *potuerit*; also, *sed et* is illogical. T. Mayer-Maly (cited n. 99) 371-372 (bibliography at p. 371 n. 50), presumes postclassical shortening. However, the verbs are acceptable if *resistit* is emended to *restitit*; and *sed et* shows how the third rule was formed by Ulpian through the analogy of Labeo's rule.

version of it) leaves unclear whether and how the tenant was expected to ascertain in advance his ability to resist what could be a frightening unknown. In any event, at the minimum he could not simply give in to his subjective fear of the worst and abandon the premises without thought of his leasehold; and it was not impossible for a *iudex* to reconstruct, albeit with the benefit of hindsight, whether a "reasonable" man would have taken flight in this situation, by using such criteria as the normalcy of the event, the size of the army, the amount of damage done by the soldiers elsewhere, the reaction of others, and so on.

If we consider a parallel passage, this interpretation gains strength. The second rule in D. 19.2.13.7 stresses the objective ability of the tenant to resist an approaching army. The concept of *vis, cui resisti non potest*, recurs in a famous and much disputed passage, D. 19.2.15.2 (Ulp. 32 *ad Ed.*, citing Servius), where the distribution of risks in farm lease is discussed;[102] an example of irresistible *vis* is (in the text as preserved) an *incursus hostium*, and here the *locator* bears the risk of catastrophic damage to the crops. Later in the

[102] (An excerpted version): ". . . Servius omnem vim, cui resisti non potest, dominum colono praestare debere ait, ut puta . . . si incursus hostium fiat: . . . si vero nihil extra consuetudinem acciderit, damnum coloni esse. idemque dicendum, si exercitus praeteriens per lasciviam aliquid abstulit. . . ."[r] The bibliography on this passage is enormous; but modern authors are not inclined to solve its problems by presupposing interpolations. See T. Mayer-Maly, *LC* 161-162, 192-193 (earlier bibliography at p. 161 n. 43); M. Kaser, *SZ* 74 (1957) 169-174; T. Mayer-Maly (cited n. 99) 368-370; E. Betti, in *St. de Francisci* I 192-193; T. Mayer-Maly, in *Fs. Steinwenter* 58-77 (on *vis*); G. Nicosia, in *Riv. It.* 9 (1957/1958) 404-415; E. Betti, *SZ* 82 (1965) 18-20; G. Provera, in *St. Betti* III 722-723; J. Miquel, *SZ* 81 (1964) 172-175; R. Seager, *SD* 31 (1965) 330-333; C. Alzon, *Lab.* 12 (1966) 312-319; A. Watson, *Obl.* 110-115; H. Ankum, *RIDA*³ 19 (1972) 223-228; A. Thomas, in *St. Donatuti* III 1271-1277; J.M.Y. Chorus, *Handelen in Strijd met de Wet* (1976) 149-156. The problems of the passage probably defy a doctrinaire solution. Note that the sentence beginning "idem dicendum" assigns liability to the tenant—against the *Basilica* and most modern commentaries.

same text Ulpian discusses what befalls the farm *nihil extra consuetudinem*, in the ordinary course. An example of such *vis* is pilferage *per lasciviam*; in this second case the risk is borne by the *colonus*. These two examples seem to fall on either side of Labeo's rule in D. 19.2.13.7. A possible explanation of the distinction is that, in the one case, a *colonus* is hardly expected to resist an enemy attack; while, in the other, he may legitimately be expected to deal with the casual violence of a passing (and nominally friendly) army.

However, if the tenant was required, where resistance was possible, to remain in the building and resist, on the pain of being otherwise liable for resultant damage, it is improbable that, where resistance was possible, there could also have been a *iusta causa timoris* for the abandonment of the premises. Indeed, the tenant's liability for resultant damage surely results from the fact that there was no such *iusta causa*. Labeo therefore required from the tenant that he make a reasonable assessment of the danger before abandoning the dwelling. To this extent Labeo objectified the *iusta causa timoris* of Servius.

This understanding of D. 19.2.13.7 seems even more likely to be correct when we consider the situation from the viewpoint of the landlord. A number of pertinent texts in D. 39.2 (*De Damno Infecto*) describe situations where an owner of an urban property, fearing the collapse of a neighbor's building, avails himself of the praetorian *cautio damni infecti*, whereby the neighbor must promise recompense for future damages resulting from the building's precarious condition.[103]

[103] Beyond the texts cited below, note also D. 39.2.43.1 (Alf. 2 *Dig.*, citing Servius): the *habitatores ex vicinis cenaculis* abandon their dwellings when a party wall between two buildings is removed; because of a private stipulation covering losses from the demolition, the owner of the other building must recompense the "mercedem, quam habitatores non redderent." As to this (at least) the text is not interpolated: cf. *Index Interp.* In general cases, the *cautio* could also be sought by neighboring *inquilini*, their wives and guests (D. 39.2.13.5); also by a *filiusfamilias* who was a tenant (D. 39.2.21).

D. 39.2.28 (Ulp. 81 *ad Ed.*) is especially relevant. The passage begins with a citation from Cassius as to the extent of damages covered by the stipulation. It concludes:

> . . . in eadem causa est detrimentum quoque propter emigrationem inquilinorum, quod ex iusto metu factum est. Aristo autem non male adicit, sicuti hic exigit Cassius, ut si iustus metus migrandi causam praebuerit, ita in eius personam qui fulsit eadem Cassium dicere debuisse, si iusto metu ruinae fulcire coactus est.[s]

The first sentence cited above is not interpolated.[104] According to Cassius, the damages included lost rents when *inquilini* left the structure *ex iusto metu.* Again in this case the text carefully specifies that the *inquilini* had to be justified in their fear of the neighbor's building collapsing; for, if the fear of the *inquilini* was "unjustified," it is surely the case that the landlord's proper recourse was to recover his lost rents by suing his tenants *ex locato.*[105]

The tenant could also legitimately abandon his dwelling if he feared that his own building would collapse. D. 39.2.13.6 (Ulp. 53 *ad Ed.*), 33 (Ulp. 42 *ad Sab.*):

> 13.6. De illo quaeritur, an inquilinis suis dominus aedium cavere possit. et Sabinus ait inquilinis non esse cavendum: aut enim ab initio vitiosas aedes conduxerunt et habent quod sibi imputent, aut in vitium aedes inciderunt et possunt ex conducto experiri: quae sententia verior est.[t]
>
> 33. Inquilino non datur damni infecti actio, quia possit ex conducto agere, si dominus eum migrare prohiberet.[u]

The first passage indicates that the *dominus* cannot be forced

[104] Though G. Beseler was suspicious: *SZ* 51 (1931) 76-77, especially as to *ex iusto metu*; so also G. Longo, *Ric.* 533 n. 12; Mayer-Maly, *LC* 217. The text is ably defended by E. Nardi (cited n. 92) 69 n. 37. In the second sentence, read *eis* for the first *si* (so Mommsen). Lost prospective rents were also recoverable: D. 39.2.29.

[105] Unjustified abandonment is considered above. It is doubtful that the landlord could pursue damages from his neighbor if his tenant's abandonment was *unjustified.*

to give a *cautio* to his own tenants,[106] because either they assumed the risk by making the contract, or, if the building "slipped into disrepair" during the term of rent, the *inquilini* can sue *ex conducto*.[107] The second passage, which was perhaps interpolated only by the substitution of *actio* for *cautio*, indicates that the purpose of a suit *ex conducto* would be: not the recovery of damages (the building has not yet collapsed), but establishment of the right to *migrare*. In other words, the suit involved the appropriateness of justified abandonment.

These texts help to illustrate why the classical jurists were both careful to objectify the causes of justified abandonment through fear, and also extremely cautious about extending the circumstances under which an *inquilinus* could justifiably abandon his dwelling.[108] When an *inquilinus* abandoned his dwelling justifiably, the lease was in effect ended, in the sense that the tenant could not be obliged to pay further rent nor to return;[109] therefore these rents were effectively lost to the landlord for the remainder of the term of lease, unless the landlord could either persuade the tenant to return or find a substitute tenant. In a way this was fair, since

[106] The text was suspected (in unimportant details) by G. Beseler, *TR* 8 (1928) 306; and *idem*, III 122; T. Mayer-Maly, *LC* 154; but defended by M. Kaser, *SZ* 74 (1957) 184 n. 120; E. Nardi (cited n. 92) 68 n. 55. We must suppose (from "quae sententia verior est") a difference of opinion which has been suppressed; it may therefore be that some jurists allowed the tenant to extract a *cautio* from the owner of his own building, perhaps when the owner was not the tenant's direct landlord. If the tenant lived in a building adjacent to another one owned by his landlord, a *cautio* could be obtained for the latter: D. 39.2.18.3.

[107] This use of the *actio ex conducto* is discussed below. On D. 39.2.33, see G. Branca, *Danno Temuto* (1937) 355.

[108] We should probably add to the preserved discussions the fear of an approaching fire (*iustus metus ignis* justifies unusual measures in another context: D. 9.2.49.1, Ulp. 9 *Disp.*, "sive pervenit ignis sive ante extinctus est"); but not the fear of ghosts, cf. E. Nardi (cited n. 92) 178-179.

[109] So much is clear from D. 19.2.27.1, and also 60 pr., concerning expulsion.

the tenant would no doubt at once seek other housing; to ask him to return to his former dwelling when the danger was past was undeniably to complicate his situation (cf. D. 19.2.24.4, farm lease). However, the "all or nothing" requirement led to the creation of what may seem like rather rigid standards, especially since the "resistibility" of a danger is apt to be clear only in hindsight.[110] The standards for measuring the objective responsibility of the tenant's conduct are not discussed by the jurists. Nor is it entirely clear why "fear" should have been taken as the common denominator in assessing a number of reasons for abandonment that are otherwise quite diverse. Perhaps the explanation is nothing more than the transparent common sense of Servius' original proposition.

Despite the difficulties in this area, jurists proved willing to extend the list of causes beyond fear, so as to include the architectural features of the dwelling. The principal text is D. 19.2.25.2 (Gaius 10 *ad Ed. Prov.*):

> Si vicino aedificante obscurentur lumina cenaculi, teneri locatorem inquilino: certe quin liceat colono vel inquilino relinquere conductionem, nulla dubitatio est. de mercibus quoque si cum eo agatur, reputationis ratio habenda est. eadem intellegemus, si ostia fenestrasve nimium corruptas locator non restituat.[v]

The text has been variously criticized,[111] but by and large

[110] Further, the danger may never have existed at all (D. 19.2.27.1): the army may have already been stopped short of the dwelling, or the building may have been proved, despite apparent evidence to the contrary, structurally sound. It should be observed that, if the parties were still willing, the lease could be resumed at a later point within the term of lease, after the "emergency" had passed. No rent was due for the interval. Cf. above at nn. 41-42.

[111] The words *colono vel* are presumably a generalizing interpolation, and *habitationem* may therefore have been altered to *conductionem*. The rest of the text is substantially genuine, cf. M. Kaser (cited n. 102) 184 n. 121; A. Rodger, *Owners and Neighbors* (1972) 87-89 (bibliography at p. 87 n. 4); *contra*: A. Last, *Jherings Jb.* 62

unfairly. Two problems are set: in the one case, a neighbor's construction has partially blocked ("obscured") the windows of the tenant's *cenaculum*; in the other, the *locator* has not (obviously, after complaints) fixed doors and windows that are broken. Light and security were perhaps the only two architectural amenities of which Roman apartments could regularly boast, and the collocation of the two is hardly accidental. Furthermore, the sequence of actions described in the text also recalls D. 39.2.13.6 and 33 (examined above): the consequences of the new circumstances are, first, that the tenant can sue *ex conducto* and can also abandon the apartment; second (here D. 19.2.25.2 goes further), the tenant can also (*quoque*) resist a suit for rent that comes due thereafter.

Some slight support for this view of D. 19.2.25.2 can probably be derived from D. 39.2.37 (Ulp. 42 *ad Ed.*). The text discusses the situation where a neighbor has demolished an allegedly unsafe but actually sound wall that belongs to another; this latter can seek recompense. Unfortunately, the text has been heavily interpolated to support the (postclassical) duty of the neighbor to rebuild the wall.[112] The last two sentences of the passage read:

> . . . sed et si qui reditus ob demolitionem amissus est, consequenter restitui eum Sabinus voluit. si forte habitatores migraverunt aut non tam commode habitare possunt, imputari id aedificatori potest.[w]

(1913) 98 n. 3, who excised "certe . . . dubitatio est"; G. Longo, *Ric.* 526, and T. Mayer-Maly, *LC* 153, who also removed the last sentence, wrongly. (On the importance of doors and windows, cf. D. 6.1.59; 19.2.19.4, both discussed below at nn. 227ff.; and note the existence of a special class of thieves specializing in house- and *cenaculum*-breaking, Ulp. D. 47.11.7.) G. Beseler sniped at the text: v 37; *SZ* 57 (1937) 44 (*nimium*); *SZ* 66 (1948) 355 (*reputatio*). It is not improbable that "certe . . . dubitatio est" replaced an earlier, somewhat more tentative sentence; cf. below at n. 222.

[112] So G. Branca (cited n. 107) 493-494. D. Medicus, 270 n. 33, calls his criticism "exaggerated," without elaboration.

The first sentence has not been attacked as interpolated; the second has, and with considerable justice.[113] However, it is surely possible to see this latter sentence, in what we can suppose was its original form, as Ulpian's illustration of the rule given by Sabinus. But there is no suggestion in the text that the *habitatores* evacuated because they felt in danger as a result of the demolition, and (though we can only hope that these vague words reflect the original) the implication of *non tam commode* is probably enough to bring this text within the ambit of the "comfort and security" rule in D. 19.2.25.2. Since the owner, as a consequence of *migratio*, lost the rents of the *habitatores*, it should be concluded that their abandonment was justified.

The two texts that deal with comfort and security are not at all specific (how much must the lights be obscured,[114] and must the entire apartment be affected? How broken-down is "too" broken-down?); it seems safe to conclude that this ground for justified abandonment, which probably developed considerably later than the "fear" rule (Gaius is the first to attest it), left rather more to the socially formed

[113] A critique especially in G. Branca, *Riv. It.* n.s. 7 (1932) 252-254; G. Beseler, III 19, 123; *SZ* 56 (1936) 97; *SZ* 57 (1937) 2, 7, 9; *SZ* 66 (1948) 373; *contra*, as to the last sentence, D. Medicus, 270, who considers it perhaps a gloss, but in substance genuine, illustrating the previous sentence. Linguistic objections are produced by Beseler and Branca against *tam*, *commode*, *imputari*, *aedificatori*, and *potest*. The original text probably allowed the plaintiff to complain of two sorts of damages: (1) lost rents due to abandonment; (2) reduced rents due to *deductio ex mercede* (see below at n. 223). The present text is an abbreviated account, not a gloss.

[114] However, comparison with D. 7.1.30 and 8.2.10, on which see A. Rodger (cited n. 111) 56-76, suggests that the tenant had more rights against his landlord than did the legatee of an adjacent building against the heir. Marcellus, in both places, remarks that the legatee cannot prevent the heir from (partially) obscuring his lights, and that the legatee must be content with "modicum lumen" (D. 7.1.30), "quantum sufficit habitantibus in usus diurni moderatione" (D. 8.2.10); for, after all, "habitare autem potest et aedibus obscuratis"[x] (D. 8.2.10, cf. 7.1.30). This latter, however, is below the standard of performance in D. 19.2.25.2.

discretion of the *iudex*. Nonetheless, this new reason for justified abandonment was also easily susceptible of "objective" analysis.

It is very probable that the preserved list of grounds for justified abandonment is not complete. Thus, it is clear from D. 19.2.60 pr., discussed above at nn. 41-42, that where a dwelling is being used both for residence and for sublease, the tenant is justified in abandoning if he cannot show the building to prospective lessees before the rental year begins; this decision, however, is better set in relation to the commercial-lease category of "frustration of evident business purpose," a category represented, for example, by the famous decision on the cheese factory at Minturnae (D. 8.5.8.5, Ulp. 17 *ad Ed.*, citing Aristo).

All of the passages on justified abandonment have in common, first, that they deal with circumstances which had arisen during the term of lease, and which might have been thought to alter in some fundamental way the conditions under which the tenant had originally adhered to the lease. In particular, D. 39.2.13.6, which argues that the *inquilinus* cannot have a *cautio damni infecti* from his landlord because: *either* he rented a building that was defective to begin with;[115] *or* the building "slipped into disrepair" during the term of lease (in which event the tenant could abandon), ignores the problem of latent defects that become apparent only after the tenant occupies the dwelling (but cf. D. 19.2.19.1, farm lease).

Second, it is noteworthy that the grounds for justified abandonment usually reflect physical circumstances that could be either directly verified or at least easily attested. The disorderliness of the *insula*, noise from neighbors, and the like (which occasion so-called "constructive eviction") are not mentioned as grounds for abandonment.

In general, it may also be observed that this subject is considered by the jurists without regard to whether or not

[115] This aspect of the text is dealt with below, at n. 217.

the landlord was in a position to have avoided the circumstances leading to the abandonment; sometimes he was, sometimes he was not. The situation, however, is invariably seen from the tenant's viewpoint: under what circumstances was he justified in abandoning? It is probably not helpful, therefore, to invoke the concept of a landlord's warranty in relation to these sources, though obviously the landlord could himself reduce, in many cases, the risk of the tenant's justified abandonment.

Tenant's Pledges and the Interdict de Migrando

The way the jurists thought about justified expulsion and justified abandonment is in one respect by modern standards remarkable, namely that it does not emphasize the importance of the term of lease. This is probably in large part a consequence of the great length of Roman leases, which often ran to multiple years. Over so long a period, circumstances could arise, on one side or the other, which might lead to a disruption of the lease through expulsion or abandonment. In a subsequent suit we would anticipate that the remainder of the term of lease would be invoked primarily as an instrument in determining the amount of damages (if any) owed to the injured party; and so in fact it was, as we have seen.

It was at this point that a major complication arose. For while the tenant was legally entitled to leave the dwelling at any time, he did not enjoy the same freedom for his furnishings, which (at first only by express agreement) were a pledge to the landlord for the tenant's payment of rent.

The principal device regulating the subsequent disposition of such pledges was the interdict *de migrando*, the text of which is given by D. 43.32.1 pr. (Ulp. 73 *ad Ed.*):

> Praetor ait: "Si is homo, quo de agitur, non est ex his rebus, de quibus inter te et actorem convenit, ut, quae in eam habitationem qua de agitur introducta importata ibi

> nata factave essent, ea pignori tibi pro mercede eius habitationis essent, sive ex his rebus est et ea merces tibi soluta eove nomine satisfactum est aut per te stat, quo minus solvatur: ita, quo minus ei, qui eum pignoris nomine induxit, inde abducere liceat, vim fieri veto."[y]

The defendant of this interdict was ordered to allow the plaintiff-tenant to remove an object (e.g. a slave): (1) *if* the object was *not* one of those things concerning which the two parties had agreed that the tenant's furnishings ("things moved in, brought in, originating or made there")[116] should serve the defendant as a pledge for the rent of the dwelling; or (2) if the object *was* one of those things, but (a) the rent had already been paid to the defendant, or (b) the tenant had provided security for the rent, or (c) the defendant himself was responsible for its nonpayment. A few questions have been raised about the text,[117] but it is basically sound.

The date of the interdict is unknown, but it must have been introduced into the Edict at least by the reign of

[116] The phrase "introducta importata ibi nata factave" occurs only here; elsewhere the jurists use "inducta (et / vel) illata," D. 20.2.4 pr., 7.1; C. 4.65.5; or "invecta (et) illata," D. 2.14.4; 11.7.14.1; 13.7.11.5; 20.2.2, 6, cf. 3; or just "invecta," D. 20.2.5. The nearest equivalent to the phrasing in D. 43.32.1 pr. is D. 20.1.32 (Scaev., farm lease): "inducta invecta importata ibi nata paratave"; this is probably a quotation from the *interdictum Salvianum*, though that suggestion is not taken up by O. Lenel, *EP* 490-492.

[117] For *actorem*, read *illum*, O. Lenel, *Paling.* II 849, cf. *EP* 490, taken up (rightly) by Krueger; while A. Berger, *RE* s.v. "interdictum" (1916) 1644, conjectured *conductorem*, followed by H. Kreller, *SZ* 64 (1944) 314. For mss. "sive ex his rebus *esset*," Mommsen, whom I follow, read "est et." For "ei, qui eum pignoris nomine induxit," Lenel, *EP* 490 n. 11, and Berger restored *illi eum*; but Kreller was content to insert *eum* before *abducere*, correctly (so also the *Basilica*, 60.19.1, = Heimb. 5.608). On the text see also F.B.J. Wubbe, *Res Aliena Pignori Data* (1960) 177-180; cf. P. Frezza, II 303-305, on whom M. Talamanca, *Iura* 15 (1964) 388. The interdict is perpetual, and is both actively and passively inheritable: D. 43.32.1.6. It presumes the existence of a valid lease.

Augustus, when Labeo (see D. 43.32.1.4) commented on it.[118]

The interdict was very closely written, but it still left open a number of questions:

(1) Granted that an agreement on furnishings as a pledge was common in Roman leases,[119] was an express agreement required? This question was at first answered affirmatively, so it appears, but toward the end of the first century A.D. Neratius described a tacit agreement to this effect as implied in every case (D. 20.2.4 pr., 1 *Membr.*), excepting apparently only leases where the opposite had been expressly provided; further, he extended the doctrine to include the contents of outbuildings on the same property (D. 20.2.4.1).[120] Thereafter the doctrine of tacit pledge appears also in other authors.[121]

[118] It should be observed that the *interdictum Salvianum* and the *actio Serviana*, both originally concerned with farm lease (M. Kaser, *RPR*² 1 472-473), are approximately contemporary with the interdict *de migrando*; this latter may have come into existence as a consequence of the thought of Ser. Sulpicius Rufus, elsewhere responsible for so much of the classical law of urban leasehold.

[119] Note above all the inclusion of such a term in the *lex horreorum*: *CIL* 6.33747, 37795 (= *FIRA* 3.145a, c); this even after Neratius had implied the pledge (D. 20.2.3, Ulpian/Nerat.; a classical controversy may be suppressed in this text).

[120] On the text, see before all W. Schuller, *Lab.* 15 (1969) 268-284, at 272-275 (with literature); Schuller rescued many important texts from exaggerated *Interpolationskritik*. See also J. De Churruca, in *Labeo* 23 (1977) 249. On silent *conventio*, see W. Mühl, *Tacere, Tacitus und Taciturnitas* (1961) 16-20; it is still rejected by H. Wagner, *Voraussetzungen, Vorstufen, und Anfänge der Römischen Generalverpfändung* (1968) 14-15. The classic attack on *pignus tacitum* was by P. Koschaker, in *Fs. Hanausek* 152, widely followed; but cf. now A. Wacke, *SZ* 90 (1973) 224, 226. J. De Churruca, *RIDA*³ 24 (1977) 189-231, unfortunately arrived too late for use in this section.

[121] D. 20.2.6 (Ulp. 73 *ad Ed.*); D. 2.14.4 pr. (Paul 3 *ad Ed.*); cf. D. 24.3.7.11 (Ulp. 31 *ad Ed.*). By contrast, the extension of the rule to lodging houses (*deversoria*) was still controversial in the late classical period; cf. D. 20.2.3 (Ulpian / Nerat.).

(2) Granted that the payment of rent was a good faith obligation bound to other contractual obligations, did the pledge of furnishings cover other tenant obligations besides the rent? By the mid-second century A.D. Pomponius was willing to maintain that the pledge covered not only the rent, but also any damages for which the *culpa* of the tenant was responsible and for which the landlord had an *actio locati* (D. 20.2.2, Marc. *Lib. Sing. ad Form. Hyp.*, quoting Pomp.).[122]

(3) Must, therefore, *at least* the contractual payment of rent (i.e. a lease) be involved? This question is answered with regard to the interdict by Ulpian (D. 43.32.1.3, 73 *ad Ed.*):

> Si tamen gratuitam quis habitationem habeat, hoc interdictum utile ei competet.[z]

The occupant who has a free dwelling can avail himself of an analogous (*utile*) form of the interdict.[123] He obviously qualifies under the first heading of the interdict: he has made no agreement with the other party, even tacitly, concerning pledges for rent. The situation described in 43.32.1.3 can arise in two ways: the plaintiff can be the guest of the defendant to the interdict; or (more interestingly) the plaintiff can be the guest of the defendant's tenant. This latter situation is specifically provided for by D. 20.2.5 pr. (Marc. *Lib. Sing. ad Form. Hyp.*, citing Pomp.):

> Pomponius libro tertio decimo Variarum Lectionum scribit, si gratuitam habitationem conductor mihi praestiterit, invecta a me domino insulae pignori non esse.[aa]

[122] On the text, W. Schuller (cited n. 120) 280; it has never been seriously suspected.

[123] Minor objection has been taken to *competet* (so already Krueger), and H. Kreller (cited n. 117) 315, suggested *redditur*. G. Beseler, *SZ* 57 (1937) 22, wrongly thought of excising *gratuitam*. On the *utile* interdict, cf. M. Kaser, *RZ* 321.

This text, which is not interpolated,[124] is very important. The *invecta* of a tenant's guest are not a pledge to the owner of the *insula*; therefore (following D. 43.32.1.3) the quest can employ an *interdictum utile* against the owner.

(4) Are all objects whatsoever that are brought into the tenant's dwelling considered as pledged furnishings?[125] This question was much more difficult to answer. However, there arose various categories of things not included in the pledge, which the tenant could therefore recover through the interdict.

(4a) Casually introduced objects were not included. D. 20.2.7.1 (Pomp. 13 *ex Var. Lect.*):

> Videndum est, ne non omnia illata vel inducta, sed ea sola, quae, ut ibi sint, illata fuerint, pignori sint: quod magis est.[ab]

Therefore, objects not introduced into the dwelling with the intention that they remain were not pledged.[126] This category would probably include, for instance, the property or slaves of the tenant[127] or of his guests when these were

[124] No serious doubts have been raised; see W. Schuller (cited n. 120) 280.

[125] To judge from D. 20.4.11.2 (farm lease), the mere promise to bring something in was insufficient, and a previous pledge on the object took priority (cf. D. 20.4.21.1). Instances of things "originating or made" in the dwelling are not mentioned and were no doubt rare: e.g. a child born to a slave, D. 43.33.1 pr. (farm lease), cf. D. 20.1.29.1.

[126] The text is not interpolated; *quod magis est* suggests, however, that the point was not yet settled. On the passage, see F.B.J. Wubbe (cited n. 117) 184-185, who compares D. 20.1.32 (Scaev., farm lease): "ut ibi perpetuo essent, non temporis causa accommodarentur."[ac] This learning may derive from that over *instrumentum*; cf. Q. Mucius, in D. 28.5.35.3 (Ulpian).

[127] But cf. D. 20.1.34 pr. (Scaev. 27 *Dig.*), where, albeit under somewhat peculiar circumstances, the stock on hand of a *taberna* is regarded as pledged; cf. F. Sturm, in *Die Rechtsgeschichtliche Exegese* (1972) 30-49. At D. 36.4.5.22 (Ulpian), a *habitatio* is leased as a storeroom for a dead man's property.

passing casually through the leasehold; and it might also include:

(4b) In many cases, other people's property. A general rule in this regard is laid down by Alexander Severus, C. 4.65.5 (A.D. 223):

> Certi iuris est ea, quae voluntate dominorum coloni in fundum induxerint, pignoris iure dominis praediorum teneri. quando autem domus locatur, non est necessaria in rebus inductis vel illatis scientia domini: nam ea quoque pignoris iure tenentur.[ad]

The text is apparently uninterpolated.[128] In farm leases the objects of others were not held in pledge unless they were brought in by the will of their owners, *voluntate dominorum*;[129] but in urban leases another principle was adopted: the *scientia domini* was not required. Therefore, in theory, other people's things could be held in pledge by the landlord. However, this rule admitted so many exceptions as to be often meaningless. D. 43.32.2 (Gaius 26 *ad Ed. Prov.*):

> Hoc interdictum inquilino etiam de his rebus, quae non ipsius sint, sed forte commodatae ei vel locatae vel apud eum depositae sunt, utile esse non dubitatur.[af]

The passage[130] affirms explicitly that the property not belonging to the tenant, but detained by him under a con-

[128] It has seemingly never been so considered. The last sentence furnishes strong support for the classicity of the doctrine of tacit pledge, as F.B.J. Wubbe (cited n. *117*) *201* n. *68*, seems to realize. It is quite another question whether the owner could vindicate his own property held as pledge for another's rent; on this, see M. Kaser, *SZ* *78* (*1961*) *216-218*, with literature, arguing that vindication was possible.

[129] To this rule on farm lease should be referred D. 20.2.5.1 (Marcianus/Pomp.): "Item: illud, inquit, videndum est voluntate domini induci pignus ita posse, ut in partem debiti sit obligatum."[ae]

[130] It has seemingly not been held to be interpolated. The words *non dubitatur* indicate that controversy was not quite over.

tractual arrangement, can be released through the interdict. It is not said that the landlord must first be satisfied as to the rent, nor is this to be assumed.[131] The *inquilinus* (and not the property's owner) has the interdict. This text can be brought into harmony with C. 4.65.5 only by close observation of its words. There were two requirements for freeing the object: (a.) it must not belong to the tenant (the question of ownership being otherwise not important); and (b.) it must be in the tenant's detention through a contract. In fact, the second requirement must have been in practice the crucial one, since the existence of the contract normally meant that the object did not belong to the tenant.[132] Therefore, in order to succeed with the interdict, the tenant must normally have been asked simply to prove the existence of the contract. But such a proof could be offered without reference to the *scientia* (much less the *voluntas*) of the object's owner—who in any case might not have been the person with whom the tenant contracted. The exception for contractually detained objects, like that for the property of guests, is to be explained primarily by analogy from the category of casually introduced objects, which were also excepted from the pledge (D. 20.2.7.1).

Not contradicting this interpretation is D. 43.32.1.5 (Ulp. 73 *ad Ed.*):

> Illud notandum est praetorem hic non exegisse, ut in bonis fuerit conductoris, nec ut esset pignori res illata, sed si pignoris nomine inducta sit. proinde et si aliena sint et si talia, quae pignoris nomine teneri non potuerint, pignoris

[131] H. Kreller (cited n. 117) 318-320; *contra*: F.B.J. Wubbe (cited n. 117) 186-187, and M. Kaser (cited n. 128) 217, the latter objecting that questions of ownership would thereby become involved in the interdictal process. That, however, is the sense of Ulpian and Gaius; and the difficulties with such involvement may be exaggerated.

[132] The texts for this proposition are collected in B. Albanese, *Bull.* 62 (1959) 121-155; on whose arguments see, however, J.A.C. Thomas, *Index* 2 (1971) 283-290; M. Kaser, *SZ* 89 (1972) 139-140.

> tamen nomine introducta sint, interdicto huic locus erit: quod si nec pignoris nomine inducta sint, nec retineri poterunt a locatore.[ag]

Ulpian describes two categories of things, both able to be freed under the terms of the interdict and hence exempted from the category of pledged things.[133] Ulpian's second category is things "not led in on the account of pledge"; this is surely a reference to the general category of casually introduced objects in D. 20.2.7.1. Such objects, states Ulpian, *also* cannot be retained by the landlord; therefore that is the meaning of the phrase "interdicto huic locus erit" with reference to the first category. Ulpian's first category consists of objects which (a.) belong to another, and (b.) are such as cannot be held on the account of pledge, but which are nevertheless moved in on the account of pledge. Qualification (a.) is the same as in D. 43.32.2. Qualification (b.) is probably the same as qualification (b.) in D. 43.32.2, but it looks at the situation from a different viewpoint. These objects quite simply cannot be held by the landlord as a pledge, even where the tenant has practiced deliberate fraud in their regard. Therefore if (e.g.) a tenant has rented his entire furnishings, they can all be released through the interdict; but nevertheless *in principle* objects belonging to another can be held by the landlord—as, for instance, objects held in bad faith, such as stolen objects.[134] For purposes of

[133] The first sentence (and esp. "sed et . . . sit") is interpolated according to A. Berger (cited n. 117) 1645: *si* is used for *ut*, *sit* for *esset*: Berger is widely followed. But the phrasing has obviously been influenced by the wording of the interdict. The text has "proinde et si aliena sint et sint alia"; Mommsen emended the last three words to "et si talia," while Kreller (cited n. 117) 317, preferred "et sint talia"—which in its context is hardly Latin. Mommsen also read "interdicto huic"; the mss. have *hoc*. On the text, P. Frezza, II 305-309, finds difficulties which, I believe, simply do not exist; M. Talamanca (cited n. 117) 388, I do not understand. On the meaning of *pignoris nomine*, see F.B.J. Wubbe (cited n. 117) 185, esp. n. 24.

[134] Again, it needs emphasis that the object's owner could probably vindicate such a pledge; see n. 128.

interpreting the interdict, the group of pledged objects is not what is *in bonis* of the tenant,[135] nor by what is specifically brought in as a pledge; so, the first and most difficult sentence of the passage.

(4c) An express exception to the general rule on tenant's furnishings was made for pledged slaves manumitted by the tenant. D. 20.2.6 (Ulp. 73 *ad Ed.*):

> Licet in praediis urbanis tacite solet conventum accipi, ut perinde teneantur invecta et inlata, ac si specialiter convenisset, certe libertati huiusmodi pignus non officit idque et Pomponius probat: ait enim manumissioni non officere ob habitationem obligatum.[ah]

A few words may have dropped out at the end of the last sentence, but otherwise the text is probably sound.[136] Manumission therefore removed the slave from the category of pledged objects. While here a tacit pledge is mentioned, the rule on manumissions probably went back to the time when only express pledges were allowed; at D. 20.2.9 (discussed below), Paul cites the elder Nerva (cos. A.D. 22) in a discussion to the same effect: *contra* Nerva, the tenant may manumit his slaves only up to the moment when his

[135] The meaning of this requirement (which was for the *actio Serviana*, see below) is disputed; but M. Kaser (cited n. 128) 197-210 (praetorian ownership), is less believable than F.B.J. Wubbe (cited n. 117) 72ff. (any having leading to usucapion); the latter is supported by F. Wieacker, *TR* 30 (1962) 68-72. On A. D'Ors, *Iura* 20 (1969) 90-97, see G. Schlichting, *Die Verfugunsbeschränkung des Verpfänders* (1973) 122-124. See now M. Kaser, *TR* 44 (1976) 240-244. In an article to be published in *SD* 45 (1979), n. 83, Kaser accepts Wubbe's view.

[136] Again, for a justification of the text, see W. Schuller (cited n. 120) 277-279. H. Wagner, *SD* 33 (1967) 168 (on the passage, 168-171), supposes that "esse servum" or the like has fallen out at the end. There was a similar rule in general pledges: D. 40.9.29 pr.; such exceptions are explained by *favor libertatis.* Text criticism in P. Koschaker (cited n. 120) 125 n. 3; G. Beseler, *TR* 8 (1928) 331 n. 1, both mainly against *tacite*; more broadly, F. Schulz, *SZ* 48 (1928) 277. Such manumissions were later held as conditionally valid (e.g. *fr. Dos.* 16).

furnishings are seized (Nerva supported manumission even thereafter). The rule was still under discussion in Nerva's time, but was obviously settled in the late classical period.

(4d) Finally, it is not unlikely that by the end of the classical period a further exception was made, on humanitarian grounds, whereby the tenant was allowed to keep property essential to life, as well as servile concubines and natural relatives in slavery.[137] This would explain the wretched possessions which an expelled tenant takes with him in a poem of Martial (12.32, examined below). For similarly humanitarian reasons the landlord was required, before satisfying himself as to the rent, to use the furnishings to pay burial costs for an indigent tenant who died lacking the means to pay for a funeral (D. 11.7.14.1, Ulp. 25 *ad Ed.*).

(5) A question could be raised as to whether only objects actually standing in the tenant's dwelling were included: that is, did the furnishings of the dwelling constitute a sort of revolving fund, to which the landlord was obliged to limit himself in recompense for rent in arrears? Actually, at least by the end of the classical period the landlord was probably also able to pursue objects removed from the dwelling, even when they were in the hands of third parties, by means of the *actio Serviana*. This suit required, however, that the objects had been *in bonis* of the tenant; objects not *in bonis* could not be sued for by this means.[138]

We come now to the second portion of the interdict. That portion allows the tenant to move out his object even if it belongs to the group of pledged objects, provided that:

(1) He has already paid the rent. By Labeo's time the

[137] This is conjectured by H. Kreller (cited n. 117) 319-320, on the basis of D. 20.1.6-8 (Ulp., Paul), which exempt such things from a general pledge; cf. also D. 42.5.38 pr.

[138] Cf. above, n. 135. It is now commonly believed that the *actio Serviana* was generalized in Julian's time: M. Kaser, *RPR*² 1 472-473; cf. W. Kunkel, *SZ* 90 (1973) 154-156; M. Kaser (cited n. 135) 240-241; if not earlier: F. Wubbe, *SZ* 89 (1972) 430-432, reviewing H. Wagner (cited n. 120), at 51-55.

pledge could be held also for rent falling due in the future (D. 43.32.1.4, discussed below); therefore it was irrelevant for purposes of the interdict whether or not the tenant was in arrears in his payment of rent, since rent was reckoned in relation to the tenant's entire contractual obligation.[139] From D. 19.2.13.11 (Ulp. 32 *ad Ed.*), we learn that when the tenant stayed in the dwelling after the end of the term of lease, previously pledged objects remained pledged also for the rent of this additional interval.[140] D. 13.7.11.5 (discussed below) concerns satisfaction by payment of rent to others than the landlord himself.

(2) The landlord and the tenant could also agree on some alternative form of security, in which case the pledge of the tenant's furnishings was discharged; see also D. 20.6.6 pr. (Ulp. 73 *ad Ed.*). There is an example of such an alternative form at D. 20.4.13 (Paul. 5 *ad Plaut.*), and an example of a discharge at D. 20.6.14 (Labeo; farm lease).

(3) Finally, the pledge was discharged if the landlord himself had prevented the tenant from paying rent.

The purpose of the interdict would be plain enough even if we did not have the explicit statement of Ulpian (D. 43.32.1.1, Ulp. 73 *ad Ed.*):

> Hoc interdictum proponitur inquilino, qui soluta pensione vult migrare: nam colono non competit.[aj]

The interdict avails the urban tenant who has already paid his rent and wishes to change residences,[141] including, obviously, moving out his possessions. What is less clear, how-

[139] Cf. also D. 20.1.14 pr. (Ulp. 73 *ad Ed.*): "Quaesitum est, si nondum dies pensionis venit, an et medio tempore persequi pignora permittendum sit. et puto dandam pignoris persecutionem, quia interest mea: et ita Celsus scribit."[ak]

[140] This passage is discussed below, at nn. 145-150.

[141] H. Kreller (cited n. 117) 315, wrongly doubted the last clause; followed by P. Frezza, II 304. We may perhaps deduce from C. 8.14.7 (Just., A.D. 532), which extends the tacit pledge from the "two Romes and their territory" to the provinces, that classical law limited the pledge to Rome; on the passage, W. Schuller (cited n. 117) 282.

ever, is the sequence of events that would have resulted in use of the interdict. A good starting point is D. 43.32.1.4 (Ulp. 73 *ad Ed.*):

> (a.) Si pensio nondum debeatur, ait Labeo interdictum hoc cessare, nisi paratus sit eam pensionem solvere.
> (b.) proinde si semenstrem solvit, sexmenstris debeatur, inutiliter interdicet, nisi solverit et sequentis sexmenstris, ita tamen, si conventio specialis facta est in conductione domus, ut non liceat ante finitum annum vel certum tempus migrare.
> (c.) idem est et si quis in plures annos conduxerit et nondum praeterierit tempus.
> (d.) nam cum in universam conductionem pignora sunt obligata, consequens erit dicere interdicto locum ⟨non⟩ fore, nisi liberata fuerint.[ak]

Of this passage, the second half of (b.) ("ita tamen . . . migrare") is certainly interpolated, and (d.) is perhaps interpolated.[142] The passage sets three cases. First, the rent (*pensio*) is not yet owed; according to Labeo, the tenant cannot succeed with the interdict unless he is willing to pay the unowed *pensio*. Second, according to Ulpian, the same is true if the tenant has rented for a year with two six-month payments; payment of only one is insufficient for use of the interdict.[143] Third, the same is true also for multiple-year leases.

[142] The second half of (b.) has been interpolated after C. 4.65.34 (Just.); cf. L. Mitteis, *SZ* 22 (1901) 138-139, who is generally followed. (The constitution allows either party to withdraw without penalty from the lease within one year, but allows them to void this rule by an express contract clause.) In the last sentence, *non* must be inserted (so the *Basilica* and the later manuscripts; F omitted the word); in this form, it summarizes the previous text; as to its language, see G. Beseler, III 63.

[143] The text is not impossible as it stands, but is improved if we either omit *sexmenstris debeatur* as a gloss (so H. Kreller, cited n. 117, 315 n. 37) or emend it to read "sexmenstris nondum debeatur" (so the *Basilica*, 60.19.1, = Heimb. 5.608). The latter course is preferable, if not obligatory.

The text leaves us more in the dark than is commonly realized. Let us begin by supposing that the tenant wishes to move out in the middle of his term of lease. It is, first of all, less than clear that he in fact owes rent for the remaining term of lease; we have already discussed this problem under the heading "Justified Abandonment." Second, even on back rent he may have a claim to deduction (see under the heading "*Deductio ex Mercede*"). The landlord's act can be conceived as a kind of self-help, to prevent the tenant's *migratio* before the rent is paid; but how could the tenant then assert his own contractual rights? There can only be one answer to this question: if the tenant believed that he owed less than the amount of rent claimed by his landlord, he had to proceed *ex conducto* in order to recover his furnishings; in the context of this *bona fide* suit, the tenant's claim and the landlord's counterclaim to the rent could be examined and determined by the *iudex*; then, if the tenant was willing to pay whatever rent was owed, the landlord could be compelled to return the tenant's furnishings through a monetary judgment (cf. below at n. 224, on D. 19.2.19.5). To this extent, therefore, the interdict *de migrando* and the *actio conducti* were conceived as alternatives available to the tenant, depending on whether or not he was willing to pay what the landlord demanded.

The following considerations favor this reconstruction of the law. First, no source hints that the interdictal procedure itself could be used to settle disputed rent, nor is such a usage *a priori* probable; the interdict was reserved expressly for the tenant "qui soluta pensione vult migrare." Second, the proper forum for disputes over the extent of rent obligations was an *actio conducti*; indeed, it is in conjunction with this suit that all juristic discussion occurs both of justified abandonment and of all other factors (such as the tenant's liability for damages to the apartment, cf. D. 20.2.2) which acted to modify the agreed-upon rent. It was on occasion even possible to sue *ex conducto* for liberation from the lease, as when the landlord no longer had grounds to enforce it: D. 19.2.10, cf. 15.9, and 33.2.30.1; 34.3.18 (farm leases). Third, the tenant's use of the *actio conducti* to secure return of his possessions is in fact attested by D. 19.2.19.4-5 (Ulp. 32 *ad Ed.*), discussed below under "*Deductio ex Mercede*"; therefore the intent of the *actio conducti* as hypothesized above is entirely consistent with our sources.

Finally, the use of the *actio conducti* envisaged above is apparently attested in two passages (D. 39.2.13.6, 33) already considered under "Justified Abandonment." In these passages, the *inquilinus* fears that his building will collapse; if the landlord refuses to let him leave, the tenant can proceed *ex conducto*. The second passage requires repetition in its *catena*. D. 39.2.33 (Ulp. 43 *ad Sab.*), 34 (Paul. 10 *ad Sab.*):

> 33. Inquilino non datur damni infecti actio, quia possit ex conducto agere, si dominus eum migrare prohiberet,[al]
>
> 34. utique si pro praeterita pensione satisfacere paratus fuit: alioquin iusta retentio pignoris domino fieri videretur, sed et si quasi pignora retinuerit et ea interierint ruina vicinarum aedium, potest dici etiam pigneraticia actione locatorem teneri, si poterat eas res in locum tutiorem transferre.[am]

The passages are not interpolated.[144] Here the content of the *actio conducti* is evident: acting on his belief that abandonment is justified, the tenant is seeking *ex conducto* the recovery of his possessions that are endangered by the impending collapse; the grounds for the landlord's retention of the furnishings are also clearly described (cf. *iusta retentio pignoris*); while the interdict *de migrando* is ignored. (The remainder of D. 19.2.34 will be considered below.) In this passage the intricacy of these legal institutions is well

144 In D. 39.2.33, read (probably) *cautio* for *actio*. G. Beseler, *SZ* 53 (1933) 38, thought D. 39.2.34 interpolated as a whole, wrongly. D. 39.2.34, unlike 33, obviously concerns danger from collapse of a neighboring structure; but for our purposes this difference is unimportant. With D. 39.2.34, compare C. 4.24.9 (Diocl., A.D. 293; *horrea*).

illustrated: for an *actio conducti* would also permit a judicial determination as to whether the tenant's fears about the building's collapse constituted a ground for justified abandonment before the abandonment was complete. The same collocation of an *actio conducti* and *migratio* occurs also in D. 19.2.25.2 (Gaius; see above at n. 111); see also D. 19.2.10 (Jul. *libro ad Fer.*).

In D. 43.32.1.1, Ulpian envisages application of the interdict to situations where the tenant seeks to change residences. In such a situation, when the landlord refuses to allow the tenant to remove his furnishings before the rent is accounted for, the refusal can be variously construed, depending on its outward form. The physical obstruction of the tenant's removal of his furnishings need not necessarily have prevented the tenant's continued occupancy of the dwelling.[145] However, the landlord could act much more forcefully. D. 20.2.9 (Paul. *Lib. Sing. de Off. Praef. Vig.*):

> Est differentia obligatorum propter pensionem et eorum, quae ex conventione manifesta pignoris nomine tenentur, quod manumittere mancipia obligata pignori non possumus, inhabitantes autem manumittimus, scilicet antequam pensionis nomine praecludamur: tunc enim pignoris nomine retenta mancipia non liberabimus: et derisus Nerva iuris consultus, qui per fenestram monstraverat servos detentos ob pensionem liberari posse.[an]

The passage is perhaps abbreviated, but is not substantially interpolated.[146] The text proceeds from the distinction be-

[145] In this connection, we might think of D. 19.2.19.5 (Ulpian), where the landlord, whether maliciously or not, has narrowed a doorway so that the tenant cannot remove his strongbox; cf. below at nn. 225-226.

[146] On the text, see H. Wagner (cited n. 136) 165-168 (reading *manifesta*, with the Italian *Digest*, against mss. *manifestari*), against interpolations discovered by F. Schulz, *SZ* 48 (1928) 276-277; P. Frezza, II 168; and others. *Manifesta* includes both express and tacit pledges (*contra*: Wagner, p. 166). The text has *percludamur*, a *hapax*

tween slaves especially in bond for the rent (whom we cannot manumit), and slaves bound in accordance with a contractual agreement. The latter we may manumit only so long as we are ourselves living in the dwelling (*inhabitantes*),[147] but not after we have been locked out (*praecludamur*); we may not free slaves that are being held on account of pledge (*retenta pignoris nomine*); the jurist Nerva was laughed at when he showed that slaves detained (*detentos*) on account of rent could be freed by calling through a window.[148]

In this case the tenant has not only been prevented from removing his furnishings, he has also been prevented from entering the dwelling. The distinction between *inhabitantes* and *praecludamur* is clearly brought home by the anecdote about Nerva: the tenant was actually standing outside his dwelling and looking in through a window. Furthermore, it is clear from D. 39.2.34 (cf. D. 13.7.11.5, considered below) that the landlord through preclusion was considered to possess the tenant's furnishings; they became a possessed *pignus*. But the landlord's act surely amounts in such cases to an expulsion of the tenant, for the landlord was obliged by the contract to permit the tenant to inhabit the dwelling. Therefore (by the rules on justified expulsion) the expelled tenant owes no rent for the period after preclusion; and the question as to whether rent in arrears is offset by any damages to the tenant resulting from the expulsion would have to be determined by examining whether or not the

---

that should undoubtedly be emended to *praecludamur* (a verb used also at D. 43.24.20 pr.).

147 The logic of this passage requires that *inhabitantes* be nominative: so G. Beseler, *SZ* 66 (1948) 277; *contra*: H. Wagner (cited n. 136) 167 n. 22 (following F. Schwarz), who may misunderstand the sense.

148 G. Beseler (cited n. 147) 277, thought it improbable that anyone could have laughed at Nerva, he is followed by H. Wagner (cited n. 136) 167 n. 25, who thinks that later authors misunderstood Nerva's point. But see already F. Schulz (cited n. 146) 277 n. 6. The tone of cold ridicule is remarkable.

expulsion is justified. Again in this case the tenant is able to resort to an *actio conducti*, or, if he does not contest the amount of rent due and is willing to pay what is owed, to the interdict *de migrando*.

A clear illustration of the operation of preclusion comes from a poem of Martial (12.32.1-5):

> O Iuliarum dedecus Kalendarum,
> vidi, Vacerra, sarcinas tuas, vidi;
> quas non retentas pensione pro bima
> portabat uxor rufa crinibus septem
> et cum sorore cana mater ingenti. . . .[20]

Vacerra has been expelled after not paying rent for two years; failure to pay rent was a ground for justified expulsion (C. 4.65.3). Most of Vacerra's furnishings, however, have been retained (*retentas*) by the landlord, who is obviously pursuing his right of preclusion. It is particularly significant that Vacerra's expulsion occurred on July 1, the day that a new tenant would presumably have taken control of the premises. Obviously, Vacerra is now penniless, and has no hope of resisting his landlord on legal grounds.

At the end of this analysis stands a simple and yet compelling point: if a preclusion had not been considered an expulsion, then surely many landlords would have seen that their advantage lay in precluding their tenants as soon as the term of lease began, thereby forcing the tenants either to pay in advance for the entire term of rent or else to forfeit their furnishings. But the result would obviously have been unacceptable.

Martial's pitiless poem, which ends by suggesting that Vacerra and his family live under a bridge (lines 23-25), amply illustrates the rough-and-tumble attitude of the Romans in these matters—not pity for the wretched expellee, but rather scorn that he had rented an apartment he could not pay for. The landlord's retention of the tenant's furnishings amounted to an act of self-help that was perhaps encouraged by his belief that the tenant's furnishings, when they were brought into the apartment, somehow also entered the landlord's sphere of control.[149] More forcefully still, the furnishings constituted the only obvious property which the landlord could lay his hands on to bring pressure to bear on the tenant.[150] Naturally, the landlord would not miss this opportunity. The jurists did not, it seems, seek directly to hinder the landlord either in his simple detention of furnishings or in his preclusion of the tenant. Rather, they first allowed this act of self-help also in cases where the parties had not expressly agreed to a pledge of tenant's furnishings; and then they wove around the act of self-help the doctrines of justified abandonment and expulsion, the clear alternatives of the *actio conducti* and the interdict *de migrando*, whereby the legal consequences of self-help could be drawn.

This body of thought does not end, however, with cases of detention or expulsion by the tenant's direct landlord (though this will no doubt have been the most frequent case); for the tenant could also be expelled by a third party. If the third party had no claim of right, then not only the tenant but also the possessor and owner of the *insula* had the usual variety of interdictal and proprietal remedies (the tenant only with regard to his possessions or through the contract). More interesting is the situation where the third party did have a claim of right. Two broad categories can be distinguished:

(1) The tenant's landlord had no right to rent the apartment, and the expeller is the building's owner. The principal source is D. 12.6.55 (Pap. 6 *Quaest.*):

> Si urbana praedia locaverit praedo, quod mercedis nomine ceperit, ab eo qui solvit non repetetur, sed domino erit

[149] So, e.g. E. Rabel, IV 634 (article publ. 1943). It should be noted that this consideration grounds a pledge to the owner/possessor rather than one to the landlord; cf. below, on D. 13.7.11.5.

[150] So, e.g. F.B.J. Wubbe (cited n. 117) 182-183, 285, who sees the interdict as an attempt to regulate a "right" preexisting in popular usage; cf. also H. Kreller (cited n. 117) 318 n. 51.

> obligatus. . . . quod si vecturas navium, quas dominus locaverat, item pensiones insularum acceperit, ob indebitum ei tenebitur, qui non est liberatus solvendo. . . .[ap]

A *praedo* (a possessor in bad faith) has rented out an urban property and collected rent from the tenant.[151] The tenant, if expelled by the owner, can collect damages from the *praedo*, who lacked the right to rent (see above at n. 59). But according to this text, the tenant owes nothing to the owner, and the owner can exact his lost "fruits" only from the *praedo* directly. Therefore the tenant the recuperatory interdicts against the owner, while the interdict *de migrando* is irrelevant, since there is no contract between tenant and owner. (However, the text continues, if the tenant contracts with the owner and then pays rent to the *praedo*, he must also pay the owner and seek recovery from the *praedo*. In this case the interdict *de migrando* is of use to the tenant only after the owner has been satisfied as to the rent.)

(2) More difficult is the situation where the expeller is the owner (or another) standing above the tenant's landlord on a contractual ladder. Here there are two related questions: Could the tenant satisfy his obligation to the landlord by paying rent to the owner, in situations where the landlord had not (or had not expressly) allowed this? Also, could the owner force the tenant to pay rent (either to him or to the landlord) by precluding the tenant, and did the tenant then have an interdict *de migrando* against the owner?[152] It would have been very tempting to answer at least the second question with a yes, and this on a variety of grounds. The same considerations were present here that had initially led to the contractual and juristic construction of a landlord's lien on tenant furnishings: namely, the sense

[151] On the passage, see F. Haymann, *Bull.* 59/60 (1956) 23-24; the text is not interpolated, but *ob indebitum* in the last sentence does not refer to the *condictio indebiti.*

[152] In farm lease this question was answered in the negative, to the extent that a subtenant's furnishings were not pledged to the owner: D. 19.2.24.1 (Paul).

that the tenant had physically set his furnishings within another's structure, and the simultaneous feeling that preclusion of the sitting tenant constituted the only certain level which the owner could utilize to secure payment of rent, since the middleman might not even live on the premises.[153] Supporting this position would be the existence of the owner's right, uncontested throughout the classical period, to expel sitting tenants whenever he so desired; and also the general doctrine that allowed the inclusion of other people's property in the body of pledged furnishings. Particularly relevant in this latter regard is the exception whereby the tenant's *guest* was allowed an *interdictum utile* against the tenant's landlord. The granting of such an interdict was a clear precedent for the situation of the subtenant.

With this background, we may consider D. 13.7.11.5 (Ulp. 28 *ad Ed.*):

> (a.) Solutam autem pecuniam accipiendum non solum, si ipsi, cui obligata res est, sed et si alii sit soluta voluntate eius, vel ei cui heres exstitit, vel procuratori eius, vel servo pecuniis exigendis praeposito.
>
> (b.) unde si domum conduxeris et eius partem mihi locaveris egoque locatori tuo pensionem solvero, pigneraticia adversus te potero experiri (nam Julianus scribit solvi ei posse): et si partem tibi, partem ei solvero, tantundem erit dicendum.
>
> (c.) plane in eam dumtaxat summam invecta mea et illata tenebuntur, in quam cenaculum conduxi: non enim credibile est hoc convenisse, ut ad universam pensionem insulae frivola mea tenebuntur.
>
> (d.) videtur autem tacite et cum domino aedium hoc convenisse, ut non pactio cenacularii proficiat domino, sed sua propria.[aq]

This passage, which comes from the portion of Ulpian's Commentary on the *actio pigneraticia*,[154] is extraordinarily

[153] See above, nn. 149-150.

[154] O. Lenel, *Paling.* II 584.

difficult, above all because it seems to begin in one place and end in another. Postclassical shortenings no doubt contribute to that impression; further, the sentence "non enim . . . tenebuntur" in (c.) is probably interpolated; and the last sentence may (or may not) be interpolated.[155] It seems best to discuss the passage sentence by sentence.

The passage begins with a generalized observation that a debt may be redeemed not only by payment to the creditor, but also to a third party *voluntate eius*, or to one from whom the creditor inherits,[156] or to the creditor's procurator, or to the creditor's servile debt-collector. The theme, therefore, is the extent of the ambit of persons, other than the creditor, to whom the debtor can successfully make payment. Behind three of the examples stands either an explicit authorization (payment *voluntate eius* to another) or a generalized authorization (payment to the procurator or the slave) by the creditor. Payment to the one from whom the creditor inherits introduces another idea—the actual enrichment of the creditor as a consequence of the payment. All these examples are met in other passages.[157]

Sentence (b.) moves abruptly to a discussion of a particular problem arising from the typical owner/middleman/

[155] On the text of the first sentence, see below n. 156. G. Beseler, *SZ* 57 (1937) 22, attacked *plane* to the end, on a variety of grounds; cf. *idem*, *SZ* 66 (1948) 284 and 302; on the fourth sentence see below n. 164. That the passage has been revised cannot be denied. In (c.) Mommsen removed the false mood by correcting *tenebuntur* to *teneantur*.

[156] The words "vel ei cui heres exstitit" were excised by S. Solazzi, *RIL* 59 (1926) 359-372, at 364 n. 1 and 368-369. Solazzi believed that this instance did not belong in a list of people receiving by the creditor's *voluntas*; however, it is not clear that the passage should be so narrowly construed (compare esp. D. 46.3.49, Marcian., a rather similar list), and it is perhaps best to assume that the original text was shortened.

[157] Cf. S. Solazzi, *L'Estinzione dell'Obbligazione* vol. 1 (2d ed. 1935) 54-80 (procurator and slave: 54-58; a third person *voluntate eius*: 58-59); on payment to one from whom the creditor inherits, cf. 80 (based on D. 46.3.96.4).

tenant arrangement in urban leasehold. The tenant can pay his rent directly to the owner, so writes Ulpian (following Julian), and if he has done so then he can win in an *actio pigneraticia* against his landlord; further, the tenant can also divide his rent between the landlord and the owner, with a similar result. In this *actio* the tenant is the plaintiff, which would mean that the pledge for rent was at the time of the *actio* possessed by his landlord.[158] However, the logic of the second sentence would also require that the tenant prevail where the pledge was not possessed: that is, either in an interdict *de migrando* against the landlord, or in an *actio Serviana* brought by the landlord for the recovery of the tenant's pledge.[159] It is not explicitly said in this passage that the tenant obeyed the landlord's will in paying the owner, nor is the basis of Julian's decision made clear.[160] However, Julian is hardly likely to have left such a statement entirely unqualified.[161]

In the third sentence (c.) it is asserted as obvious that the tenant's furnishings are held only to the total of his own rent. But now the ambiguity of the text increases: a discussion begins of the tenant's furnishings (*invecta et illata*), properly a possessionless pledge; to whom does Ulpian consider them as bound (*tenebuntur*): to the landlord, or to the owner, or to both?[162] The author of the last half of this sentence was obviously prepared to believe that they were

158 Cf. M. Kaser, *RPR*² I 536-537, for sources. We should perhaps suppose that the landlord has (through preclusion) taken possession of the tenant's pledge. An *actio pigneraticia* in this situation is envisaged by D. 39.2.34.

159 Cf. M. Kaser, *RPR*² I 472-473.

160 We should therefore be cautious about subsuming this case under the heading *voluntate eius*, as S. Solazzi (cited n. 156) 368-369, wished.

161 Cf. E. Bund, *Untersuchung zur Methode Julians* (1965) 52-53, who compares the rather harsher doctrine of D. 46.3.34.6 (Jul. 54 *Dig.*).

162 The first alternative, however, is trivial.

bound to the owner, though not of course for the entire rent of the *insula*.[163]

In the fourth sentence (d.) the ambiguity is nearly complete.[164] Here the text moves from the theory of tacit pledge of furnishings, a theory that (as we have seen) was already well developed by Ulpian's time. The owner of the structure is seen as the beneficiary of a tacit pledge; however (*autem*), the other party to that pledge is not the tenant himself but rather the middleman with whom the owner has contracted (*convenisse*). This passage *could* mean that the tenant should not be thought of as pledging to the owner directly, but only indirectly and through the pledge of the middleman; it is this latter pledge to which the owner must always refer.

We should perhaps not attempt to explain away all the ambiguities of a clearly doubtful passage. This much, however, can be said:

(1) D. 13.7.11.5 offers only limited support for the view that a tenant could, without regard to or despite the will of his landlord, pay rent directly to the owner.[165] The broad phrases of the second sentence would probably appear less

[163] So also the *Basilica*, 25.1.11.5 (= Heimb. 3.59; Schelt. BT 1190).

[164] The linguistic objections to this sentence in G. Beseler, *SZ* 57 (1937) 22, seem unconvincing: the sentence is allegedly unclear as it stands; *hoc convenisse* is suspicious (untrue); and *ut non* is postclassical (Beseler ignored the *sed*). It should be observed that the author of this sentence knew the vocabulary of tacit pledge in D. 20.2; *convenire ut* derives from the Edict (D. 43.32.1 pr.).

[165] This view was taken by the Pandectists, e.g. H. Dernberg, *Das Pfandrecht* vol. 1 (1860) 308; P. A. Östergren, *Das Gesetzliche Pfandrecht* (1905) 71-72; revived in part by F.B.J. Wubbe, *TR* 26 (1958) 190-191 (who rightly stresses that in any case no *subpignus* is involved here); *idem* (cited n. 117) 190-192, 286; accepted by M. Kaser (cited n. 128) 217 n. 149; *RPR*² 1 637 n. 14; and in part by P. Frezza, II 307-308. Wubbe observes that the tenant might prefer to pay the owner so as to avoid the risk of having to pay twice in the event that the owner seized his furnishings after the middleman's insolvency; but it is unclear why such a double payment would be necessary.

sweeping if the linking element between the first two sentences had survived postclassical abbreviation; still, the word *unde* must imply at least some resemblance between the tenant's payment to the owner and the situations described in the first sentence. There are other reasons for not interpreting the second sentence too broadly: the tenant's debt to his landlord was a *bona fide* debt which was often but not always measurable by the agreed-upon rent (cf. D. 20.2.2, discussed above); further, the tenant's debt was in any case incommensurable with the *bona fide* debt of the middleman to the owner. Perhaps it is enough to construe the passage as saying that if the tenant paid the owner in the belief that this was what his landlord desired, and if the landlord was enriched by this payment, then the tenant's debt was discharged to the extent of the enrichment.[166] Because of the *bona fide* relationships linking the three parties, and because of the very unusual pyramidal structure of their obligations with regard to one single piece of property, it may have been possible to infer the middleman's consent in circumstances where that would normally have been impossible.

(2) On the other hand, the passage is distinctly more favorable to the position that the tenant's furnishings constituted, at least to some extent, a pledge also to the owner. Further, it might be supposed that the passage envisages a rather precise situation, in which *the owner* has precluded the tenant in order to recover an outstanding portion of the middleman's rent. In this situation (which was tantamount to the tenant's expulsion *by the owner*), the tenant's primary aim would be to settle up any money due as swiftly as possible;[167] where the amount was disputed, preclusion by

[166] The view of S. Solazzi (cited n. 156) 368-369, thus seems to me correct in a modified form. Arrangements for dividing a tenant's payments between a landlord and his creditor are described in D. 31.88.15.

[167] It will be recalled that expulsion by the owner frees the tenant from the obligation to pay further rent for the period after expulsion, but does not entitle the tenant to damages from his landlord; cf. above at nn. 60-63.

the owner could of course be followed by an *actio conducti* against the landlord. However, the tenant's payment to the landlord did not automatically free his furnishings from the owner's preclusion. Within the framework of the contractual ladder, there were at least three possible ways out of this problem:

(a) the tenant's furnishings could be regarded as pledged only to the landlord and *not* to the owner; but in that event the owner's preclusion was from the outset resistible by the tenant, and the owner was left in a difficult position as against a middleman whose rent was not otherwise secured; or:

(b) the tenant's furnishings could be regarded as pledged to the owner *for the middleman's payment of rent*; in which case the tenant's furnishings were rather awkwardly bound up with the middleman's satisfaction of the owner, and the tenant was obliged to await this satisfaction; or:

(c) the tenant's furnishings could be regarded as pledged to the owner *for the tenant's payment of rent either to the middleman or to the owner.*[168]

It is this final view which D. 13.7.11.5 seems to take; or, at any rate, such an interpretation fits extremely well both with the text and with the practicalities of the problem posed above, in which the owner had precluded the tenant in order to recover the middleman's rent. Let us suppose that the owner's preclusion could be considered legitimate; such a legitimacy would have to be founded on the belief that the tenant's furnishings were pledged to the owner, that is, that the owner was to be regarded as a sort of secondary creditor standing alongside the tenant's immediate landlord. In accordance with this view, Ulpian's

[168] There are other possibilities: the tenant's furnishings were pledged to the owner only for the tenant's payment to the owner (but that is ruled out by the fourth sentence); or only for the tenant's payment to the middleman (but then the owner is not a creditor of the tenant).

analysis begins with the (admittedly, not unqualified) ability of the tenant to pay the owner directly; nothing more than the possibility of payment is involved,[169] not the desirability or probability.

The remainder of the analysis follows almost automatically. After preclusion, the tenant could free his possessions from the owner by paying rent either to his own landlord or to the owner. However, if he paid to the owner, he was obliged (as we have seen) to take at least some account of his own landlord's will in the matter; since if the landlord forbade such a payment, the tenant would not necessarily satisfy the landlord by payment to the owner, and thus might be unable to free his furnishings *from the landlord.* Therefore, the tenant would normally find it in his best interests to pay the landlord rather than the owner; and certainly, if the tenant disputed the amount of rent owed, it was the landlord that he had to sue *ex conducto.* But once the tenant had settled with the landlord, he was able to use the interdict *de migrando* (or an *utile* variant) against the owner, so as to free his furnishings.

Here the third and fourth sentences become relevant. The tenant's possessions are a pledge only for the amount of his own rent (and not for the rent of the entire building); upon this consideration is founded the tenant's use of the interdict against the owner. This arrangement results from the reciprocal obligations binding the parties together in good faith; for "it had been tacitly agreed upon with the owner (*scil.* by the middleman and the tenant) that the owner would profit (*scil.* directly) only from his own *pactio* with the middleman, and not from the tenant's *pactio.*" The owner benefited indirectly because the tenant's rent payment enabled the middleman to pay his rent to the owner; it was therefore in any case decidedly not in owner's interests to allow the expelled tenant to depart with his furnishings before the tenant had accounted to his own landlord for the rent.

[169] So F.B.J. Wubbe (cited n. 165) 190.

Ulpian's line of reasoning therefore legitimized the owner's preclusion, and so gave the tenant access to the interdict *de migrando* against the owner.[170]

The meaning of the rule in D. 13.7.11.5 can be further explored in three variants. In the first variant, the middleman has absconded during the term of lease; in this situation, where the tenant *cannot* pay his landlord, it would be equitable to hold the tenant's furnishings in tacit pledge to the owner for the middleman's rent, so that the tenant could not be unjustly enriched at the owner's expense.[171] In the second variant, an owner-landlord has sold the property in the middle of the term of lease; in this situation, the former owner has continued as the tenant's landlord, but the tenant's rents might accrue to the new owner.[172] The complexly interlocking interests thus set up were perhaps best solved by reference to the logic of D. 13.7.11.5. Many versions of this variant can be imagined.[173]

In the third variant, a number of tenants have rented an apartment together; such an arrangement is known from D. 9.3.1.10 (Ulp. 23 *ad Ed.*). Several texts suggest that under certain circumstances the landlord could proceed against any one of these tenants for the whole debt.[174] In early

[170] H. Kreller (cited n. 117) 314 n. 30 had already contemplated this use of the interdict, but in doing so he had to rely on his emendation of D. 43.32.1 pr. (above, n. 117).

[171] This proposition cannot be proven, and I do not mean to suggest it as anything more than a possibility.

[172] Rent acceded to the buyer only by express agreement (D. 19.1.53 pr.; 19.2.58 pr.; cf. 18.1.68 pr., farm lease). By juristic construction it remained with the seller in the absence of an express agreement (D. 19.1.13.11, farm lease; a division of *pensiones*: D. 20.4.13); on these texts, see T. Mayer-Maly, *LC* 56-58, with literature, and add A. Torrent, in *Homenaje—C. Sánchez del Río y Pequero* (1967) 263-271. On the right of the new owner to expel a sitting tenant, see C. 4.65.9 (Alex., A.D. 229; farm lease).

[173] Consider the complex security arrangements in D. 20.1.20 (Ulp. 63 *ad Ed.*), where the landlord's creditor, who is to be paid *ex pensionibus*, has a *utilis* lien against the tenants.

[174] The matter is very unclear; but see D. 13.6.5.15; 19.2.13.9, 47;

classical law it is probable that a tenant who paid the whole debt could recover shares from the remaining tenants through an *actio societatis*; but a postclassical constitution of A.D. 259 proposes (in the preserved text, at least) that the landlord could cede his rights to the tenant.[175] Surely, these rights would include the landlord's rights over the pledges of the other tenants.

Despite the steady development of law surrounding the tenant's pledge of furnishings, the use of self-help against the tenant remained a potential flashpoint for violent controversy. The last stage in the development was therefore the decision, which perhaps originated with the emperor, to assign controversies regarding tenant's pledges to the Praefectus Vigilum, who (unlike the Praetor) had police power in the settling of disputes.[176] By Ulpian's time the extraordinary procedures before this Praefectus had virtually replaced the interdict *de migrando* (D. 43.32.1.2, Ulp. 73 *ad Ed.*).[177] This change seems to have involved no drastic alteration in the law regarding tenant's pledges; a passage from Paul (D. 20.2.9, quoted above), which derives from his monograph on the Praefectus Vigilum, shows the reception into extraordinary procedure of the rule governing manumissions.

C. 4.65.13; M. Kaser, *RPR*² 1 657 n. 12, with literature; add D. Liebs, *Konk*. 184-188.

175 An *actio societatis* against one's co-tenants is mentioned at D. 9.3.4 (Paul; the aftermath of a suit *de effusis* is envisaged). On C. 4.65.13 (Valer., A.D. 259), which seems to me to concern a dwelling rather than a farm, see E. Levy, *Konk*. 1.238 n. 2; D. Liebs, *Konk*. 188.

176 See in general A. dell'Oro, *I Libri de Officio* (1960) 250-254, esp. 253-254. Note the similar authority of the Praefectus Vigilum to investigate break-ins into urban dwellings: D. 1.15.3.1-2. D. 47.10.20 (Modest.) almost surely has nothing to do with the Praefectus Vigilum or preclusion; cf. F. Raber, *Grundlagen Klassischer Injurienansprüche* (1969) 150-152, with bibliography, *contra*: D. A. Musca, *Lab*. 16 (1970) 309-310.

177 This sentence was willfully considered interpolated by H. Niedermeyer, in *St. Riccobono* 1 216-217; on it, see A. A. Schiller, *AHDO-RIDA* 3 (1949) 357-358.

Tenant's Pledges

Another passage from the same book may indicate one change in the law. D. 19.2.56:

> Cum domini horreorum insularumque desiderant diu non apparentibus nec eius temporis pensiones exsolventibus conductoribus aperire et ea quae ibi sunt describere, a publicis personis quorum interest audiendi sunt. tempus autem in huiusmodi re biennii debet observari.[ar]

This text,[178] which does not directly concern preclusion, involves the consequences of a prolonged disappearance of an urban tenant (or of a lessee of a storeroom in a *horreum*); after a certain interval, the tenant's locked room can be opened and the contents inventoried under the supervision of relevant officials (the Praefectus Vigilum in the original text). The reference to a *biennium* in the second sentence is troublesome, for it contrasts with the temporal vagueness of the first sentence.[179] Nor ought we lightly to suppose that the owner of an *insula* had to hold a dwelling unused for so long a period of time. It is, of course, entirely possible that the second sentence is interpolated; its wording is certainly postclassical. Still, it is tempting to suppose (or at least to suggest) that the last sentence originally completed the analysis in the text, by stating a requirement imposed through the Praefectus Vigilum whereby the landlord was required to hold the tenant's pledges for two years before selling them up. During this period of grace the urban tenant

[178] On it, see esp. F. Eisele, *SZ* 18 (1897) 22, followed by most scholars; cf. esp. T. Mayer-Maly, *SZ* kan. 22 (1955) 412-415; J.A.C. Thomas, *RIDA*[3] 13 (1966) 356-357. Independent objection to the last sentence was taken by C. Ferrini, *Manuale di Pandetti*[3] (1908) 703 n. 1; on *observare*: G. Beseler, *SZ* 66 (1948) 335. Too uncritical, in any event, are C. Alzon, *Location des Entrepôts* (1960) 118-120, and D. A. Musca (cited n. 176) 307 n. 75. For a classical core, M. Kaser, *RPR*[2] II 406 n. 42.

[179] Very similar in its vagueness is D. 20.4.21.1 (Scaev.; *horrea*). T. Mayer-Maly (cited n. 178) 414-415, cites other postclassical legislation imposing two- or three-year time limits on expulsion; and it is admittedly easy to discard the second sentence altogether.

could pay any rent that was due and recover his pledges. In any event, it is clear from D. 39.2.34 (Paul., quoted above) that the landlord was required to hold the pledges in safekeeping for at least some time after preclusion; indeed, he was liable to the tenant if he failed to keep them in a safe place and they were destroyed. A century earlier, by contrast, Martial's unfortunate tenant apparently reckoned on the irremediable loss of his furnishings.

Three final observations may be made on this portion of Roman lease law. First, the law as to the tenant's pledge presupposes that his furnishings were likely to have a considerable commercial worth. Although the landlord was not confined to the tenant's furnishings in seeking to recoup rent in arrears (he also had the *actio locati*), still, the considerable development of the law in this area shows how frequently landlords must have relied, more or less exclusively, on the pledge of furnishings. It is therefore obvious that the tenants to whom this law applied were normally of some wealth.[180]

Second, the law as to tenant's pledge (or at least the law as I have interpreted it) apparently relies on the relative swiftness of the Roman judicial system. Especially relevant here is the *actio conducti*, which a tenant might bring to recover his furnishings when he disputed the amount of rent due; it would be obviously unfair (at least, in a modern appreciation) to deprive the tenant of his furnishings during protracted litigation. However, it is far from clear that the Roman procedural system, despite its simplicity, was sufficiently speedy to fulfill this requirement.[181] The conse-

[180] M. Kaser, *RPR*² I 472, argues from the form of the interdict *de migrando* (it is the tenant who must bring it) that it envisages a socially dependent tenantry. However, the form of the interdict seems to me much more strongly influenced by the *physical* relationship between the two parties; further, the tenant's bringing of the interdict, which was anyway not especially onerous, also implies nothing nearly so strong as social dependency. So also W. Kunkel, *SZ* 90 (1973) 153 n. 4; still doubtful, M. Kaser, *TR* 44 (1976) 239 n. 32.

[181] See J. M. Kelly, *Roman Litigation* (1966) 118-131, with litera-

quence would be that a tenant, even where he had a legitimate claim against his landlord, might well feel pressured into settling on unfavorable terms.

Third, the law on tenant's pledge is nevertheless no negligible achievement on the part of the jurists. The evenness and clarity of it, its responsiveness to the varied claims of the parties to the pledge, above all its drive toward legal control of the situation, all of these characteristics display the consequence of deep and sustained thought by the jurists. Indeed, in perhaps no other area of Roman lease law are the principal interests of Roman landlords and tenants so precisely articulated over so long a period of time.

Tenant's Liabilities to His Landlord

Occasionally the tenant may have become liable to his landlord for payment of more than the rent,[182] especially because he inhabited a dwelling belonging to another and was therefore obliged to take care of it. By the late classical period the tenant's duties appear as highly generalized; but it is not easy, because of the state of the sources, to trace the development leading to this position.

Two principal sources state a generalized doctrine. D. 20.2.2 (Marc. *Lib. Sing. ad Form. Hyp.*):

> Pomponius libro quadragesimo Variarum Lectionum scribit: non solum pro pensionibus, sed et si deteriorem habitationem fecerit culpa sua inquilinus, quo nomine ex locato cum eo erit actio, invecta et illata pignori erunt obligata.[183]

---

ture. It does not seem likely that extraordinary cognition was materially faster.

[182] We may leave to one side the tenant's liability for interest on overdue rent; see above n. 49. The section below partially reproduces my article in *SZ* 95 (1978) 232-269. Many of these texts are reconsidered now by D. Nörr, in *Festschrift für Franz Wieacker* (ed. O. Behrends *et al.*, 1978) 115-144.

We should compare this text, which as far as we know is authentic,[183] with D. 19.2.11.2 (Ulp. 32 *ad Ed.*), which deals with *locatio conductio rei* in general:

> Item prospicere debet conductor, ne aliquo vel ius rei vel corpus deterius faciat vel fieri patiatur.[at]

This passage is also uninterpolated.[184] The doctrine in these two sources is essentially identical. According to Pomponius in Marcianus, the tenant is liable if he makes the dwelling worse through his *culpa*, and his furnishings are pledged for whatever amount his landlord could then realize in a suit *ex locato*; according to Ulpian, the lessee has the duty to see to it that the rented object does not become worse either in its physical or its legal condition as a consequence of the tenant's action or acquiescence.[185]

From these passages can be derived three characteristics of the later classical doctrine: first, the dwelling must be "worsened" (that is, its worth to the landlord must deteriorate to an extent that is measurable in monetary terms); second, the damage must result from the act (or the acquiescence) of the tenant; third, the tenant's conduct must be characterized by *culpa*, blameworthiness, which in the commonest case means negligence.[186] A number of generalized passages attest that the liability of both parties in *locatio*

[183] Cf. W. Schuller, *Lab.* 15 (1969) 280.

[184] It has apparently never been so considered. Note the extremely broad phrasing; the concept of *culpa* is latent in the duty of care.

[185] What does "facere ius rei deterius" mean? Is the tenant liable if he does not keep up a servitude (cf. e.g. D. 8.6.20, farm lease)? So, A. Pernice, II.2.1 256.

[186] See, with bibliography, M. Kaser, *RPR*² I 504-505 and 511-512; II 350. As D. 19.2.30.4 (Alfen.; farm lease) shows, originally only the personal conduct of the lessee was thought of; cf. A. Watson, *Obl.* 120-121. Note esp. D. 19.2.57 (Jav. 9 *ex Post. Lab.*): dirt dumped by lessee on rented lot results after rainstorm in damage to landlord's abutting house; ruling: contractual but no delictual liability, which shows that the duty of care was higher under the contract, to the extent that it could suffice when the lessee's negligence enabled the damage to occur.

conductio was for *dolus* and *culpa*.[187] *Dolus* shades into intentional doing of damage.

It is important to observe that (with the exception of D. 9.3.5.4, discussed below) no source goes further than the standard set by these two sources. By contrast, the liability for tenant farmers reached into other, quite different areas, as is established by Paul. *Sent.* 2.18.2: blameworthy conduct (*culpa*), for which the tenant is liable, consists not only in damage to the property, but also in failure to cultivate and in failure to repair the buildings.[188] This latter duty is especially significant; the urban tenant had, so it seems, no general duty to repair his dwelling. As we shall see in the next section, that duty (together with the liability for failure to perform) was assigned to the landlord.

It is perhaps helpful, before examining further classical sources, to contrast the late classical doctrine with a post-classical constitution, C. 4.65.29 (Diocl.):

> Cum conductorem aedificia, quae suscepit integra, destruxisse proponas, haec heredes etiam eius praeses provinciae instaurare aedificiorum inter vos habita ratione iubebit.[au]

The lessee, since deceased, has allegedly destroyed buildings which he received undamaged; if the allegations are true, the tenant's heirs can be made to recompense the damage. Here the circumstances leading to the destruction are not

[187] Cf. esp. D. 13.6.5.2 *in fine* (Ulp. 28 *ad Ed.*), perhaps genuine, but cf. D. Nörr, *SZ* 73 (1956) 103-106, with bibliography; also, D. 13.6.5.15; 50.17.23 (both revised). Liability runs down to *culpa*: D. 4.9.3.1; 39.2.18.4. *Custodia* is first mentioned for tenants of immoveables in generalized postclassical sources: D. 13.6.5.15; C. 4.65.28 (A.D. 293); *Inst.* 3.24.5. At D. 19.2.29 (Alfen.), 41 (Ulpian/Marcell.), *custodire* is not technical. A co-tenant was probably solely liable for his own negligence: D. 13.6.5.15 (Ulpian/Celsus).

[188] The list of duties is not different in D. 19.2.25.3 (Gaius; probably abbreviated), which, however, as the text stands does not mention *culpa*. The development is from a list of duties to the concept of *culpa* as an embracing term for them; cf. D. 19.2.25.4, a clear illustration.

emphasized, and only the imputability to the deceased tenant is stressed.[189] This standard of liability is cruder than the classical one.

One should not consider the few early classical sources as illustrating the doctrine in D. 19.2.11.2 and 20.2.2; rather, they represent the case law out of which the later classical doctrine evolved. Only one source deals with the urban tenant's personal liability for property damage (in the absence of a lease provision); but it is an extremely good one: D. 19.2.13.7 (Ulp. 32 *ad Ed.*), discussed above at nn. 99-102. This source requires the tenant to resist pilferage by a passing army (according to Labeo); or else, presumably if resistance is evidently pointless, to notify the owner (if possible, adds Ulpian) before abandoning the structure. Failure to perform this duty subjected the tenant to liability for damage done by the soldiers.[190] The clear thrust of the passage is that the tenant was liable for the pilferage of the owner's property only if his blameworthy conduct made the pilferage possible. The extension here is interesting: in Labeo's time, the tenant's liabilities already reached beyond his own direct doing of harm, and included also any conduct of his that made possible the doing of harm by others not

[189] The text is uninterpolated. I do not mean to press the point; perhaps *culpa* is implied. That is certainly the case in D. 19.1.13.30 (Ulpian/Tubero), where a *colonus* is liable to his landlord if he does damage.

[190] The text, discussed above at n. 101, is little altered. Is the *conductor* in this case actively legitimated for the *actio furti*? The generalized sources on *locatio rei* (e.g. D. 19.2.6; 47.2.14.12, 59) seem to regard only the lease of moveables; D. 47.2.26.1 (Paul) gives the *colonus* the *actio furti* for theft of standing grain (cf. D. 47.2.83.1, = Paul. *Sent.* 2.31.30; so also D. 47.2.14.2?), while D. 47.2.52.8 (Ulpian) allows him the action only indirectly, through a kind of cession, when a thief removes earth from a sulphur mine on the leasehold (cf. D. 19.2.60.5, Labeo; very confused). Since the tenant farmer's interest in fruits was higher than that in fixtures, the answer to the question above is therefore probably no. Similar logic underlies Celsus' grant to the *colonus* of the Aquilian action for damage to fruits, D. 9.2.27.14 (partially interpolated).

under his control, provided that this specific harm was both foreseeable and preventable.

It was established above (after n. 102) that the standard of conduct required in D. 19.2.13.7 was an objective one: the tenant was required *qua* tenant to consider rationally the gravity of the situation and to act responsibly so as to protect (if possible) the landlord's property, or (if that was not possible) to notify the landlord of the danger; the tenant was not required to exercise a superhuman effort of thought or valor. But if he failed to meet the minimum standard, then he was held liable for the resultant loss; and if he was competent to make the contract in the first place, then it would carry no weight for him to say that he did not realize he had a duty to his landlord, or that he was (for instance) too stupid or too nervous to foresee the danger and to carry out protective measures. It may be that in Labeo's time the jurists were inclined to provide numerous detailed rules of conduct for different cases; in the late classical period, at any rate, the tendency was to allow for wide variations in cases; hence the general and discretionary phrasing usual in most sources.

From D. 19.2.30.4 (Alfen.; farm lease), we may perhaps conclude that the tenant was not liable for normal wear and tear (*vetustas*), although this source admittedly discusses a lease clause (cf. Cato, *Agr.* 144.6).

An example of tenant *culpa* drawn from daily life shows, however, that the tenant's duties were sometimes not narrowly limited to the avoidance of damage to the landlord's property. D. 9.3.5.4 (Ulp. 23 *ad Ed.*):

> Cum autem legis Aquiliae actione propter hoc quis condemnatus est, merito ei, qui ob hoc, quod hospes vel quis alius de cenaculo deiecit, in factum dandam esse Labeo dicit adversus deiectorem, quod verum est. plane si locaverat deiectori, etiam ex locato habebit actionem.[av]

In this excerpt Ulpian concludes his discussion of the vicarious liability of the resident of a dwelling (*habitator*) by including liability for things dropped or poured from the dwelling's windows, thereby causing damage to the plaintiff on the common way beneath.[191] Under many circumstances the resident could be held liable, even if he is faultless, also for the acts of others in the dwelling, such as guests (D. 9.3.1.9, 5.1), co-lessees (D. 9.3.1.10, 3; but cf. 5 pr.), and subtenants (D. 9.3.5.1-2). Analogously, the *horrearius* and the lessee of a shop or schoolroom could also be vicariously liable in such circumstances (D. 9.3.5.3).

In D. 9.3.5.4, Ulpian allows the resident, when he has been held vicariously liable, to sue the actual culprit. Unfortunately, the text, which is meaningless, probably suffers from the loss of a few words followed by a misguided attempt to "improve."[192] The clearest emendation is Lenel's:

> Cum autem legis Aquiliae actione propter hoc quis damnas est, merito ei, qui ob hoc condemnatus est, quod hospes . . .

The text, so emended (and the form of the emendation is certain), means that an Aquilian action for negligent damage lay against the culprit; and that therefore, if the resident had been held vicariously liable, according to Labeo he should have an analogous Aquilian action against the culprit. If the culprit was a tenant of the resident, he was liable also under a suit on the contract.[193] In this case, the "damage" to the resident involved his subjection to the quasi-dilectual

[191] Cf. W. Wolodkiewicz, *RIDA*[3] 12 (1968) 371-379; M. Kaser, *RPR*[2] II 428 nn. 24, 27. Compare also D. 44.7.5.5 (Gaius).

[192] Scholarship on this very interesting passage is virtually nonexistent, though E. Levy, *Konk.* I 328, seems to adopt the interpretation given here. E. Seidl, in *St. Volterra* I 76, offers a truncated version; G. Beseler, *SZ* 66 (1948) 276, had some needless alterations. Already the Byzantines saw the problem with the transmitted text: B. 60.4.5 (= Heimb. 5.330), which means that the corruption probably antedates Justinian. Lenel's emendation is in *Paling.* II 550-551, improving on that of Mommsen; it is accepted by L. Mitteis, in *Index Interp. ad loc.*

[193] This extreme extension of the idea of *damnum* presents more difficulty for the Aquilian action than for contract.

suit *de deiectis*; through the tenant's *culpa* resulting in property damage, the landlord is forced to pay money not otherwise due, and thus his estate is diminished—a concept of damage notably broader than the property damage discussed above. Probably, as in the other cases of concurrence, the resident's use of one suit exhausted the other.[194]

The measure of damages due to the landlord *ex locato* because of the tenant's *culpa* is not discussed in any classical source.[195] In D. 9.3.5.4, the landlord is presumably seeking the amount lost in the suit *de deiectis*—an amount which would normally be double the actual damage to the passer-by, or a large fixed sum if a freeman had been killed (so the Edict, D. 9.3.1 pr.). In D. 19.2.13.7, it might make a difference, depending on whether the landlord could recover the cost of the pilfered items, or the cost of replacing them, or the amount by which his dwelling had been reduced in value through the pilferage.

The tenant's liabilities can be further illustrated through classical discussions of his duties under special contract provisions, and of his vicarious liability for the acts of others.

A contract provision regulating the tenant's conduct within the dwelling obviously clarified the standard against which his conduct was measured. A tenant was obliged to perform according to the *lex locationis* (D. 19.2.25.3, Gaius; farm lease). A frequent contract clause limited his right to have a fire.[196] One source on this subject states that the effect of prohibiting a fire was to make the tenant liable for any accident that might ensue if he did have one (D. 19.2.11.1,

[194] See below, n. 203. My article cited above (n. 182) discusses other cases where tenants are liable *ex locato* for monetary losses to third parties; the main text (D. 19.1.13.30, Ulpian/Tubero; farm lease) involves damage to a leasehold not owned by the landlord.

[195] As is observed by D. Medicus, 185.

[196] To the sources cited below, add D. 19.2.9.3 (Ulpian; farm lease); on which, J. Miquel, *SZ* 81 (1964) 170-173, who emends to *conductor(is)*, is preferable to J.A.C. Thomas, *SZ* 79 (1962) 334-339, who retains *locator(is)*.

Ulpian).[197] As we might put it (though ancient sources avoid this formulation), the tenant's violation of the contract clause already constituted a blameworthy act, as a result of which he was obliged to accept even the unexpected consequences. This line of reasoning is clear in D. 19.2.11.4 (Ulp. 32 *ad Ed.*), 12 (Hermog. 2 *Iur. Epit.*):

> 11.4. Inter conductorem et locatorem convenerat, ne in villa urbana faenum componeretur: composuit: deinde servus igne illato succendit. ait Labeo teneri conductorem ex locato, quia ipse causam praebuit inferendo contra conductionem.[aw]
>
> 12. Sed et si quilibet extraneus ignem iniecerit, damni locati iudicio habebitur ratio.[ax]

The tenant of an urban villa has a haystack despite a prohibition in his contract; his slave (or a stranger) sets fire to the haystack; the tenant is liable *ex locato*. The *quia* clause at the end of D. 19.2.11.4 is probably at best a postclassical summary of Ulpian's reasoning,[198] which, however, is clear in any case; as D. 19.2.12 also shows, the decision hinged not on the tenant's vicarious liability for the acts of others, but rather on his duty to observe the contract. His failure to observe it made the damage possible, and this is the basis of his liability.[199] The rule goes back to Labeo. The addition

[197] The text is widely contested (cf. *Index Interp.*), but the essential point is not in doubt; cf. T. Mayer-Maly, *LC* 179; J. Miquel (cited n. 196) 172. (The second sentence of D. 19.2.11.1 has doubtless strayed from the context of D. 19.2.9.3.) Violation of a contract clause is wrongly brought into relation with *culpa* by C. A. Cannata, *Colpa* 311 ("colpa contrattuale pura").

[198] For text criticism, see *Index Interp.*, and add H. H. Pflüger, *SZ* 65 (1947) 195, who nonetheless considers the last clause to be substantially genuine; *contra*: e.g. J.A.C. Thomas, *SZ* 79 (1962) 337 (citing D. Daube at n. 12).

[199] So F. Haymann, *SZ* 40 (1919) 238; H. H. Pflüger (cited n. 198) 195; M. Sargenti, *SD* 20 (1954) 158; C. A. Cannata, *Colpa* 302 n. 2 and 311 n. 2 (if I understand him); and cf. D. 19.2.57 (above n. 186), also from Labeo, with a similar analysis of causation. T. Mayer-Maly,

by Hermogenianus reflects the ambiguities that arose in Labeo's decision at a time when the tenant had become more frequently liable for the blameworthy acts of his slaves.

This vicarious liability of the tenant for the conduct of others is a decidedly complex matter. D. 19.2.11 pr. (Ulp. 32 *ad Ed.*):

> Videamus, an et servorum culpam et quoscumque induxerit praestare conductor debeat? et quatenus praestat, utrum ut servos noxae dedat an vero suo nomine teneatur? et adversus eos quos induxerit utrum praestabit tantum actiones, an quasi ob propriam culpam tenebitur? mihi ita placet, ut culpam etiam eorum quos induxit praestet suo nomine, etsi nihil convenit, si tamen culpam in inducendis admittit, quod tales habuerit vel suos vel hospites: et ita Pomponius libro sexagesimo tertio ad Edictum probat.[ay]

The text opens with three questions. First, is the tenant liable (1a) for the *culpa* of his slaves, and (1b) for the *culpa* of "those he admitted into the property"? Second, if the answer to (1a) is yes, is the tenant liable noxally or *suo nomine*? Third, if the answer to (1b) is yes, can the tenant escape liability by ceding to his landlord the actions against the guilty party, or is he liable as if the *culpa* were his own? The text that follows has been drastically pared and probably confused.[200]

LC 196-197, seems to me a bit stiff (why should the lessor's purpose in inserting the provision matter?). According to our texts (all very early), a contract clause imposing a duty meant that the tenant was not to violate the term himself (D. 19.2.11.1, 4; 12; 29); and, when relevant, that he had to see to it that others under his authority did not violate the term (D. 19.2.30.2) or make it impossible for him to carry out the term (D. 19.2.30.4), this latter duty being virtually a strict liability in the era before vicarious liability became known. Measurable damage was always required, though the parties could probably substitute liquidated damages (cf. D. 19.2.54.1).

[200] The mass of authority against this text in the *Index Interp.* should not mislead; most of the objection is doctrinaire. We may

As the text stands, Ulpian's answer to the third question (the only answer that survives) is that, even without a contractual agreement, the tenant is liable *suo nomine* for the *culpa* of "those whom he has admitted to the property," but with the proviso that the tenant must himself have shown *culpa* in "admitting" such persons. This proviso, which imposes a requirement sharply limiting the general rule, is written in poor Latin and is usually regarded as interpolated.[201] In any event, the text shows that Ulpian's answer was controversial (cf. "mihi ita placet," and the support drawn from Pomponius). The reasonableness of Ulpian's answer depends, at least in part, on the extensiveness of *induco*. "Members of his household" (*sui*)[202] and "guests" are mentioned as examples in the exception; but were, for instance, subtenants also included? The alternative in the third question, that the tenant's "actions" (in which the *actio locati* must be included, cf. D. 19.1.13.30, Ulp.) might be ceded to the landlord, surely suggests that at least subtenants were also discussed in the original.

Such answer as we have to the second question in D.

---

dismiss the extreme excisions in G. Beseler, III 186; followed to some extent by H. H. Pflüger (cited n. 198) 193-194. The text is not limited to urban lease.

[201] See *Index Interp.*, esp. A. Pernice, II.2.1 257 n. 2; F. Schulz, *GrünhZ.* 38 (1911) 26 and 33ff. It is, however, sometimes asserted that the interpolation summarizes the original: L. Chiazzese, *APal.* 16 (1931) 421; P. Krückmann, *SZ* 63 (1943) 39; T. Mayer-Maly, *LC* 200-202; G. MacCormack, *RIDA*[3] 18 (1971) 540-541. While this may be true (the general rule is too broad), it must be stressed that a summary does not suffice to reproduce the thought of the original; what meaning e.g. did Ulpan give to "*quasi* ob propriam culpam"? MacCormack, like C. Alzon, *Location des Entrepôts* (1964) 69 and 142, is altogether too sanguine; and his summary on this theme (pp. 543-545) is intolerant of legal subtlety and historical analysis.

[202] Cf. D. 9.3.6.2 (Paul. 19 *ad Ed.*), on the *actio de posito vel suspenso*: "Habitator suam suorumque culpam praestare debet.[az]" *Sui* also includes slaves, but that question is better left to one side for the moment.

19.2.11 pr. comes from two parallel versions of Ulpian, 18 *ad Edictum*. First, *Coll.* 12.7.9:

> Sed et si qui servi inquilini insulam exusserint, libro X Urseius refert Sabinum respondisse lege Aquilia servorum nomine dominum noxali iudicio conveniendum: ex locato autem dominum teneri negat. Proculus autem respondit, cum coloni servi villam exusserint, colonum vel ex locato vel lege Aquilia teneri, ita ut colonus servos posset noxae dedere et si uno iudicio res esset iudicata, altero amplius non agendum.[ba]

A distinction between schools is drawn. If an urban tenant's slaves have burned down the *insula*, Sabinus accorded the owner a noxal action *lege Aquilia*; his younger contemporary Urseius added that the contract action was excluded. If a tenant farmer's slaves burned down a *villa*, Sabinus' contemporary Proculus also gave a "pro-noxal" action on the contract, either action however exhausting the other.[203] A pro-noxal action is one of the possibilities mentioned for the *culpa* of slaves in D. 19.2.11 pr. (considered above). The second text is D. 9.2.27.11:

> Proculus ait, cum coloni servi villam exussissent, colonum vel ex locato vel lege Aquilia teneri, ita ut colonus possit servos noxae dedere, et si uno iudicio res esset iudicata, altero amplius non agendum. sed haec ita, si culpa colonus careret: ceterum si noxios servos habuit, damni iniuria teneri, cur tales habuit. idem servandum et circa inquilinorum insulae personas scribit: quae sententia habet rationem.[bb]

[203] Concurrence causes no difficulties: D. Liebs, *Konk.* 209-210; it does not seem probable that all the passages on concurrence are interpolated, *contra*: U. von Lübtow, *Untersuchungen zur Lex Aquilia* (1971) 70-72. The "pro-noxal" action on the contract is more problematic; see n. 206, esp. as to E. Levy, *Konk.* II 70-78. Against attempts to find post-Ulpianic elements in this text, see F. Wieacker, *Textst.* 246; D. Liebs, *Konk.* 210 n. 82.

This text omits the views of Sabinus and Urseius, and adds to the rule of Proculus an exception, that this rule is true only if the *colonus* is free from *culpa*; but if he has "noxious" slaves, he himself should be held liable for the wrongful loss. Proculus, approved by Ulpian, urged extension of this rule to urban leasehold.

However probable it may be that the wretchedly written exception in D. 9.2.27.11 is interpolated,[204] it is clear that the discussion in this fragment is governed by the second question in D. 19.2.11 pr. The doctrine of the two passages as preserved is, furthermore, apparently a single one: the tenant is fully liable (1) if he has shown *culpa* in his choice of slaves or in his admission of freemen into his dwelling, and (2) if as a result of their *culpa* damage has been done to the owner; but where condition (1) is not fulfilled, the tenant is liable *on the contract* only "pro-noxally" in the case of slaves, and for no damages at all (only a cession of actions, if relevant) in the case of free persons.

On the basis of these passages, I believe that, despite elements of inevitable obscurity, four stages can be discerned in the development of the classical doctrine as to the urban tenant's vicarious liability. The first and narrowest state is the opinion of Sabinus, whereby the landlord has only the noxal action on the delict. This view presupposes a symmetry with the doctrine whereby the landlord was liable only for a noxal action on the delict when his slaves damaged or stole the tenant's property (D. 19.2.45 pr.,

[204] The probability is very high; in addition to the *Index Interp.*, see the massive bibliography in S. Schipani, *Responsibilità "ex Lege Aquilia"* (1969) 426 n. 32 (generally, 424-426), and G. MacCormack (cited n. 201) 538 nn. 31-32; and add, just on language, F. Eisele, *SZ* 13 (1892) 122-123; G. Beseler, v 12, 24; *idem*, *SZ* 66 (1948) 314, 332; F. Pringsheim, *SZ* 69 (1952) 292 n. 253. The same authors cited above (n. 201) are also optimistic about recovering some content here (Chiazzese, 420-421; Krückmann, 20; Mayer-Maly, 200; MacCormack, 536-539); add W. W. Buckland, *Yale LJ* 33 (1923/1924) 350; G. MacCormack, *SD* 41 (1975) 51. Against this view, J.A.C. Thomas, *Lab.* 17 (1971) 18; M. Kaser, *RPR*² I 513 n. 81; II 431 n. 53.

Paul).[205] Essentially, this degree of liability was no more than any Roman presented to another for the actions of his slaves.

The second stage involves Proculus' recognition that in the tenant's case something more than a mere delict was involved; the tenant's slaves lived in the dwelling with the tenant, and the tenant incurred through the contract a certain responsibility for them. But while Proculus gave the landlord a contractual action, he allowed the tenant to escape that action by surrendering the guilty slave, so that the tenant's liability was no higher than under a noxal Aquilian action.[206] This construction came dangerously close to admitting delictual principles into a *bona fide* action. Therefore, Proculus' "pro-noxal" action on the contract was perhaps more significant for its theoretical affirmation of a relevant contractual consideration than for its practicality.

In the third stage, subsequent jurists began to explore circumstances in which the tenant's contractual liability for acts of his slaves might be extended to include the full value of the damage. Ulpian, 18 *ad Ed.* (D. 9.2.27.9, = *Coll.* 12.7.7), preserves a decision of Neratius, where a tenant

[205] This passage is discussed below, at n. 242. Compare, on the reluctance to allow concurrence, D. 9.2.27.34 (Ulpian/Mela). A lease clause, however, could dramatically alter the situation: D. 19.2.30.4 (Alfen.), with A. Watson, *Obl.* 118-121, giving literature, esp. U. von Lübtow, in *St. Betti* III 369-373.

[206] That is, the Proculian ruling should be limited to the wording where *Coll.* 12.7.9 equals D. 9.2.27.11, plus the final sentence of the latter (sense only). On the basis for the Proculian ruling, see D. Liebs, *Konk.* 123 n. 217; on "pro-noxal" liability in contractual actions, p. 121, and p. 210 n. 82 against E. Levy, *Konk.* II.1 70-71; see also J.A.C. Thomas, *Lab.* 17 (1971) 16-32; M. Kaser, *RPR*[2] I 633 (it is not frequent); both with bibliography. G. MacCormack, *RIDA*[3] 19 (1972) 364, is unconvincing. The views of Sabinus and Proculus were plainly seen as opposed (cf. *autem*); this against Thomas, pp. 17-19, and G. MacCormack (cited n. 204) 60-61. The *Basilica* scholia (60.3.27.11, = Heimb. 5.292), followed by Levy, admit noxal liability only for the Aquilian action; but this mistranslates the Latin. The *Basilica* text itself (= Heimb. 5.291) gives the interpretation in my text.

farmer's slave, a stoker set to tend a furnace, fell asleep and let a *villa* burn down; the tenant was liable *ex locato* if he was negligent in choosing the servant.[207] Here the issue centered on the suitability of one particular slave for one particular and very dangerous task. In this case, the negligence of the tenant raised his liability above the normal degree. Though the decision comes from another area of *locatio*, we might compare D. 19.2.25.7 (Gai. 10 *ad Ed. Prov.*): the transporter of a column is liable for the *culpa* also of his employees; presumably, this profession demanded considerable skill.[208]

The fourth stage is represented by the doctrine in Ulpian. Here we may recognize the contribution made by Pomponius, whereby the tenant had a certain vicarious liability also for the free persons admitted to his dwelling.[209] While the two "exceptions" in D. 9.2.27.11 and 19.2.11 pr. are surely interpolated, it *may* be that Ulpian's own view was close enough to suggest these postclassical paraphrases: as, for instance, that when his slave (or a freeman) did damage to the landlord's property, the tenant was liable *suo nomine* in a contractual action if he had allowed this person to dwell in the premises even though he knew (or ought to

[207] Only the first part of the text is relevant here; its genuineness is generally accepted; on it, cf. e.g. C. A. Cannata, *Colpa* 299-302; G. MacCormack (cited n. 201) 539, with bibliography. (Compare Marcellus in D. 19.2.41.) This doctrine does not seem to appear before Neratius in sources on hire; contrast Labeo's decision in D. 19.2.13.1, where the doctrine is avoided. D. 19.2.60.7 (Labeo) involves warranty of a leased slave, and so is irrelevant.

[208] The exact basis of the decision is unfortunately unclear; cf. C. A. Cannata, *Colpa* 281-286, *contra*: G. MacCormack, (cited n. 201) 541-542 (both with further literature); add I. Molnar, *Lab.* 21 (1975) 42-43, and G.C.J.J. van den Bergh, *TR* 43 (1975) 68-69 (both missing the point).

[209] Note the rule against third-person liability for (some?) lessees in Julian, D. 13.6.19 (1 *Dig.*), cf. D. 19.2.41 (Ulp. 5 *ad Ed.*); and the exception taken to it by Marcellus in the latter passage. On these texts, W. Hoffmann-Riem, *SZ* 86 (1969) 400, with bibliography. Some form of liability for subtenants is, under my reasoning, probable.

have known) that the person's presence was likely to result in damage of this specific type; for example (to take an extreme case), the admitted person was a known arsonist who then set fire to the dwelling. Such a hypothetical generalization of the doctrine in D. 9.2.27.9 would amount to no more than saying that also in this area the tenant should not by his negligence endanger the landlord's property. Whether this doctrine is to be designated *culpa in eligendo* or not (probably not), I am unconvinced that classical jurisprudence was incapable of reaching such a position by the aid of its own doctrinal tenets. In any event, however, it should be recognized that Ulpian's doctrine (whatever it was) remained controversial even in Ulpian's time, and that its application was perhaps not common.

Much about vicarious liability remains obscure. Nonetheless, it seems certain that toward the end of the classical period a tendency was emerging to unite this form of liability with other liabilities under the general heading *culpa*. Unless this view is accepted, it is hard to reconcile sources such as D. 20.2.2 (Marcianus, quoting Pomponius), which assign to the tenant only an undifferentiated *culpa*-liability, with sources such as D. 19.2.11 pr. (Ulpian, citing Pomponius), which even when stripped of the commonly alleged interpolations make the tenant liable for the acts of those in his household. However, the *culpa*-liability does not appear in our sources (or at least not in those for *locatio conductio rei*) as a unified concept from which the various rules of liability can be neatly derived; and it may be that attributing to the tenant a *culpa*-liability meant in the late classical period very little more than saying that he was liable for the sum of all the various liabilities hitherto established for him in juristic writings.[210] *Culpa* would

[210] At least, I am unconvinced by the schema in C. A. Cannata, *Colpa*, esp. p. 317. There are lines of cases for lessee's liability other than those mentioned in the text: e.g. liability when a rented or loaned object is used in a way other than originally intended (cf. D. 13.6.5.7, 18 pr.; 19.2.13.3; cases restricted to moveables); liability for

therefore be incomprehensible without reference to the rich body of case law in particular areas. Something like this may be meant by Pomponius in D. 20.2.2 when he writes that the tenant was liable for damage done by *culpa* "when there is a contractual suit on this count."

All the same, *culpa* was perhaps coming to be recognized as a useful tool in discussing questions such as vicarious liability, and therefore as a conceptual source of liability. Vicarious liability greater than "pro-noxal" liability was plainly not unknown to early classical jurists; but they tended to reach it through the interpretation of special contract clauses (cf. D. 19.2.30.2, 4, both from Alfenus), sometimes with results that may seem to us more than a little harsh. Even though a text such as D. 9.2.27.9 (Neratius' decision) is bound now to seem isolated, the breakthrough for which it stands should not on that account be underestimated; at last a way was being discovered to isolate particular circumstances under which a tenant could be reasonably held as vicariously liable for the full damage. We ought not to speak, in this connection, of the invention of a new type of *culpa*, but rather of the extension of the idea of *culpa* into a new and different area.

Deductio ex Mercede and Alternatives

In certain situations, and particularly (we may suppose) where a condition adversely affecting tenancy was nevertheless not severe enough to justify abandonment, a tenant might unilaterally reduce his rent so as to reflect his diminished enjoyment. In the Justinianic *Digest* this form of relief did not find favor, it seems, and there are signs that the compilers have deliberately altered or omitted classical passages concerning *deductio*. Therefore it is admittedly not easy to determine the exact classical character of *deductio*.

---

one's own defective equipment that results in damage to a loaned object (D. 13.6.5.7; a slave); and so on. M. Kaser, *RPR*² I 511 n. 67, observes the need for a comprehensive study of non-Aquilian *culpa*.

Deductio ex Mercede

The principal text derives from the teachings of Servius. D. 19.2.27 pr. (Alf. 2 *Dig.*):

> Habitatores non, si paulo minus commode aliqua parte caenaculi uterentur, statim deductionem ex mercede facere oportet: ea enim condicione habitatorem esse, ut, si quid transversarium incidisset, quamobrem dominum aliquid demoliri oporteret, aliquem partem parvulam incommodi sustineret: non ita tamen, ut eam partem caenaculi dominus aperuisset, in quam magnam partem usus habitator haberet.[bc]

There are undeniably serious difficulties with this text, difficulties that begin with its first sentence.[211] These difficulties include: the odd placement of *non*; the peculiar expressions "ea . . . condicione habitatorem esse," "si quid transversarium incidisset," and "in quam magnam partem usus habitator haberet"; the vagueness of the repeated forms of *aliquis*, and of the various evaluatives ("paulo minus commode," "aliquem partem parvulam incommodi," "magnam partem usus"); the repetition of *pars*; the switch from direct to indirect discourse; the oddness in tense and sense of *aperuisset;* and so on. None of these objections is in itself fatal to the text, and counterarguments can be found;[212] but still the sum of the objections is not without considerable weight.

As the text stands, its logic runs: tenants should not deduct at once from the rent if their use of some portion of an apartment is only slightly impaired; for they are subject to the condition that they put up with the minor inconveniences caused by the landlord's repairs to the structure; but

[211] Here, for once, the interpolationists have not been critical enough. See the authors in the *Index Interp.*; add F. Albertario, v 300 n. 3 (article publ. 1922); G. Beseler, *SZ* 57 (1937) 10; *idem*, *SZ* 66 (1948) 345; G. Longo, *Ric.* 527-528 (article publ. 1953); T. Mayer-Maly, *LC* 154; but see also M. Kaser, *SZ* 74 (1957) 183 n. 15, who observes that the defects in the text cannot be healed by brackets.

[212] E.g. A. Watson, *Obl.* 115-116 (*parvulam* a characteristic diminutive). The switch to indirect discourse probably indicates a citation from Servius.

this rule does not bind them if a much-used part of the structure is affected by the repairs. Probably implicit in this text are the following rules:

(1) if the tenant's use of the apartment is seriously impaired, he is permitted to compensate by deducting from the rent (*arg. e contrario*);

(2) impairment of use means the objective reduction in the tenant's ability to use the apartment;[213]

(3) this impairment of use must arise after the start of the term of lease (cf. "si quid . . . incidisset");

(4) the owner is permitted to make repairs to the structure (an idea already encountered in relation to D. 43.17.3.3),[214] and despite a small resultant impairment of use, no deduction of rent is allowable while these repairs are being made;

(5) however, larger repairs, which in themselves constitute serious impairment of use, justify the tenant in taking counteraction.[215]

I suspect that all five points were made, more or less explicitly, in the original text, and that the passage has been abbreviated and rewritten by the compilers so as to stress (note the emphatic *non*) that the tenant was not ordinarily able to deduct from the rent.

If the view above is correct, three further points may have dropped out of the text. The first is the proper measure of deduction; but nonetheless the text at least suggests that this was conceived in direct relation to the loss of use (i.e. 75% use, 75% rent), so long as some "threshhold level" of impairment had been reached. The second point is more difficult:

[213] Again, this rule is similar to the "comfort and security" rule discussed above at n. 111 in relation to D. 19.2.25.2 (Gaius). In both cases it is unclear whether the tenant's protection extends to "common" areas like staircases and entryways.

[214] Discussed above at nn. 77-79.

[215] We should think here not only of a deduction from the rent, but also of abandonment.

was the tenant obliged to put up indefinitely with minor impairments of use? There are signs in the text that the answer to this question was no: the word *statim* (the tenant should not "at once" deduct), and the discussion, immediately after the initial sentence, of the owner who is in fact making repairs. The suggestion is that, at least where the minor repairs were correctable, the tenant could after a sufficient time deduct if the landlord had not made the necessary repairs.[216] But this second point implies a third: that the tenant was obliged to inform the landlord as to the need for repairs (see D. 19.2.11.2, Ulp. 32 *ad Ed.*).

The scheme that emerges from D. 19.2.27 pr. is remarkably complete, despite the mangled condition of the text. In several points this scheme can be supported from other texts:

First of all, it is plain that the jurists were very reluctant to "rewrite the contract" for the parties: that is, they operated on the general assumption that the tenant had leased what he desired to lease for the rent that he wished to pay. This principle (which is less obvious and often less true than it seems) supports their refusal to allow deduction in the case of impaired use commencing from the outset of the contract; the principle is specifically affirmed by D. 39.2.13.6 (Ulp. 53 *ad. Ed.*):[217] if a house was out of repair from the start of the lease, the tenant could not request a *cautio damni infecti* from his landlord, since the tenant had himself assumed the risk in making the lease; and the *actio conducti* was available only where the house subsequently "slipped into disrepair." Latent defects are not dealt with in the sources for urban lease, but one source on farm lease suggests that, where the landlord was also unaware of the defects, the tenant could avoid rent; and that where the

[216] The *actio conducti* for a landlord's failure to repair a *villa* is mentioned in D. 19.2.15.1 (Ulpian), in a part of the text that is probably interpolated (cf. *Index Interp.*), but may reflect classical sources (it is contained already in *PSI* 1449, *verso* line 1).

[217] Examined above at n. 106.

landlord had been aware of them, this constituted bad faith and a suit for *id quod interest* was therefore permitted.[218] However, this rule cannot be brought over directly into urban lease, since the defects crucial to a farm lease were normally those which affected its profitability, and not just its use (as in urban lease). In any event, no source directly states that the tenant was required to inspect the premises for defects before entering a lease; but the law as to impaired use made it clearly in his interests to do so, and we know from D. 19.2.60 pr. (considered above at nn. 41-42) that such inspection was normal.

Second, a text from Labeo clarifies the requirements as to impairment of use. D. 19.2.28 pr.-1 (Labeo 4 *Post. Epit. a Iav.*):

> Quod si domi habitatione conductor aeque usus fuisset, praestaturum (1) etiam eius domus mercedem, quae vitium fecisset, deberi putat.[bd]

The lessee dwells in a house which has fallen out of repair; if the lessee's use of the dwelling continues unimpaired, he must pay the full rent.[219] The key word is *aeque*: that is, the overall habitability of the house must not have been af-

[218] The main source is D. 19.2.19.1 (Ulpian/Serv., Lab., Sabin.), with D. 19.1.6.4 *in fine* (Pompon.), on a rented jar. The suggestion in the former source is that, if the landlord was unaware, the farm must be extremely unfit for its purpose, and that the tenant must suffer measurable economic loss. See on these sources M. Kaser (cited n. 211) 164-166, 176-177; P. Stein, *Fault in the Formation of Contract* (1958) 101-103; D. Medicus, 154-156; A. Watson, *Obl.* 113-114; H. Honsell, *Quod Interest* (1969) 134-135. A similar rationale may underlie the decision in D. 8.5.8.5 (Ulpian/Aristo): inability to use a rented cheese factory results in an *actio conducti*.

[219] A. Pernice, I 72, wrongly excised *praestaturum* to the end; followed by G. Longo, *Ric.* 534; but the subject of *putat* is Labeo, as usual in this work. We should probably read *partis* for *praestaturum* (so Mommsen, following the *Basilica*, 20.1.28, = Heimb. 2.354, Schelt. BT 990); cf. M. Kaser, (cited n. 211) 183 n. 119. Otherwise the text is acceptable.

fected.[220] But the sentence's protasis suggests a deeper thought as well: that if the lessee continues to use the structure (without, for example, complaining to the lessor about the defect), his conduct can be taken as evidence that the dwelling's habitability is undiminished.[221]

Third, two texts considered earlier were perhaps altered by the compilers so as to delete explicit reference to *deductio ex mercede*. In D. 19.2.25.2 (Gaius 10 *ad Ed. Prov.*), a sentence provides that if a neighbor darkens the tenant's windows, it is legal for the tenant to abandon his dwelling; this sentence, which has long been suspected of interpolation,[222] may have replaced an earlier and somewhat more tentative sentence that allowed *either* deduction *or* abandonment, depending on the severity of the case. In D. 39.2.37 *in fine* (Ulp. 42 *ad Sab.*), a neighbor has demolished a wall under the false belief that it was unstable; the wall's owner can recover lost rents for tenants who, because of the neighbor's act, abandon or "live less comfortably" ("non tam commode habitare possunt"). This latter phrase, which may represent a postclassical summary of the original,[223] in any event seems to refer to losses sustained as a result of deduction.

It goes without saying, finally, that rent deduction must be considered in close conjunction with the tenant's pledge of furnishings, which was the principal Roman device for forcing rent disputes into court.

As far back as the early classical period, the jurists began experimenting with alternative methods of handling the minor problems of urban leasehold. Their considerations began with the observation that a tenant has a contractual

[220] The meaning "rightly, justly" is entirely inappropriate for *aeque* here, *contra*: *VJR* s.v. "*aequus*" col. 292 line 19, and *TLL* s.v. "*aequus*" col. 1046 line 29; see, for a proof, P. Meylan, in *St. Riccobono* IV 307 n. 84.

[221] So, as it seems, T. Mayer-Maly, *LC* 154-155.

[222] The source is considered above at n. 111.

[223] See under n. 113 above.

right to remove his furnishings.[224] D. 19.2.19.5 (Ulp. 32 *ad Ed.*):

> Si inquilinus arcam aeratam in aedes contulerit et aedium aditum coangustaverit dominus, verius est ex conducto eum teneri et ad exhibendum actione, sive scit sive ignoraverit: officio enim iudicis continetur, ut cogat eum aditum et facultatem inquilino praestare ad arcam tollendam sumptibus scilicet locatoris.[be]

An owner-landlord has narrowed a doorway, thereby preventing a tenant from removing his strongbox. The tenant might bring a contract action or the *actio ad exhibendum* to force widening of the door, at the landlord's expense. In this situation, the interdict *de migrando* was not appropriate, since the obstruction was physical and not just a matter of the landlord's will, and thus the question arose as to who should pay for alterations to the door. The words *verius est* indicate a controversy, which has probably been suppressed by the compilers; and there may be other signs of postclassical editing.[225] But it is not easy to reconstruct the original text. This passage is one of several that allows the *actio ad exhibendum* in situations where what is clearly one person's property is for some reason located on or in another's property; the strongly phrased recuperative wording of the second sentence (virtually specific performance) also points toward this *actio*. We need not suppose, however, that

[224] Obviously, this contractual right is related to the interdict *de migrando*, which, at the (relatively late) date of its introduction, was intended to speed up the tenant's removal.

[225] The text has been variously attacked. G. Beseler secluded "et ad . . . locatoris," thus removing reference to the *actio ad exhibendum* (this type of usage was thought to be postclassical); followed by B. Frese, in *ACIR* II 253; T. Mayer-Maly, *LC* 171; and in substance by G. Longo, *Ric.* 536-537. By contrast, M. Marrone, *Actio ad Exhibendum* (1958) 300-301, = *APal.* 26 (1958) 472-473, defended the use of the *actio* against Beseler, but excised the contractual suit. Neither of these alternatives is convincing.

Ulpian did not deal with the *actio conducti* in the original text;[226] it is enough to say that he probably found the *actio ad exhibendum* more suited to the purpose than the *actio conducti*, which had the disadvantage of opening (or re-opening) contract questions. Nonetheless, there can be little doubt that the original text recognized the contractual duty of the landlord as regards removal of furnishings.

With this background we may consider two parallel texts. First, D. 19.2.19.4 (Ulp. 32 *ad Ed.*):

> Si inquilinus ostium vel quaedam alia aedificio adiecerit, quae actio locum habeat? et est verius quod Labeo scripsit competere ex conducto actionem, ut ei tollere liceat, sic tamen, ut damni infecti caveat, ne in aliquo dum aufert deteriorem causam aedium faciat, sed ut pristinam faciem aedibus reddat.[bf]

A tenant has added a door (or something else) to a house, and he later wishes to remove it. In the text as preserved,[227] Ulpian approves Labeo's solution as the better one, whereby the tenant has an *actio conducti* for removal, but must fur-

[226] So, rightly, M. Kaser, *Lab.* 5 (1959) 224 n. 3, reviewing Marrone (who discusses this use of the *actio*); cf. also D. Medicus, 161-162.

[227] This passage has attracted much criticism, centered mainly on the association of the *actio conducti* with the so-called *ius tollendi*. The final clause ("sed ut . . . reddat") may safely be excised (a duty to restore is not reflected in the *Basilica*, 20.1.19, = Heimb. 2.346-347; Schelt. BT 988); cf. *Index Interp.*, esp. S. Riccobono, II 248-249 (article publ. 1917); also G. Branca, *Danno Temuto* (1937) 311 n. 4, 506; T. Mayer-Maly, *LC* 170-171. On linguistic grounds we need go no further, as was wished by C. Longo, *Locatio Conductio* (1920/1921; not seen) 506, removing "et est verius" to the end; followed by, e.g. G. Longo, *Ric.* 536; while F. P. Bremer, *Iurisprudentia Antehadriana* vol. II.1 (1898) 253, removed "ut ei tollere" to the end, and others copied him. The text is rightly defended by G. Melillo, *Tignum Iunctum* (1964) 80-82, 86-90; but I certainly cannot agree with him (p. 89 n. 126; so also Mayer-Maly) that the passage does not refer to the *actio conducti*, but rather to a property action (an extraordinary construction of "competere ex conducto actionem"); and Melillo contradicts himself at p. 87.

nish a *cautio* against damage resulting from the removal. Second, D. 6.1.59 (Jul. 6 *ex Minic.*):

> Habitator in aliena aedificia fenestras et ostia imposuit, eadem post annum dominus aedificiorum dempsit: quaero, is qui imposuerat possetne ea vindicare. respondit posse: nam quae alienis aedificiis conexa essent, ea quamdiu iuncta manerent, eorundem aedificiorum esse, simul atque inde dempta essent, continuo in pristinam causam reverti.[bg]

The inhabitant (a tenant)[228] has installed windows and doors in another's building; he may vindicate them if the owner removes them; otherwise, after their connection to the structure, they belong to the building so long as they are joined to it. Nothing is known about Minicius, whose work Julian commented on (cf. D. 6.1.61); but the parallel passages D. 12.1.22 and 19.1.6.4 show that he recorded the responses of Sabinus, who is therefore probably the subject of *respondit* in our text.[229] The last sentence of D. 6.1.59 removes from the tenant the right to vindicate the fixtures before the owner removes them. There is at least a strong suggestion in this text that the tenant had not been able to reclaim his doors and windows by any legal means during the interval before the owner removed them.[230]

The doors and windows in these passages are (evidently) not new openings, but rather the wooden fixtures that were

[228] The passage, which presents a common classical view, has apparently never been considered interpolated. *Habitator* equals *inquilinus* in a number of early jurists: e.g. D. 19.2.27 pr., 30 pr. (both Alfen.); 19.1.53.2 (Labeo); cf. D. 39.2.37 *in fine* (Ulp. 42 *ad Sab.*). It makes no difference in this passage whether or not the tenant is still in residence.

[229] So S. Riccobono, I 133-134 (article publ. 1894). O. Lenel, *Paling.* I 489 n. 3, preferred Minicius as the respondent, on the doubtful analogy of D. 6.1.61.

[230] At least, the passage should not be interpreted as limited solely to the case where the owner has removed and appropriated the tenant's fixtures; the response reflects much broader issues. Far too literalistic is G. Melillo (cited n. 227) 86-90.

set into preexisting apertures in the masonry. To judge from the remains at Ostia, they could be removed, but ordinarily only with some difficulty.[231]

In D. 19.2.19.4, Labeo allows the tenant to make a calculation: the value to him of the door he has installed, as against the costs that he will incur (through the *cautio*) for damages which the removal causes to the building. If this balance is sufficiently in his favor, then he will be likely to remove the door. If it is not, he will abandon the door, at least for the time being.

The so-called *ius tollendi*, referred to in this and other passages, was in classical law an equitable remedy for situations where expenditures attributable to one person (the claimant) had improved another person's property; by this remedy the claimant was allowed to recover at least some of the improvement. It was part of the *officium iudicis* to determine the appropriateness of the remedy, as a famous discussion in D. 6.1.38 (Cels. 3 *Dig.*) demonstrates.[232] The jurists suggest the following interrelated criteria:

(1) The *ius tollendi* was not accorded save in specific situations, therefore it was a privilege and not a true right; only as to dowries was it frequently envisaged;

(2) Its award normally depended on the absence of any

[231] The detachability of windows (and doors) is clear in D. 46.4.13.2; on the other hand, D. 30.41.9 shows the difficulty of detachment. As for Ostian windows, see J. E. Packer, *The Insulae of Imperial Ostia*, *MAAR* 31 (1971) 27.

[232] On interpolationist criticism of D. 6.1.38, see E. Nardi, *Studi sulla Ritenzione* vol. I (1947) 326-334; G. Beseler, *SZ* 66 (1948) 299; F. Wieacker, *Iura* 13 (1962) 20 n. 41; but now D. Liebs, *Konk.* 187 n. 326 ("von Anfang bis Ende echt," perhaps exaggerating); and see also E. Seidl, in *Fs. Lehmann* (1956) 103. On the *ius tollendi*, there is no really modern treatment; see the bibliography in M. Kaser, *RPR*² II 296 n. 34; and add esp. J.-P. Levy, *Les Impenses Dotales* (1937) 223-275 (the best account hitherto); and *idem*, in *Synt. Arangio-Ruiz* I 97-103. Suffice it to say that I am convinced that all the references in the passage below are classical in content if not in form.

viable alternative whereby the claimant could recover the expenditures (e.g. D. 6.1.38);

(3) The *iudex* considered the degree of hardship which a suit involved for either party; the *ius tollendi* could alleviate hardship on one side or the other (again, D. 6.1.38);

(4) The good faith of the claimant and his relationship to the other party were also taken into account (D. 6.1.27.5, 38); extreme bad faith probably weakened the claim (see D. 41.1.7.12, but also the possible exceptions of D. 5.3.39.1, and 6.1.37);

(5) One source suggests that the claimant should not have been under a positive legal duty not to build (D. 7.1.15 pr.: a usufructuary), and the *ius tollendi* could probably be removed by contract (e.g. *CIL* 6.37795, = *FIRA* III no. 145c);

(6) The claimed property should be separable from the main property (D. 6.1.38; 25.1.9)—in this respect an entire building might be more favored than a fixture within a building;[233]

(7) Almost all sources stress in one way or another the necessity either of doing no damage to the main property or of not leaving it worse than it was before the expenditures;

(8) Malicious use of the *ius tollendi* was not allowed; the claimed property, when separated, ought to be of some use to the claimant (D. 6.1.38; 24.1.63; 25.1.9; 30.43.1).

Finally, it must be stressed that the *ius tollendi* was equitable, not a series of hard and fast rules; the weakness of the claim by one criterion might not necessarily doom it. As an equitable claim, it was in some cases available even where the claimant had never owned or possessed the things he sought to remove; it was sometimes enough that his money had ultimately been used for these expenditures (D. 15.3.3.4,

[233] However, separability is plainly not the sole criterion in D. 19.2.19.4; *contra*: e.g. S. Riccobono, II 247-259; H. Siber, II 59; S. Riccobono, *Bull.* 47 (1940) 7-10; G. Melillo (cited n. 227) 80; but cf. T. Mayer-Maly, *LC* 171. The text says nothing about separability.

Ulpian).[234] The *ius tollendi* thus stood in no strict dogmatic relationship to principles of property accession, like *tignum iunctum* or *superficies solo cedit*, as these principles emerge in sources like D. 6.1.59; the *ius tollendi* was an equitable exception to the principles of accession.

Therefore D. 19.2.19.4 and 6.1.59 do not contradict each other, but rather speak to different aspects of the installation of fixtures. In the first passage Labeo is ascribing to the tenant a contractual right to remove the fixtures, subject to certain conditions; in the second passage, Julian asserts the revival of the tenant's full ownership after the owner's removal of the fixtures.

From among the criteria for the *ius tollendi* that are listed above, it was undoubtedly the fourth that Labeo considered to most favor the tenant's case, since the tenant's right to remove his effects was a well-established part of the *actio conducti*;[235] while the sixth, seventh, and eighth criteria were indirectly expressed in the *cautio*. For us, however, the most important criterion is the second, namely that, at least in Labeo's time, the tenant could not obtain direct recompense for his expenditures in installing the door. Behind this

[234] A creditor has lent money to a slave, who has used it for lavish, unauthorized decoration of his master's house; the creditor cannot recover the loan directly from the master by the theory that the money has been turned to the master's benefit (*actio de in rem verso*), but he does have the *ius tollendi*. The text is clearly revised (cf. *Index Interp.*), but the core is salvageable; the comparison with the unauthorized procurator and the granting of the *ius tollendi* seem to allude to D. 17.1.10.10 (Ulpian/Labeo), note references to Labeo at D. 15.3.3.3, 5. The text of D. 17.1.10.10 has recently been defended against exaggerated dogmatism (cf. *Index Interp.*) by P. Angelini, *Il "Procurator"* (1971) 101-103; it is probably abridged. The difficulties of combining the sources on the *ius tollendi* with the sources on accession to immoveables are clearly illustrated by J. P. Meincke, *SZ* 88 (1971) 153-156, esp. 155 n. 82.

[235] What was the action which Ulpian rejected in D. 19.2.19.4 (cf. "et est verius")? Probably the *actio ad exhibendum*, as in D. 19.2.19.5. But we need not suppose, with S. Riccobono, 1 222-223, that Ulpian originally preferred the other action.

rule lies the reasonable principle that urban tenants should not be encouraged to alter the structure of their dwellings significantly. The force of this rule made it in the tenant's interest to make alterations light and easily removable. Otherwise, the tenant was obliged to await the owner's separation of the fixtures from the structure.

The problem arises, however, that not every expenditure by a tenant for a new fixture is to be regarded equally. Of the many reasons that a tenant might have for inserting new windows and doors in his dwelling, surely the commonest has to do with personal security; as we saw above (at n. 111, on D. 19.2.25.2), excessive dilapidation of these fixtures was sufficient to justify the tenant's abandoning the dwelling. In many cases, however, a tenant might himself repair the old fixtures or install new ones. Were these necessary expenses also irrecoverable, even in the later classical period? Some later classical sources allow the tenant farmer to collect not only necessary but also useful expenditures which improve the farm property;[236] but a tenant farmer, unlike an urban tenant, is in part the employee of his landlord (see his duty to cultivate: D. 19.2.25.3, 54.1; Paul. *Sent.* 2.18.2), and thus in a sense the manager of an economic enterprise. Therefore, the doctrine of farm lease cannot without qualification be transferred to urban lease (though it does have an analogous sphere of application in the lease of a middleman). Perhaps the urban tenant could by the end of the classical period recover necessary expenses for his dwelling, or could repair and deduct from the rent; the sources fail us. One (possibly postclassical) source pertaining to public law allows a tenant to repair the roadway beside his dwelling when the landlord has failed to do so; the tenant can then deduct the cost of the repair from his rent.[237]

[236] D. 7.1.34.1 (Julian); 19.2.61 pr. (Scaevola), 55.1 (= Paul. *Sent.* 2.18.4). The literature on these passages, which is unsatisfactory, includes S. Riccobono, II 142-149 and T. Mayer-Maly, *LC* 170-172. On the *colonus* as an employee, see before all A. Pernice, *SZ* 19 (1898) 90-91; and above at n. 51.

[237] D. 43.10.1.3 (Papin. *Liber de Cura Urbium*, in Greek), on which

Deductio ex Mercede

Finally, under unusual circumstances the landlord might be expected or compelled to remit the rent altogether, even though the tenant continued to enjoy the dwelling. D. 19.2.5 (Ulp. 28 *ad Ed.*):

> Si tibi habitationem locavero, mox pensionem remittam, ex locato et conducto agendum erit.[bh]

The landlord has (apparently voluntarily) remitted the rent; nonetheless the contract continues, and the two parties are required to fulfill all other contractual duties to one another.[238] This type of voluntary remission appears to have occurred most frequently through legacy (D. 34.3.18, cf. 16-17; 19.2.24.5), and occasionally in the form of an outright gift (see D. 2.14.56). Twice in the late Republic public remissions of urban rent were enacted, both in circumstances that were virtually revolutionary.[239] It appears, however, that the remission of urban rent never became a part of imperial policy; with the consequence that the well-developed body of private law concerning remission of farm rent has no counterpart in the sources for urban leasehold.[240] Nonetheless, it is likely that (as in farm lease, see esp. Plin. *Ep.* 9.37) the landlord was socially expected to remit rent in

---

see T. Mayer-Maly, *LC* 172-173 (with bibliography), who seems to accept the idea as classical. The text is misunderstood by A. dell'Oro, *I Libri de Officio* (1960) 267 (cf. generally pp. 263-268).

238 The text is not interpolated. On it, see J. Michel, 256-257, and 307ff., where the difference between remission and "leasehold" *donationis causa* is discussed; H. P. Benöhr, *Das Sogennante Synallagma* (1965) 105-106.

239 Remissions occur in 48 B.C. (*CIL* 14.4531, from Ostia; Suet. *Caes.* 38.2; Dio 42.41.1) and in 41 (Dio 48.9.5); see above all M. Frederiksen, *JRS* 56 (1966) 128-141, at 133-135; Z. Yavetz, *Plebs and Princeps* (1969) 45, with bibliography. On the revolutionary nature of these remissions, see Caes. *BC* 3.21.1; Dio 42.22.3-4, 32.2; and, for the reaction of landlords, Cic. *Off.* 2.83.

240 The question of *remissio mercedis* is tangled up, in the sources and in the scholarship, with the more general one of *periculum locatoris*; see the full bibliography given above at n. 102.

order to counter unexpected and unusually severe economic hardships among his tenants.

No juristic source discusses the extent of the urban landlord's liability to his tenant (beyond his liability in making the premises available), as when (for instance) the landlord damages the tenant's property.[241] D. 19.2.45 pr. (Paul. 22 *ad Ed.*) indicates that where the landlord's slaves caused the tenant a loss or stole something, only a noxal action on the delict was allowed, but no action on the contract.[242]

No source discusses the balance of liabilities for losses to the tenant caused by *vis maior* (save as it affects the habitability of the premises);[243] nor is there discussion of the landlord's liability for express or tacit warranties lying beyond the implied "warranty" of continued habitability.[244]

Holding Over and Leases Without Term

Holding over occurs when a tenant continues to detain the premises beyond the end of the term of lease, with either the explicit or the tacit consent of his landlord. I have combined discussion of this topic with a discussion of leases originally

241 Cf. M. Kaser, *RPR*² I 566 n. 34, for bibliography; additions in II 602. The texts do not really deal with this point, probably because contract protection was not required.

242 On the passage (not interpolated), see esp. P. Stein, (cited n. 218) 104-105; D. Liebs, *Konk.* 122-123. G. MacCormack, *RIDA*³ 18 (1971) 542-543, misunderstands the text.

243 All the discussion of this point centers on farm lease, where it is obviously more relevant, cf. esp. D. 19.2.15.2, with M. Kaser, *RPR*² I 566 n. 37 (bibliography). Still, the sources on farm lease do not imply that (e.g.) the landlord was liable for damage caused by *vis maior* to a tenant's personal property. C. 4.65.12 (Philip, A.D. 245) exempts the owner, in the absence of complicity, from liability for damage caused to tenant's property from a break-in by thieves; cf. also D. 9.2.27.8 (Ulpian, = *Coll.* 12.7.3). Nor had the owner a liability for damage from the collapse of neighboring buildings, cf. D. 39.2.13.5, 21.

244 But the validity of such warranties is to be presumed from normal Roman lease law; cf. M. Kaser (cited n. 211) 161-166, for sources.

without term because the law was probably similar for both cases.

Only one text speaks clearly to the problem of holding over in urban leasehold. D. 19.2.13.11 (Ulp. 32 *ad Ed.*):

> Qui impleto tempore conductionis remansit in conductione, non solum reconduxisse videbitur, sed etiam pignora videntur durare obligata. sed hoc ita verum est, si non alius pro eo in priore conductione res obligaverat: huius enim novus consensus erit necessarius. eadem causa erit et si rei publicae praedia locata fuerint. quod autem diximus taciturnitate utriusque partis colonum reconduxisse videri, ita accipiendum est, ut in ipso anno, quo tacuerunt, videantur eandem locationem renovasse, non etiam in sequentibus annis, etsi lustrum forte ab initio fuerat conductioni praestitutum. sed et si secundo quoque anno post finitum lustrum nihil fuerit contrarium actum, eandem videri locationem in illo anno permansisse: hoc enim ipso, quo tacuerunt, consensisse videntur. et hoc deinceps in unoquoque anno observandum est. in urbanis autem praediis alio iure utimur, ut, prout quisque habitaverit, ita et obligetur, nisi in scriptis certum tempus conductioni comprehensum est.[bi]

There are some difficulties with this text,[245] but our attention centers primarily on the first sentence (which is not interpolated) and on the last (of which only the *nisi* clause has a probably postclassical form).[246] The first sentence establishes

[245] Its core is rightly defended by F. Gallo, in *Synt. Arangio-Ruiz* II 1198-1211, at 1202-1203, against the authors in the *Index Interp.*, and also e.g. G. Donatuti, in *St. Bonfante* IV 476-477; F. Pringsheim, *LQR* 7 (1933) 380 n. 6; F. Wieacker, *Societas* vol. I (1936) 102 n. 3; G. Longo, *Ric.* 540-541 (article publ. 1953); T. Mayer-Maly, *LC* 220. G. Beseler, in *Scr. Ferrini Mil.* III 296, thoroughly rewrote the text.

[246] Cf. *Index Interp.* The phrase *in scriptis* is obviously not classical if it means that a written lease was required in order to establish a term of lease; cf. T. Mayer-Maly, *LC* 89. However, it is perhaps best to take the *nisi* clause as an inaccurate postclassical summary; the original text probably voided the rule in the main sentence during

the rule that when a tenant remains in the leasehold beyond the term of lease, he is considered to have re-leased the premises (*reconduxisse*) and his previous pledges (for payment of rent) still hold for this new interval.

The last sentence describes a special rule for urban leasehold: the tenant is obligated only for the period during which he is in residence. In conjunction with the first sentence, this means that not only does the contract continue at its old rate of rent, but also that the tenant's pledges are held for this new period until the tenant ceases to live there.[247] Could the tenant therefore abandon the dwelling at any time during the holdover period, without incurring a liability for rent beyond the time of actual occupancy? Likewise, could the landlord expel the tenant at any time during the holdover period, without incurring a liability for damages because of his failure to provide the structure?

The answer to these two questions, which is surely yes in both cases, is perhaps best established through the comparison which Ulpian draws with farm lease. Here the consequence of holdover is that *both* parties are considered to renew for a full year: that is, during this new interval the landlord must provide the farm, and the tenant must pay the rent.[248] By contrast, in urban leases Ulpian clearly envisages no implication of a new term of lease. But if the period of holdover could end at any time, it is surely most reasonable to assume that either party was free to terminate

---

the term of lease established by the parties expressly. If this view is correct, the main rule was relevant not only to cases of holdover but also to cases of lease without term.

[247] Compare C. 4.65.16 (Valer., A.D. 260; farm lease).

[248] Observe that this is *not* the case when the *colonus* remained on the farm against the express will of the landlord; in that case, e.g. detachment of fruits was *furtum*: D. 12.1.4.1; 47.2.68.5. Further, the landlord must have been competent to renew: D. 19.2.14 (farm lease). Probably any tenant who held over against the landlord's will was liable for damages in a suit on the contract; see above at nn. 73-74. There was apparently no "*furtum usus*" of immoveables, however.

it; and this must be the implicit meaning of "prout quisque habitaverit."

What this interpretation means is that the concept of unjustified expulsion and abandonment was no longer applicable past the end of the term of lease. Unjustified abandonment resulted, as we have seen, in the tenant's having to pay the agreed-upon rent for the remaining term of lease;[249] but here no such term existed, as Ulpian clearly states. The consequence of unjustified expulsion was, in the typical case, that the landlord had to pay as damages the cost of equivalent housing for the remainder of the term of lease;[250] but again, no such term existed. In this situation, the distinction between "justified" and "unjustified" expulsion and abandonment ceased to be legally meaningful.

Up to this point I agree substantially with Filippo Gallo.[251] What is more difficult to understand is Gallo's reluctance to apply these same rules to leases that originally had no fixed term. Instead, he argues that the time-interval envisaged for payment of rent was construed by the jurists as a term of lease (e.g. monthly payment of rent meant a monthly term of lease),[252] with the consequence that in most instances the

[249] Cf. esp. D. 19.2.24.2, 27.1, 55.2; 43.32.1.4; all discussed above under "Justified Abandonment."

[250] Cf. above all D. 19.2.28.2, discussed above at n. 56. The middleman could obtain *id quod interest* damages; cf. esp. D. 19.2.30 pr.

[251] F. Gallo (cited n. 245) 1202-1206. Gallo, however, needlessly invents a day-to-day renewal of the holdover; what is the utility of such a device? Why not an hour-to-hour renewal? The true reason seems to be Gallo's unwillingness to admit any leases without a term.

[252] *Ibid.* 1201-1208; followed by R. Knütel, *Contrarius Consensus* (1968) 122-123. Gallo supports his views by reference to the *Codice Civile* (pp. 1207-1208). If I am not mistaken, no classical source actually discusses a lease in which a term of lease had not been set by the parties. In C. 4.65.10 (Gord., A.D. 239), *perpetua conductio* probably refers to a permanent lease of public land (cf. Gaius 3.145), and not to a lease without fixed term as S. Perozzi, II 290, thought; cf. M. Kaser, *RPR*² I 568 n. 54, with literature. On the other hand, a lease without fixed term was certainly possible, since only *merces certa* was required for a valid lease (Gaius 3.142).

tenant could be expelled or abandon only as the rent fell due. There is, of course, nothing legally impossible about this view; the major objections to it are that it presupposes an improbable asymmetry with *reconductio tacita*, and that it lacks support in ancient texts. Gallo, it is true, cites D. 43.32.1.4 (Ulp. 73 *ad Ed.*), a text we have already considered in relation to the interdict *de migrando* (at nn. 142-143). The first two sentences run:

> Si pensio nondum debeatur, ait Labeo interdictum hoc cessare, nisi paratus sit eam pensionem solvere. proinde si semenstrem solvit, sexmenstris debeatur, inutiliter interdicet, nisi solverit et sequentis sexmenstris, . . .[bj]

Here the tenant is seeking to abandon his dwelling; he must account to his landlord for the full rent. Gallo argues that the first sentence better accords with a lease lacking a fixed term; and certainly no term is mentioned.[253] But Gallo fails to reckon with the second sentence (linked to the first by *proinde*), where there must have been a term of one year; otherwise, by Gallo's own rules, the tenant would have been able to depart without liability from the building after six months. The continuation of the cited text (the next case concerns lease "in plures annos") makes it even clearer that a term of one year was understood in the first two cases—or, at least, that one was understood by Ulpian. In sum, there seems to be no reason to doubt that a contract with an indefinite term could be unilaterally ended by either party at any time.

It may therefore be observed, in conclusion, that Roman jurists did not favor urban leases without a fixed term, nor were they willing to construe a term of lease where the parties had failed to provide one for themselves. In such cases, where the tenant's rent was payable at fixed intervals, the termination of the lease would simply result in a *pro rata*

253 However, a one-year term of lease is mentioned in the *Basilica* (60.19.1, = Heimb. 5.608; a term of lease: 609).

portion of the rent becoming due.[254] The parties themselves did not enjoy in the meantime the protection of the rules on unjustified abandonment and expulsion. All of this amounted to strong legal pressure on the parties to agree in advance on a term of lease. On the other hand, where the parties wished (or where one was too weak to prevent it), it was entirely possible to construct a lease without a definite term. Toward the end of the classical period such a lease form was partially supplemented by the growth of a doctrine relating lease without definite term to *precarium*.[255]

Mitigation of Damages

As we have seen, urban leasehold not infrequently terminated through abandonment or expulsion, whether for justified reasons or not. If the active party had no justification, he thereby opened himself to an immediate suit on the contract, by means of which the injured party could obtain a legally ordained relief. In such a situation, it sometimes occurs that a legal system, instead of forcing the "guilty" party to pay the full measure of relief, will instead seek alternatives whereby the ostensible desires of the aggrieved plaintiff are satisfied in a manner that requires the minimum from the defendant. This seeking for alternatives is called mitigation of damages. It is a relatively sophisticated way of looking at a contractual relationship, and, as we might have forecasted, it enjoys only limited development in Roman law.

Suppose, for example, that a landlord is evicted through no fault of his own, with the consequence that his tenants

[254] Payment of rent owed to date: D. 19.2.9.1, 21; 39.2.34; cf. 19.2.9.6. Where rent was paid in advance, the refund of a *pro rata* portion was required: D. 19.2.7-8, 19.6, 30 pr.-1, 33.

[255] Cf. esp. D. 19.2.4 (Pompon.), with M. Kaser, *SZ* 89 (1972) 104-111 (on the passage, pp. 109-110); the considerations in F. Gallo (cited n. 245) 1208 n. 32, are unconvincing.

are expelled; but the landlord is willing to offer them alternative and equivalent housing. D. 19.2.9 pr. (Ulp. 32 *ad Ed.*):

> Si quis domum bona fide emptam vel fundum locaverit mihi isque sit evictus sine dolo malo culpaque eius, Pomponius ait nihilo minus eum teneri ex conducto ei qui conduxit, ut ei praestetur frui quod conduxit licere. plane si dominus non patitur et locator paratus sit aliam habitationem non minus commodam praestare, aequissimum esse ait absolvi locatorem.[bk]

This text establishes, more clearly than any other, the rule whereby a landlord owes *id quod interest* damages for lack of right.[256] The text, indeed, goes to great lengths to specify the *locator*'s innocence; he purchased the house (or farm) *bona fide*, and then rented it out and was evicted "sine dolo malo culpaque eius." Any view of this text that sees in the landlord's actions anything less than complete good faith is surely misconceived.[257] In this situation, it was obviously very tempting to ameliorate the landlord's damages by allowing him to offer the tenant an equivalent dwelling. Thereby the landlord was relieved from a situation where he could be compelled not only to pay the higher cost of the tenant's alternative dwelling under another landlord (D. 19.2.28.2) but also to undergo the risk of having his own alternative dwelling go unused. The specification "non minus commodam," which has sometimes made this sentence suspect of interpolation,[258] is in any event crucial to the

[256] Cf. before all M. Kaser, *SZ* 74 (1957) 168, and in general 166-169.

[257] *Contra*: N. Palazzolo, *Bull.* 68 (1968) 286-292, who ignores the chiasmus "locaverit mihi isque sit evictus" and (against all authoritative editions) interpunctuates after *mihi*; he then argues that "sine dolo malo culpaque eius" applies only to the eviction (but note that *eius* is used, not *sua*). This is a good illustration of the difficulties of expressing oneself so as to remove all equivocations, and it voids the complaint of S. Solazzi, *L'Estinzione dell'Obbligazione* vol. 1 (2d ed. 1935) 81, that the text is repetitious.

[258] Most commentators until recently deleted "plane si . . . loca-

development of the idea: the tenant should not be forced to accept a less than fully equivalent dwelling (even when the landlord offers a reduced rent), and the landlord must, because of his original lack of right, bear all the risk. But no more than the risk; a judicial finding that the proffered alternative is equivalent relieves the landlord of further liability for damages if the tenant declines the offer.

The same idea recurs in D. 19.2.60 pr. (Labeo *Post.* 5 *a Iav. Epit.*), discussed above at nn. 41-42. In this text a middleman is regarded as justified in renouncing the lease of a *domus* when (due to repairs that are being made) he is unable to show the apartments to prospective sublessees as late as one month before the start of the rental year; nor can he himself be compelled to live in the structure when the rental year begins:

> . . . nisi si paratus fuisset locator commodam domum ei ad habitandum dare.[bl]

As it appears from the text, the middleman had envisaged living in the *domus* himself, as well as subleasing parts of it. He cannot be held to the contract to the extent that he must live in the house himself, even though the house may well be ready for him at the start of the rental year. There follows the *nisi* clause quoted above, which (on purely formal grounds) can be unhesitatingly rejected as not belonging to the original text.[259] But the situation in D. 19.2.60 pr., and even the language of the *nisi* clause ("commodam domum"), are so close to D. 19.2.9 pr. that we are perhaps justified in supposing the *nisi* clause to be not an innovation,

---

torem," see *Index Interp.*; but see now T. Mayer-Maly, *LC* 156; M. Kaser (cited n. 256) 168; D. Medicus, 100 n. 15. On *commodus*, see G. Beseler, *SZ* 57 (1937) 11-12 (often interpolated, but not always); on *aequissimum*, *idem*, *SZ* 45 (1925) 456 (the word may replace a milder one).

[259] Cf. *Index Interp.*, and esp. F. Eisele, *SZ* 10 (1889) 312-313, who supposes interpolation following D. 19.2.9 pr. On the rest of the text, see above at nn. 41-42.

but rather a summary of a passage which raised the possibility of an alternative house. Here, to be sure, the landlord was (in the absence of any fault) not liable to the middleman, who was taking advantage of the unavailability of the *domus* as a ground for renunciation of the entire contract;[260] nor is there anything "unjust" about such a solution. Nonetheless, in this case the repairs to the building obviously had not at first diminished the wish of the two parties to resume the contract as soon as feasible, and it was only the delay past the last reasonable date for obtaining sublessees that caused the middleman finally to back out. In such a situation there is something to be said for allowing the landlord to offer alternative housing.

Beyond this point the sources do not go. They do not extend the right of offering alternative housing to a landlord who because of his own fault, however slight, was forced to expel a tenant—as, for instance, where the landlord has accidentally leased the same premises to two tenants.

Similarly, it is unlikely that mitigation was recognized in the case of tenants who abandoned "unjustly"; as we saw above (at nn. 92-95), the landlord was entitled to seek forthwith, not damages, but outstanding rent;[261] nor is there a hint in the classical sources that he was obliged to minimize his damages by seeking a substitute tenant. Indeed, it appears that in principle the landlord could pocket both the "rent" of the extenant and whatever he received from a substitute tenant.[262]

[260] See esp. M. Kaser (cited n. 256) 183 and n. 113; accepted by D. Medicus, 100 and n. 16.

[261] D. 19.2.24.2, 28.2; 43.32.1.4; cf. 19.2.55.2 (farm lease); all discussed above at nn. 92-95. The final *quatenus* clause in D. 19.2.55.2, which limits the landlord's claim to *id quod interest*, is interpolated, cf. n. 95.

[262] At least, no source opposes this view, though I find it very difficult to believe. I suspect, however, that the tenant could at least demand that he be allowed to occupy the dwelling if he had paid the rent; but if his rent was owed only as it fell due (cf. above at n. 95), this would in effect mean that the contract remained in force. The

Such a doctrine is extremely harsh. The explanation for it is perhaps twofold: the jurists wanted tenants to think very seriously before abandoning;[263] they also knew how easy it was for them to disappear afterwards in the maze of a city like Rome. More generally, the jurists seem in principle to have preferred not to modify payments of money due under a contract;[264] either all the money was due, or none of it. In any event, their insistence on the tenant's payment of the remaining rent did not allow the development of a doctrine governing mitigation of damages in this area of the law.

---

sources seem to suggest that, after an unjustified abandonment, the landlord had his choice between ending the lease (hence seeking only the rent up to the abandonment) or enforcing the lease to the end of its term (hence seeking all rent as it fell due). In the latter case, the major difficulty arose when the tenant no longer wished to occupy the structure and could not find a subtenant; could the landlord then rent to another tenant?

[263] Cf. above, under "Justified Abandonment."

[264] See esp. D. Medicus, 332-333.

V

Recognition of Interests in Roman Lease Law

IN THE preceding chapter I set out the system of law by which, so I implied, urban leasehold was governed during the High Roman Empire. In three important respects, however, this implication is incorrect.

First of all, we do not read our juristic sources in anything like their original form and fullness; rather, we read them mostly in a Byzantine version: highly excerpted, often compressed, and at least to some extent reworded. Admittedly, scholars have not yet arrived at a consensus in evaluating the significance of this Byzantine redaction,[1] nor, in the nature of things, is a consensus likely to emerge. However, even if the substance of our sources were virtually intact (and that is improbable), the loss of the great bulk of juristic writings would still leave us with only a fragmentary idea of the content of classical law.

Second, my attempt to restore a classical law of leasehold was to some extent misleading. In recent years, many scholars have turned away from the notion that classical law constituted a unified body of law; instead, they have recognized how often the jurists disagreed, and they have accepted the possibility of a "classical law" that was formed

[1] Compare M. Kaser, *Zur Methodologie der Römischen Rechtsquellenforschung* (1972), with A. Guarino, *Sulla Credibilità della Scienza Romanistica Moderna* (= *Atti Acad. Pont.* 20, 1972), on which Kaser, 102-109; and cf. F. Wieacker, *SZ* 91 (1974) 1-40.

slowly, in tentative and uneven stages, and with considerable disagreement at every stage.[2] This change in scholarly attitude raises the question of whether we may validly speak of a single Roman law of urban lease; in reality, the "system" assembled above is a composite drawn from sources varying widely in date and nature, and it would be ingenuous to suggest that the whole of this "system" was ever simultaneously in force.

Third, even if these difficulties could be overcome, juristic sources still cannot be dealt with as if they described a body of positive law similar to a modern code. Roman jurisprudence operated differently. At least in the early Empire,[3] and probably (as I think) throughout the classical period, Roman trials were "agonistic" in character. The *iudex* was not normally a law-trained judge in our sense, but rather a layman attempting to resolve as best he could arguments pro and con. The ambience of a *iudicium* was rhetorical: the direct confrontation of conflicting interests, the clash of advocacy and persuasion. Within this setting, juristic writings constituted one source of law among many, albeit a powerful source and probably an increasingly powerful one over time; still, the *iudex* retained a considerable reserve of discretion.[4] These considerations suggest that we should not try to equate juristic law with the actual law administered in Roman courts.

[2] Compare F. Schulz, *Principles* 106-108, with M. Kaser, *Meth.* 19-31; mainly a difference of emphasis, but with dramatic consequences for legal history.

[3] Cf. D. Nörr, *Fs. Felgentraeger* 353-366 (who may not distinguish juristic pretensions from reality, however). Not until the reign of Hadrian were *iudices* required to follow juristic opinions, and then only if the jurists were unanimous; where jurists disagreed, the *iudex* could pick and choose; cf. Gaius 1. 7, with M. Kaser, *RPR*² 1 211 n. 7 (literature). Granted the degree of disagreement among the jurists (above n. 2), all Hadrian probably meant was that the *iudex* had to judge within the general framework of Roman law.

[4] On the role of discretion in undermining a system of positive law, see L. M. Friedman, *The Legal System* (1975) 32-39; on the *iudex*, W. Kunkel, *Herkunft*² 370, and M. Kaser, *RZ* 273-274.

These three points combine to make me a "rule-skeptic";[5] the known juristic rules on urban leasehold were doubtless influential in the Roman judicial system, but are not likely to describe precisely the law applied by that system at any given time.

From one point of view, however, it need not matter to a legal historian that the known rules on urban leasehold were not in fact invariably applied within the Roman judicial system; from this viewpoint, which I shall pursue below, it is sufficient that the jurists at least intended them to be applied and had some confidence in their influence on the legal system.

When a conflict about substantive law arises within a judicial system, a legal rule disposing of that conflict implies at least a *de facto* discrimination between the competing sets of interests advanced by two parties who, in a typical suit,[6] are arguing about that point of law; as a result of a dispositive rule, one party wins and the other party loses.[7] Because of this, rules of substantive law by their nature cannot be interest-neutral. But the juristic rules of Roman lease law, although they normally did not arise (unlike judge-made law) in the context of actual adjudication, did enjoy some considerable measure of official backing and authority; and as such these rules constituted, at least *de*

[5] I also doubt that *any* system of rules can accurately describe the content of a living legal system; cf. L. M. Friedman (cited n. 4) 25-44, for a discussion.

[6] On the significance of legal typification ("the recurrent problem-situation"), see K. Llewellyn, *The Common Law Tradition: Deciding Appeals* (1960) 43-44. There seems no reason to suppose that the hypothetical cases in the jurists arose from thin air.

[7] In reality, the relation of interests to law is of course considerably more complicated than I suggest; cf. J. Stone, *Social Dimensions of Law and Justice* (1966) 168. Interests are defined more exactly in Chapter VI below (at n. 18). For the moment it suffices to isolate them in the rhetorical context of trial debate (cf. D. Nörr's article cited n. 3). At least this amount of social information was beyond all question available to the jurists; it would be instructive, for instance, were Cicero's private orations analyzed in terms of interests.

facto, the Roman government's major response to and evaluation of the various interests regularly asserted by the parties to urban leases. It is worth the effort, I think, to attempt to set out schematically the principal interests protected within Roman lease law, and to describe briefly how and to what extent they were protected.

We may approach the matter of interests from two points of view. First of all, we may assume that the two litigants are each concerned only with their own private or individual welfare, and that they are advancing a conflict of purely individual interests for adjudication by the State as a theoretically impartial arbiter. In this situation, each party is seeking legal protection for his own advantage. In the following pages, I have attempted to discover the major personal or individual interests protected by Roman lease law.[8]

An analysis of personal interests may begin with a generalized description of the institution of urban lease:

(1) a property owner (*dominus/locator*), who seeks to exploit his urban property for personal gain, unites with

(2) a tenant (*conductor* or *inquilinus*), who seeks shelter for his household, in

(3) a contract whereby their respective desires can be simultaneously satisfied.[9]

This basic pattern provides an initial structure for analyzing the personal interests in urban lease law.

[8] In the following pages I have normally relied on the interpretation given the cited passages in Chapter IV, and thus have avoided extensive footnotes. Ideally, an interest analysis of Roman lease law should be historically differentiated; but in the present state of our knowledge this is hardly possible.

[9] This "Interessenlage" is described by e.g. K. Larenz, *Methodenlehre der Rechtswissenschaft*[3] (1975) 187. One must observe that: (1) the similarity between the ancient and modern legal institutions has no special significance in assessing the former; (2) an Interessenlage is only a description of an abstract legal institution, and does not purport to give an accurate description of social reality (though the similarity in this case may be reasonably close).

(1) The owner's fundamental interest (and indeed his reason for concluding the contract) was his desire to exploit the property for profit.[10] There were several sides to this interest, however.

(1a) For the Romans, latent in the owner's right to dispose of his property to others through contract was the (at first sight contradictory) idea that in general he did not thereby lose control of his property. This interest is witnessed especially in his continuing possession of the premises.[11] Gaius 4.153:

> Possidere autem videmur non solum si ipsi possideamus, sed etiam si nostro nomine aliquis in possessione sit, licet is nostro iuri subiectus non sit, qualis est colonus et inquilinus; . . .[a]

The tenant was *in possessione* for the landlord, even though he was not subject to the landlord's control. In this sense the owner continued to enjoy an active interest in the physical dwelling; his absolute power to expel the tenant at any time and thereby to resume direct control of the premises (at most he subjected himself to a suit for damages) was a clear expression of his interest. Equally germane to his interest was the right of preclusion, since this right assumed (especially after the implication of a tacit pledge: D. 20.2.4 pr. *et al.*) that the owner's sphere of control might extend, in some circumstances, also to the tenant's furnishings within

[10] On the support given this interest by Roman law, see F. Schulz, *Principles* 151-153. The owner's right to exploit his property by contract is affirmed and justified by Cicero, *Off.* 2.83-85, as part of his property rights (73, 78); Cicero's essay, a classically Roman (though Stoic-influenced) defense of private property, is discussed by M. Frederiksen, *JRS* 56 (1966) 138-140, with literature. On the individual's interest in control of property in modern law, see J. Stone (cited n. 7) 244-254.

[11] Again, it needs emphasis that this is a general rule, not the result of the unfavorable social position of the urban tenant in particular; though the general rule no doubt worked hard consequences. Cf. M. Kaser, *RPR*[2] 1 389-390, 567; below, n. 22.

the physical perimeter of the dwelling; Ulpian's apparent extension of the owner's right of preclusion past the middleman directly to subtenants (D. 13.7.11.5) forcibly brings home the power of this interest. Some similar view of the owner's interest in having "what is his" may have underlain his right to expel the tenant if he required the dwelling for his own purposes (C. 4.65.3).

(1b) Exploitation of the premises obviously implied, in the case of leasehold, the reception of rent from tenants.[12] The tenant's failure to pay rent was a justification for his expulsion (C. 4.65.3); and the tenant was responsible for seeing to it that the rent reached his actual landlord (D. 12.6.65). The landlord's strong interest in the collection of rent helps to explain why a tenant who abandoned his dwelling unjustifiably was liable for the entire outstanding rent, and not just for damages (D. 19.2.24.2, 28.2); and the tenant's furnishings were a pledge for the entire outstanding amount (D. 43.32.1.4). The juristic construction of the tenant's tacit pledge of furnishings (D. 2.14.4; 20.2.4 pr.-1, 6) and the jurists' approval of the stark right of preclusion (D. 20.2.9) were equally motivated by protection of this interest; the possessions could be held until the landlord was satisfied as to the rent.[13] Finally, various tenant rights were modified in favor of the owner's interest in receiving rent; good examples are the restrictions on justified abandonment (D. 19.2.13.7; 39.2.13.6, 28, 33) and on deduction from rent (D. 19.2.27 pr., 28 pr.-1), and the construction of the owner's limited opportunity to mitigate damages after a breach (D. 19.2.9 pr., cf. 60 pr.).

(1c) From the owner's interest in exploiting his property also sprang his interest in maintaining it so that its earning

[12] Cicero particularly stresses this interest at *Off.* 2.88. On Cicero's management of his urban properties, see my article, *CJ* 74 (1978) 1-6: he insisted on punctual payment of rent: *Att.* 12.32.2. Compare Ulpian, *Frag. Vindob.* 1.2.

[13] The late classical extension of the *actio Serviana* to cover these pledges was discussed at Chapter IV n. 138.

capacity was not diminished. The owner could justifiably expel a tenant not only if the building had to be demolished (D. 19.2.30 pr., 35 pr.) but also if it required serious repair (C. 4.65.3). For purposes of repair he could enter the premises with the power of an interdict *uti possidetis* behind him (D. 43.17.3.3); and small repairs could not be made the excuse for a tenant's deduction from the rent (D. 19.2.27 pr.).

(1d) Allied to the owner's interest in maintaining his property was his interest in preventing harm to it. The owner could justifiably expel the tenant for gross misconduct with regard to the premises (C. 4.65.3). Further, the growth of the tenant's *culpa* liability, and especially of his liability for the *culpa* of others (D. 9.2.27.11; 19.2.11 pr.), vividly illustrates the persuasiveness of this interest, which also acted to impose limits on the tenant's right to abandon (D. 19.2.13.7); not only was the tenant to be deterred through this liability from unthinking negligence, but the landlord was also to receive compensation for resultant damage whenever possible. Similar logic extended the tenant's pledge of furnishings so as to cover his negligent damage (D. 20.2.2).

(1e) These interests were contractual, and so adhered not only to the owner but also in part to a middleman. This introduced some problems; for instance, the middleman did not have possession (D. 43.16.20), though there is no evidence that this lack hindered him in expelling or precluding an *inquilinus* (cf. D. 13.7.11.5). Further, it seems clear that he also acted as a "stand-in" for the owner when the *inquilinus* negligently damaged the dwelling (cf. D. 19.1.13.30); in classical law the middleman seems to have been expected to cede the resultant action to the owner (cf. D. 19.2.11 pr.), though he probably became liable himself for his tenant's *culpa* if he had been negligent in choosing the tenant (decisive evidence is lacking). We will return below to the problem of the middleman.

(2) On the side of the tenant were ranged a group of interests derived from or related to the tenant's basic interest

in obtaining a dwelling. Shelter is obviously a fundamental human need. However, the upper-class Roman tenant, like his modern counterpart in all classes, understood far more by this than merely a roof over his head.

(2a) The tenant's interest in his dwelling obviously implied his interest in enjoying unabatedly its physical security and comfort.[14] He could not enjoy this if he had reason to fear staying there (D. 19.2.27.1, cf. 13.7; 39.2.33), particularly if he feared the collapse of his own structure (D. 39.2.13.6); in that event he could justifiably abandon the structure, without regard to the landlord's ability to prevent the cause of fear (D. 19.2.27.1). So, too, if the physical condition or the amenities of the building declined to the extent that the tenant's enjoyment appreciably diminished; depending on how bad it was, the tenant could in some cases justifiably abandon (D. 19.2.25.2) or deduct from the rent (D. 19.2.27 pr.). Further, the tenant was also protected against unjustified expulsion from the dwelling during the term of lease; in that event, he could demand the payment of damages (esp. D. 19.2.28.2), and so also if he was expelled by a third party because his landlord lacked the right to lease (esp. D. 19.2.9 pr., 15.8). When the owner-landlord disposed of the property through sale (D. 19.2.25.1) or otherwise (e.g. through legacy; cf. D. 30.120.2, = *Frag. Vat.* 44, on farm lease), he was obliged to provide for the tenant's continued occupancy. Finally, that the tenant's interest was conceived generally and not just in relation to a specific dwelling is shown by the juristic construction of the landlord's limited right to mitigate damages through the offer of alternative housing (D. 19.2.9 pr., cf. 60 pr.).

(2b) But the tenant's interest in the dwelling was not limited to the physical habitation of it; the dwelling was

[14] The classic exposition of a tenant's desires is Juv. 3.190-211. The corresponding social interest in guaranteeing minimum conditions of welfare is mentioned by Cicero, *Off.* 2.74; such minimums are in the main culturally determined, cf. F. Heichelheim, *Wirtschaftliche Schwankungen* (1930) 100. Compare J. Stone (cited n. 7) 353-357.

also his home, and he had an interest in finding within it a place of privacy where he could lead the domestic life that pleased him.[15] The last clause of D. 43.17.3.3, though its authenticity is contested, apparently required a landlord, if he wished to enter and repair a dwelling, to state his purposes publicly before obtaining an interdict *uti possidetis*; and indeed no source ascribes to the landlord any arbitrary right to enter the dwelling in circumstances short of expulsion. The one source which suggests the landlord retained a key (D. 19.2.56) also allows him to use it only with permission from the Praefectus Vigilum.[16] No sources imply that the landlord had an interest, by virtue of his position, in his tenant's private life; reasons of this sort are not given as grounds for expulsion in C. 4.65.3. The list of exceptions to the category of pledged furnishings is also relevant;[17] these exceptions reflect, at least in part, the tenant's interest in leading a social life distinct from his landlord's claims. The property of guests is not included (D. 20.2.5 pr.; 43.32.1.3), nor are things detained by the tenant under a contract (D. 43.32.1.5, 2). To be sure, the interests of third parties are also bound up in these exceptions; especially the exception made for slaves manumitted by the tenant before preclusion (D. 20.2.6, 9), where *favor libertatis* is involved. Nonetheless, in some cases even the tenant's own property did not constitute part of the pledge, as when it was only casually within the dwelling (D. 20.2.7.1). Finally, the tenant's general contractual right to remove his property at the end of the lease (D. 19.2.19.4-5), and the particular applications of this right in the option between the interdict *de*

[15] On privacy in Roman law, see now M. D. Blecker, *TR* 43 (1975) 279-296; on modern law, compare J. Stone (cited n. 7) 212-218. On Roman "individualism," the classic treatment is in F. Schulz, *Principles* 146ff., esp. 160.

[16] Cf. G. Rickman, *Roman Granaries* (1971) 208-209. This may be the meaning of D. 39.2.34, that the precluding landlord retains furnishings "as if" (*quasi*) they were *pignora*.

[17] On "rule and exception" as illustrative of interest patterns, see N. Luhmann, *Rechtssystem und Rechtsdogmatik* (1974) 32ff.

migrando and a suit *ex conducto* (D. 19.2.25.2; 39.2.33-34), is but a slight extension of this interest; just as the tenant could dwell in his home without disturbance, so too he could depart from it in orderly fashion, provided his contractual obligations had been met. An aspect of this interest is the imposition on the landlord of a duty to protect for a time even legitimately precluded pledges (D. 39.2.34). (But the jurists do not go further, by providing a "period of notice" before expulsion.) The jurist's tendency to treat each tenant's apartment as a little world governed by him is complemented by their refusal to allow his justified abandonment if (e.g.) a tenant's neighbors are a source of annoyance to him; all have equal rights in this respect.

(2c) The concession to the tenant of the right to sublease, in the absence of a contractual provision to the contrary (C. 4.65.6), somewhat complicates the picture. This concession created for the tenant, if he exercised his right, an economic interest in the exploitation of the leasehold. (Roman law did not clearly distinguish between middlemen who sublease for profit only, and tenants who both dwell and sublease.) Where the intention to sublease was clear, the tenant was justified in abandoning if sublease was impossible, even though he might be able to live in the structure himself (D. 19.2.60 pr.). Further, if his subtenant was evicted due to his landlord's lack of right to lease, the tenant could recover *at least* an amount equal to what he had to refund to the subtenant (D. 19.2.7-8). The complexity of this area of law is clearly illustrated by the difficult relationship between sublease and pledge of furnishings (D. 13.7.11.5).

(3) An interest on the part of either party in contractual security was also protected; the parties could reasonably expect to receive what they had contracted for.[18] Thus, in addition to the various enforcements of the contract discussed above, it is to be observed that Roman jurists generally advocated enforcing all agreed-upon clauses of a

[18] This is "freedom of contract"; compare J. Stone (cited n. 7) 251-254, with F. Schulz, *Principles* 225-227.

lease, even where these seriously weakened the position of one party (D. 19.2.11.1; cf. 19.2.9.2, 30.4, farm lease). So also the tenant was held to have received the dwelling he had bargained for (D. 39.2.13.6), with the result that only impairment of use arising thereafter was a ground for deduction from rent (D. 19.2.27 pr.): the problem of latent defects is not faced in our texts. The tenant was held automatically liable for damage resulting from his violation of a clause in the lease (D. 19.2.11.1, 4; 12). Deviations from the principle of contractual security are always easily explained in terms of a conflicting interest of one party or the other; variations that are more difficult to justify, such as the remission of rent introduced to preserve economic balance in farm lease, are not found in urban lease. Equally, the jurists refused to recognize an automatic renewal of the term of lease after expiration of the contractual term (D. 19.2.13.11).

While an analysis of Roman lease law in terms of personal or individual interests is entirely adequate if we assume that a State (in the person of its representative or appointee) is primarily an impartial arbiter or umpire, such an analysis is inadequate if the State is taken to be not impartial, but rather an active party concerned with obtaining a socially "acceptable" outcome to private litigation. This second viewpoint is involved when (as often occurs)[19] litigants cease to base their claims for legal protection on their individual interests, and instead argue about what *social* interests the State should protect. A litigant who appeals to social interests is not merely arguing about the relative priority of individual interests; rather, he is advancing differently conceived interests, ones that are "involved in or looked at from the standpoint of social life in civilized society and asserted in title of social life."[20] The very ambiguity of the State's role

[19] Thus, in the *pro Caecina*, Cicero defends his interpretation of the interdict *de vi armata* by emphasizing the State's interest in upholding property rights (73-77).

[20] R. Pound, *Outlines of Jurisprudence*[5] (1943) 97.

in private litigation—an ambiguity probably latent in all developed systems of private law—in and of itself encourages both litigants and us to reexpress the individual interests described above in terms of social interests which Roman lease law seems designed to further or protect.[21] Obviously, such a reexpression does not involve a one-for-one correlation; social interests involve a different kind of argumentation, they overlap with individual interests and are not determined solely by the conflicts of private parties. The following sketch serves to bring out the principal points:

(i) Roman juristic decisions strongly favor exploitation of urban properties through lease; indeed, Roman law was "landlord-friendly," decidedly too much so by modern standards. This is so even if we leave to one side the tenant's absence of possession, which was an inherited element.[22] Otherwise, the owner was allowed to retain a very strong interest in his property (above, Categories 1a, 1c), an interest which is clearly manifested in his powers of expulsion and preclusion; nothing definitely indicates that the jurists ever sought to limit these powers,[23] and preclusion was in fact legitimized generally through the implication of a tacit pledge of furnishings. Ulpian's further extension of the owner's power of preclusion past the middleman and directly to subtenants (D. 13.7.11.5) is a particularly arresting, though not unproblematic, example of the favor accorded the owner's position. Furthermore, the owner's interest in

[21] In any event, for purposes of legal discussion personal interests must be sharply divided from social interests: J. Stone (cited n. 7) 181-182. A distinction of interest levels is clearly recognized in Ulpian D. 1.1.1.2 ("sunt enim quaedam publice utilia, quaedam privatim"),[b] on which see Chapter VI at n. 16; compare Paul D. 1.1.11 (*ius civile* is "quod omnibus aut pluribus in civitate utile est").[c]

[22] The system of possessory interdicts sprang up in response to quite different problems, cf. M. Kaser, *RPR*² 1 396-397. L. Labruna, *Vim Fieri Veto* (1971), tried to isolate the historical factors involved; the result was perhaps overly monocausal.

[23] Though there is some search for legal alternatives to expulsion by self-help; cf. Chapter IV at n. 88.

the rent (Category 1b) is also firmly protected in principle;[24] and the right to *remission* of rent was apparently never accorded the urban tenant. However, elimination of the tenant's duty to pay rent is also the jurists' commonest method of securing the tenant's interests against the landlord (see Category iv below)—though Ulpian's attempt to limit damages (D. 19.2.7-8) should also be remembered. Further, the landlord's dwelling was protected against the damages arising from rental by a gradually increasing *culpa*-liability for tenants (Category 1d). There is every reason to understand the high degree of legal protection accorded landlords in terms of the strong social position occupied by Roman property owners;[25] at the same time, however, encouragement of this particular form of property exploitation can doubtless also be related to the imperative need to house Rome's burgeoning population. In this regard, we should note the implication of the tenant's right to sublease and the general protection accorded that right (Category 2c); and, in another area of law, the allowance of renewal of a lease after breach of contract and the development of amelioration of damages through the offer of equivalent housing (D. 19.2.9 pr., 60 pr.).

(ii) Roman jurisprudence displays, in urban leasehold as elsewhere, an emphasis on enforcement of the agreed-upon terms of contracts (Category 3). Such emphasis can be defended as support for the security of the marketplace, and in most cases this is a strong and reasonable defense.[26] Modern law tends to focus on problems resulting from un-

[24] Also through the *cautio damni infecti*: D. 39.2.28-29; and cf. D. 39.2.37.

[25] On the general legal importance of maintaining the social order, see D. Nörr, *SZ* 88 (1971) 413-417, rev. P. Garnsey, *Social Status and Legal Privilege* (1970); on the importance of regular rents to the ancient "economic" system, see M. I. Finley, *The Ancient Economy* (1973) 116-118. No profound point is involved here; the matter is obvious.

[26] Compare J. Stone (cited n. 7) 336-339.

equal bargaining power; not so in Roman law.[27] While there was probably no great economic or social "gap" between landlord and tenant in upper-class lease cases (cf. Chapter III), Roman jurisprudence shows no inclination to extend protection to those less fortunate. On the other hand, it should not be forgotten that the Roman economic system was relatively simple, and that the Roman world knew neither "landlording" as an occupation nor the professional drafting of "ironclad" leases.[28] Landlords of that period do not seem to have enjoyed an advantage of professional expertise over their tenants.

(iii) The social interest in the preservation and upgrading of housing was promoted only indirectly.[29] The law in this area depended for its success on the existence of an economic impulse to maintain housing for the sake of profitability; however, the extent to which that impulse operated is difficult to measure. If the landlord wished to make light repairs during the term of lease, he was allowed to do so without prejudice as to the rent; and the need of extensive repair or demolition was grounds for justified expulsion (Category 1c). The tenant's legal interest in adequate housing was not defined with regard to a list of minimum conditions (e.g. minimum light), but only in terms of conditions existing when the lease was entered upon (Category 2a). Within the term of lease, the individual tenant was

[27] Cf. F. Schulz, *Principles* 225-227. The doctrine of *laesio enormis* is foreign to classical law: M. Kaser, *RPR*² I 550, and II 389-390: so also in lease: D. 19.2.22.3-23.

[28] This was considered above (Chapter II), but it is worth stressing again, that modern references to capitalism in the Roman rental market are very misleading.

[29] In this regard, one may recall the "building codes," though their scope is largely limited to appearance, stability, and fire prevention; cf. Chapter III n. 19. On laws to discourage destruction of existing housing, see E. J. Philipps, *Latomus* 32 (1973) 86-95; P. Garnsey, in *Studies in Roman Property* (ed. M. I. Finley, 1976) 133-136. Note also measures to encourage construction of upper-class housing: e.g. Gaius 1.33.

relatively well protected through the legal devices of justified abandonment and deduction from the rent, both of which were not dependent on absence of the landlord's "good will." However, the effectiveness of these devices in encouraging repairs must have largely depended on whether keeping a building in good repair was necessary for its profitability; thus, if after a justified abandonment the landlord could readily find substitute tenants at the same or nearly the same rent, he had no economic motive to correct a defect. In addition, the tenant was not encouraged to make repairs himself; the tenant's right to deduct for necessary repairs is not attested except in the area of public law (D. 43.10.1.3), and his *ius tollendi* (D. 19.2.19.4) was so narrow as not to be a completely adequate substitute. Finally, the tenant's *culpa*-liability (Category 1d) resulted in direct financial compensation to the landlord, who *could* use the money for repairing the damaged dwelling but did not have to do so. Much therefore depends upon unknowns about the operation of the rental market, and we must also probably reckon with differences over time.[30]

(iv) The jurists tried hard to make leasehold attractive to upper-class tenants. Perhaps precisely because the tenant lacked any property right in his leasehold, the jurists were especially ingenious in devising alternative means to secure the tenant's tranquil enjoyment of the premises and to prevent the illegitimate use of expulsion (Category 2a); it is characteristic of these doctrines that they recognized the tenant's interests without regard to the landlord's fault, and in the case of expulsion allowed the landlord to escape payment of damages only if he was in no way responsible for it or could find a justification. So long as the tenant was not actually expelled, his privacy (Category 2b) was accorded a measure of the protection which Roman law normally

[30] It is worth comparing the form of disaster relief preferred by the Caesars for urban property owners: normally direct compensation, though Tac. *Ann.* 15.43.2 is an exception; cf. R. F. Newbold, *Latomus* 33 (1974) 861-863.

bestowed on the home.[31] Against intruders he had, like any other householder, the *actio iniuriarum* (D. 47.10.5.2); against his landlord, he had contractual rights that seem to have prevailed until the landlord could bring compelling counter-interests to bear against them. (The *testatio* in D. 43.17.3.3 is probably a good example of juristic ingenuity.) While the jurists therefore seem to have recognized that the tenant's interest in his dwelling was not trivial, there were definite limits to their support of this interest. We may single out two problem areas: the tenant was given almost no rights as a "neighbor" (not even against fellow tenants), save *ex conducto* against his landlord, and even that on a limited basis;[32] and the position of a middleman who subleased for profit remained unsatisfactory. As to the latter, only the contractual ladder seems at first to have been recognized, so that the owner stood to the middleman as the middleman to the tenant (Category 1e); but there are signs in later law that the tenant was gaining, through *bona fides*, a direct relationship with the owner. Particularly relevant, of course, is the legitimation of the owner's preclusion and thereby the probable granting to the tenant of the interdict *de migrando* against the owner (D. 13.7.11.5). The probable limitation of the owner's liability for damages when he expelled subtenants, which may also be a late development (D. 19.2.7-8), is inconsistent. The jurists seem disinclined to regard the middleman as the owner's manager (or *negotiorum gestor*),[33] so as to strengthen the tenant's

[31] Cf. n. 15 above.

[32] The major exception is the concession to tenants of the *cautio damni infecti* against neighboring landowners: D. 39.2.13.5, 21, cf. 18.3—a good indication of how strong the tenant's interest had to be before he gained a neighbor's rights. The urban tenant could not make an *operis novi nuntiatio*: Ulp. D. 39.1.3.3.

[33] The stark limits on such theory in Roman law are observed by the scholarship; cf. M. Kaser, *RPR*[2] 1 586-588. If we knew more about the legal handling of the tenant's negligence (cf. Category 1e above), or about the handling of problems arising from tenant's abandonment or deduction from rent, the problem with the middleman might seem less acute.

position as against the owner. On the whole, therefore, it seems fair to say that the jurists strove to make tenancy legally attractive, but that there were definite limits to this effort. Undoubtedly, however, the law was partially supplemented in this area by social pressures and sanctions.[34]

(v) While the tenant's liability for *culpa* was subject to a steady growth during the classical period, nonetheless the jurists' caution in regard to liabilities requires emphasis.[35] The tenant's personal *culpa*-liability (in the absence of a lease provision) was rarely more extensive than his Aquilian liability (an example: D. 19.2.57, lease of a lot); his vicarious liability, while it is difficult to define precisely, was in any event undoubtedly not so high as the generalized and quasi-ethical doctrine of the postclassical period.[36] As for the liability of the landlord, one source excludes any form of vicarious liability under normal circumstances (D. 19.2.45 pr.). Otherwise, the landlord had no liability for break-ins if he was not implicated (C. 4.65.12), and was liable only under an *actio pigneraticia* for negligent safekeeping of seized furnishings (D. 39.2.34). In general, the landlord's personal liability seems also to resemble his Aquilian liability. This matter of liabilities, it should be observed, was not an insignificant one in an era before insurance; imposition of liability because of any degree of "blameworthiness" whatsoever could result in making certain enterprises simply uneconomical. We find in this area, therefore, much the same considerations at work as we observed elsewhere (Categories i, iv). As a parallel, note the jurists' clear, if somewhat conservative, estimate of the technological realities underlying a landlord's liabilities: structural failures are mentioned (D.

[34] This point is rightly emphasized by A. Pernice, *SZ* 19 (1898) 92 n. 3 (on Martial 12.32).

[35] I might observe that some modern works have inclined to ignore the reasons for this caution. By contrast, see J. M. Kelly, *Studies in the Civil Judicature* (1976) 72-73.

[36] On postclassical *culpa*, see M. Kaser, *RPR*² II 346ff., esp. 351-352.

19.2.27 pr., 28 pr.-1; 39.2.13.6, 33), also access to light and the security of doors and windows (D. 19.2.25.2), but not the condition of wall plaster or the plumbing.

(vi) Finally, a variety of common public interests are observable in the formation of urban lease law. The late classical intervention of the Praefectus Vigilum in the handling of preclusion stresses the maintenance of public order;[37] the Praefectus may also have had a special competence in investigating break-ins into apartments (cf. D. 1.15.3.2), and he certainly played a role in preventing fires in *insulae* (esp. D. 1.15.3.1, 4). The law of expulsion, which featured the use of self-help, remained a somewhat archaic feature in classical leasehold; here, however, we can perhaps discern the encouragement of nonviolent alternatives to self-help.[38] Other public interests appear in special circumstances; the *favor libertatis* that allows a tenant to manumit a slave before preclusion (D. 20.2.6, 9) is a good example. At varying points in the law a public interest in efficiency of administration is clearly expressed: as, for instance, in the requirement that the tenant's grounds for abandonment through fear (cf. D. 19.2.27.1) be objectively demonstrable; or in the well-articulated action-sequence of the interdict *de migrando* and the action *ex conducto*.

It should be clear by this point that, while analyses in terms of individual and social interests are complementary rather than mutually exclusive, an analysis in terms of social interests has both advantages and disadvantages. The main disadvantage of reexpressing Roman lease law in terms of social interests is that we thereby move one step further from the terms in which particular decisions are framed. The main advantage is that we are thereby enabled to think of Roman lease law in legislative terms, as part and parcel of public policy with regard to the Roman rental market.

[37] Cf. A. dell'Oro, *I Libri de Officio* (1960) 250-254. On the interest, compare J. Stone (cited n. 7) 293-296.

[38] See Chapter IV at n. 88.

Were we to formulate Roman lease law in terms of public policy, its priorities would seem clear: first and foremost, to encourage Roman property owners to exploit their property through rental to the upper classes; second, to encourage the upper classes to avail themselves of the opportunity to rent. These priorities seem to remain remarkably stable over time.

The process of striking balances between competing interests was a dynamic one, occurring in both the short and the long run. Each new rule struck a new balance of its own, but simultaneously altered slightly the balance of the whole body of urban lease law. For example, Servius' decision to justify abandonment due to fear (in D. 19.2.27.1) was a clear victory for the tenant's interest in unabated enjoyment of his rented dwelling; this interest was secured at law and hence established a "right." Later jurists, while apparently accepting Servius' ruling, moved to interpret it so that the landlord's interests in the rent and in the protection of his property were also protected: the tenant's fear had to be objectively provable, it had to be the fear of a reasonable man confronted with a threat which he could not physically resist (cf. esp. Labeo in D. 19.2.13.7). Gradually a legal doctrine developed out of such repeated balance-striking; this doctrine was then extended, beyond cases of abandonment justified through fear, to cases where the tenant's basic comfort and security were adversely affected (Gaius D. 19.2.25.2).

On the level of social interests, the ceaseless back and forth of these rules tilted State policy now a little in favor of the tenant, now a little toward the landlord. The social debate underlying these patterns of continually restruck balances must always be at the back of a legal historian's mind. The consequences of the debate are found again and again in every area of lease law: the intricate rules governing tenant's pledges, the forms of and justifications for expulsion, or the remarkable complexity of rent deduction already in Alfenus

(D. 19.2.27 pr.). Through this interplay the law lived on, and as a consequence its work could never be completed.

The broader context of the jurists' balancing reflected their acceptance of the Roman rental market as the starting point in the discussion of lease law. Landlords and tenants were assumed to have struck a bargain as equals within the market, and it was not the purpose of Roman law to undo or undermine their bargain; in principle, demands were not imposed in excess of what the parties had expressly or tacitly agreed to do for one another. The jurists were concerned not with the bargain but with its fulfillment. The making of a lease represented the commitment of landlord and tenant to a lengthy future relationship, upon which, however, unforeseen happenings might impinge. Roman lease law operated to ensure that, during the run of the lease, the complex interests of both parties continued to receive, in the face of unforeseen happenings, a full and fair protection within the Roman understanding of those words. Therefore Roman lease law was characterized, so it appears to me, by a belief that the interests of landlord and tenant could not be analytically isolated from one another and then given separate consideration or even enforcement; in this respect, Common Law, both in its ancient and more modern forms, differs sharply from Roman law. The jurists preferred to see the sets of interests as strictly interrelated throughout the length of the contract.

The impact of Roman lease law on the Roman rental market cannot, of course, be precisely determined. The effects, in any event, could only have occurred in the long run.[39] Clearly, ownership of leasable urban property remained a not unattractive form of investment throughout the classical period; and rental among the upper classes appears to have become more rather than less popular. It is well worth pointing to the extensive Trajanic and Hadrianic

[39] See N. Luhmann (cited n. 17) 50-51, on the "absorption of smaller pushes."

building projects for the housing of the "commercial class" at Ostia, and to the provision for a *cenaculum* on the first floor of the *Casa di Via Giulio Romano* in Rome (Chapter I). In Rome of the High Empire, investment in housing rested on a delicate balance between high profits and high risks (Gell. 15.1.3). The law of urban leasehold could have made the difference. In any event, even though its influence on the rental market was limited to the small sphere of upper-class housing, nonetheless the Roman law of urban leasehold does not seem in any way an unreasonable or irresponsible law, especially in a world where public housing and other modern impulses to socialization of the rental market were entirely unknown.

In summary, then, the suggestion in the pages above is that the rules of Roman lease law reflect discernible patterns in the balancing of interests. For the purposes of the present chapter, it is immaterial whether this balancing occurred unconsciously or consciously. The jurists' balancing would occur unconsciously if their "discovery" of new legal rules nevertheless followed patterns of which they were unaware; it would occur consciously either if they deliberately set out to weigh interests in the modern fashion, or if they deliberately set out to do something else which amounted to a weighing of interests—as, for instance, if they set out to obtain the lease law that was of the highest possible social utility.

Which of these alternatives should we choose? What should we infer about the formation of Roman lease law from the apparent pattern of its interests? The honest answer to this question is that different people will probably infer different things, some people, perhaps, nothing at all. For at this juncture we must take into consideration the motives of the jurists in proposing their rules, and this is a subject on which, it is generally accepted, we have almost no other evidence than the rules themselves, so that modern interpretations are bound to vary. In the next chapter, however, I want to explore the possibility that the "adjustment of interests" discernible in Roman lease law was not due to chance, or to the jurists' following patterns of which they were unaware, but rather that this pattern was consciously developed. My argument will be exceedingly indirect, suggestive rather than demonstrative, and I advance it in full anticipation of the inevitable objections.

VI

Roman Jurisprudence as an Instrument of Social Control

THE CONSTRUCTION of this book is obviously intended to suggest an answer to the question: how did the jurists go about creating Roman lease law? The first three chapters are designed to show that it was based on the upper-class rental market of the capital city of Rome. There are good reasons for limiting analysis of lease law more or less exclusively to upper-class leaseholds (Chapter III); but, within this socially defined area, Roman lease law takes into account every known feature of the market, including architectural as well as social and economic features (Chapters I-II). Further, the resultant law (Chapter IV) clearly reflects an "adjustment of interests" that by no means appears to be out of tune with the realities of the Roman rental market (Chapter V). Indeed, Roman lease law, although it would scarcely be "acceptable" in any modern context, does not seem at all implausible or unreasonable within its Roman context, whether the law is treated from the viewpoint of the individuals involved or from that of social policy.

My concluding chapter is intended to tie together the argument in earlier chapters and to give some suggestion of what I think this argument implies concerning the genesis, operation, and purposes of Roman lease law.

The texture of Roman juristic writings differs from most modern jurisprudence. One primary difference is the absence of surface urgency in the Roman sources: the absence of any clearly expressed sense that "law-jobs" cannot be put off until tomorrow, and that society stands in pressing need of new rules and new legal institutions. Instead, page after page of juristic writings is filled with a dry, rather unrhetorical prose that for the most part simply declares the law, offering no intellectually sufficient explanation or justification; arguments are not common, and when they do appear, they seem to conceal more than they disclose about the foundation of juristic decisions.[1] Under the circumstances, it is hardly surprising that some scholars have attributed to the jurists a highly intellectualized "mathematics of concepts"[2] divorced from the daily life of law. We may name this characteristic of Roman jurisprudence the "illusion of timelessness."[3]

One consequence of the extreme, almost stylized flatness affected by the jurists is that we often do not find it easy to

[1] On this controversial matter, I agree completely with F. Wieacker, in *Fs. Kaser* (1976) 3-27, who cites much recent bibliography. Wieacker observes (p. 4) that the postclassical tendency to strike out legal reasoning probably should not affect our judgment of the overall character of their argument. On the general failure of the jurists to seek and obtain ethical grounding for their decisions, cf. T. Parsons, *Societies* (1966) 27, 89. This failure is (or ought to be) evident to any scholar of comparative law.

[2] This famous idea is ascribed to Savigny; on the problems it entails for its (few) modern defenders, see F. Horak, in *Fs. Kaser* (1976) 29-55. The impression of timelessness is also promoted by the jurists' free mixing of "real" and "hypothetical" cases, and by their easy movement from one theme or case-group to another.

[3] By which is also meant, that when certain clearly temporal elements in Roman law have been ignored (e.g. the existence of slavery, and the absence of capitalism), what remains can be held to constitute the jurists' contribution to a "timeless" fund of legal ideas. Some such notion lies at the basis of an approach to Roman law through Natural Law, an approach which even today has its persuasive advocates; e.g. W. Waldstein, in *ANRW* II.15 (1976) 3-100, esp. 98-100, on whom see F. Wieacker, *SZ* 94 (1977) 320-324. By contrast, N. Luhmann, *Rechtssystem und Rechtsdogmatik* (1974) 49-54, rightly changes the focus to "gesellschaftsadäquate Rechtsbegriffe."

state with authority the factors impelling a jurist to any particular decision.[4] Within the limits of an historical discussion, it is possible to describe with certainty only the (partially self-imposed) parameters delimiting the jurists' freedom of decision. In Roman lease law the major parameters are two:

First, there can be little doubt (although we lack absolute proof) that the structure and preexisting social institutions or practices of the rental market were in the main adopted by the jurists as the basis and framework for the *legal* institutions of urban leasehold; the fundamental conceptions of justified expulsion and abandonment with the accompanying rules on rent abatement or damages are especially relevant in this connection, but so also are preclusion and the tenant's pledge of furnishings,[5] perhaps also such subsidiary elements as deduction from rent and amelioration of damages through the offer of alternative housing. Furthermore, the basic characteristics of Roman leases, such as the long terms of lease, long payment periods, and the practice of payment at the end of the payment period, also obviously influenced the pattern of juristic thought about lease law:

[4] The modern resort to "intuition" is, in my opinion, a symptom of despair; for bibliography on "intuition," see F. Wieacker (cited n. 1) 12 n. 37. Intuition appears to be a modern psychological substitute for *auctoritas.*

[5] Four examples can be given of the relation of contract clauses to the developing law: clauses providing for pledge of furnishings (cf. Chapter IV, n. 18) and the implication of a tacit pledge of furnishings (Neratius D. 20.2.4 pr.; *et al.*); clauses providing for the tenant's vicarious liability (cf. Ulp. D. 19.2.11 pr.) and the implication of his vicarious liability (D. 19.2.11 pr.; D. 9.2.27.9, 11); clauses restricting the tenant's right to sublease, and the implication of his right to sublease in the absence of specific provision (on both points, cf. Alex., C. 4.65.6); and clauses eliminating the right to remove fixtures (cf. Chapter IV, n. 19) and the implication of a right to remove fixtures in some circumstances (Labeo D. 19.2.19.4). In none of these cases do the ensuing juristic implications allow us to draw any conclusion about the frequency of a clause's occurrence in actual leases; all these implications are better explained through reference to public policy. However, the *idea* for the rules may have originated in social practice.

for instance, the absence of stress on the significance of the term of lease, or the tendency to emphasize deduction from rent rather than its refunding. Finally, the normal, socially determined expectations of tenants and landlords in Rome surely influenced, at least to some extent, the general juristic expectations as to the conduct of the two parties. From these viewpoints, the broad lines of Roman lease law might fairly be understood as based on preexisting social institutions, even though, to be sure, a legal system necessarily involves much higher degrees of abstraction and internal organization than do social institutions.

Second, it is also plain that the development of particular rules in lease law was influenced by the development of legal doctrines or of analogous rules in areas outside of urban leasehold; good examples are the rules on justified expulsion and those on the tenant's *culpa*-liability, both of which stood in obvious relation to farm lease.[6] A specific example of such influence is found in *Coll.* 12.7.9 and D. 9.2.27.11: Sabinus and Urseius denied that the urban tenant had contractual liability for damage done by his slaves; against Sabinus, Proculus established for *coloni* a "pro-noxal" liability on the contract, which he then applied to *inquilini*; his position was approved by Ulpian. The legal problems occasioned by urban and farm lease were obviously to some extent similar, and the two situations were often discussed together;[7] much less frequently, the *inquilinus* was discussed

[6] I have discussed tenant's liability in the broader perspective in *SZ* 95 (1978) 232-269. I intentionally leave to one side the tenant's absence of possession, which was in effect determined by the Roman procedural system before the development of lease law; cf. Chapter V, n. 22. We must also reckon with influences from the structure of the procedural system and from the development of broad underlying concepts (like *bona fides*).

[7] The following examples can be noted: Gaius 4.153; *Coll.* 12.7.9; D. 9.2.27.11; 11.7.14.1; 19.1.13.11, 30; 19.2.9 pr.-1, 13.11, 24.2, 25.1-2, 33, 35; 20.2.4 pr., 6; 24.3.7.11; 30.39.1; 34.3.18; 41.2.25.1, 37; 41.3.31.3; 43.16.20; 43.26.6.2; 43.32.1.1; 50.15.4.8; 50.16.166 pr.; C. 4.65.5; 7.30.1. This list (28 *loci*) is surely incomplete.

in relation to other legal "types," such as the *conductor* of a storeroom (cf. D. 19.2.56).

These two sources, namely the organized rental market and the generalized rules on *locatio conductio*, clearly exercised considerable influence on the development of lease law; but usually they can scarcely be described as determining factors. In fact only a small portion of Roman lease law can be "explained" through reference to these sources alone. Therefore, if we are to understand Roman lease law more completely, we must seek another source; and it is the theory of this chapter that a consideration of "interests" provides the missing source.

In Chapter IV above, I discussed juristic lease law as an analytical subsystem within the larger system of Roman private law. Because all historians of Roman law are familiar with this kind of discussion, I did not inquire into the purpose and utility of an analytical treatment, save to indicate (at the outset of Chapter V) certain ways in which such a treatment would not be enough if its aim were to describe a law actually in force. But what, then, is the purpose of analytical jurisprudence? It is "concerned with problems such as clarification of the nature of law, the meaning of terms used in its propositions, the classification of these terms and of the propositions containing them, and the study of the degree of logically consistent arrangements of which they are capable."[8] In short, it looks upon law as a coherent system of rules, theoretically complete in itself and susceptible to logical testing. The law of the jurists has long been studied, at times almost exclusively, from this viewpoint.[9]

[8] J. Stone, *Legal System and Lawyers' Reasonings* (1964) 18-19 (and *passim*). On the theories of Hans Kelsen, see now R. Moore, *Legal Norms and Legal Science* (1978); Moore rightly emphasizes the "reconstruction" which analytical jurisprudence involves (pp. 31-34). Also interesting, though less profound, is N. MacCormick, *Legal Reasoning and Legal Theory* (1978).

[9] On the "unity" of the Roman legal system, see F. Wieacker (cited n. 1) 8-10. I have a higher opinion of the jurists on this score than do most modern scholars.

When modern scholars treat Roman private law in this fashion, they are thinking of the jurists as practitioners of a highly specialized "science" largely inaccessible to most Romans,[10] practiced rather in the quiet of the study or in exclusive and professional "schools."[11]

For a legal historian, the utility of analytical jurisprudence lies in its ability to elucidate the logical web tying together diverse propositions of law within a single historical "system." Within a living system of law, analytical jurisprudence is also an important element in the decision-making process that leads to new rules of law. Analysis assists in isolating and stating a problem, in obtaining solutions logically consistent with the inherited legal system, and in framing and justifying a legal decision. If indeed we should suspect that all this is of ultimately limited usefulness to actual law finders,[12] the reason is probably that, as Oliver Wendell Holmes often observed: "The life of the law has not been logic: it has been experience."[13] For this reason, no doubt, a living system of law almost inevitably either fails to obtain complete logical coherence or attains it only at such a high level of analytical abstraction and complexity that a complete and accurate description is virtually impossible.

"The life of the law," on the other hand, directs our attention to quite a different forum for the systematic dis-

[10] Ordinary Romans received at best a training in "red letter" rules: cf. Petron. *Sat.* 46.7; Persius 5.90; Quint. 12.3.11; Juven. 14.92.

[11] On the "schools" (which should perhaps be conceived as professional debating clubs), see esp. W. Kunkel, *Herkunft und Soziale Stellung der Römischen Juristen* (2d ed. 1967) 341; and now D. Liebs, in *ANRW* II.15 (1976) 197-286, at 223ff., with bibliography.

[12] J. Stone, *Legal System* (cited n. 8) 55-61. We must learn not to think of *Digest* decisions as having been reached by some inevitable process. Compare the neo-realism of W. Twining and D. Miers, *How to Do Things with Rules* (1976).

[13] O. W. Holmes, *The Common Law* (Harvard ed. 1963) 5; cf. *Collected Papers* (1920) 50. On American realism, cf. esp. K. Llewellyn, *Yale Law Journal* 49 (1940) 1355-1400, a famous statement; and W. Twining, *Karl Llewellyn and the Realist Movement* (1973). The problem is well discussed in N. Luhmann, *Rechtssystem* (cited n. 3).

cussion of Roman law, namely (in the typical case) the proceedings *apud iudicem.* During these trial proceedings, seasoned advocates advanced sharply opposing cases for determination by a lay judge; the advocates debated law's application from the viewpoints of the affected parties. To judge from Cicero's private orations,[14] which alone survive to represent this type of legal discussion, advocates tended to speak of law much less in terms of its overall logical coherence, and much more in terms of its concrete effects. When the occasion demanded, advocates readily employed a broad range of instruments for persuasion; they summoned up every convenient weapon of social sensibility,[15] and in the process sometimes even called into question fundamental legal propositions when these worked to the disadvantage of their clients and the social categories their clients could be held to represent.

No doubt the jurists observed these discussions at the courtroom or forensic level with decidedly mixed feelings. On the one hand, many sources attest to the inevitable professional rivalry, even the hostility, between jurists and advocates;[16] and recent studies of the way jurists reached de-

[14] Several of these are newly analyzed by W. Stroh, *Taxis und Taktik* (1975), with bibliography; Stroh, however, following the lead of some legal historians, is far too aggressive in criticizing Cicero for "misrepresenting" juristic law (e.g. pp. 82ff., on the *pro Caecina*)—as if the jurists had legislative power! See also F. Wieacker, *Cicero als Advokat* (1965). On advocates in imperial *iudicia*, see Chapter III n. 6; on their education, S. F. Bonner, *Education in Ancient Rome* (1977) 288ff., only adequate.

[15] In this context a large role must be reserved for the employ of various theories of justice, both in motivating and in justifying new rules of law; cf. J. Stone, *Human Law and Human Justice* (1965) 345-355. Many theories of justice also set standards of consistency and coherence for analytical jurisprudence; cf. e.g. Stone, pp. 241-245 ("formal justice"), on Gerhard Radbruch; and in general N. MacCormick (cited n. 8).

[16] Cf. F. Schulz, *Roman Legal Science* (1946) 108-109, modified by W. Kunkel (cited n. 11) 325. For rhetorical and other criticism of juristic law, see D. Nörr, *Rechtskritik in der Römischen Antike*

cisions suggest that they tried to keep almost self-consciously aloof from their forensic colleagues in their methods of legal reasoning.[17] On the other hand, the hurly-burly of the courts, however it may at times have annoyed or embarrassed the jurists, nevertheless provided them with an indispensable laboratory for the creation and testing of law. Within the courts, jurists could witness new legal problems constantly arising and new legal ideas struck off in the heat of controversy; simultaneously they were allowed to see something of their rules at work. It seems reasonable to try to discover, within the intensely competitive arena of forensic discussion, many of the impulses toward breadth and equity which gave to Roman private law its vitality as a living system and its vast influence as a dead one.

The difficulty, however, is that for Roman law it is not easy for us to deal with such impulses on a systematic basis; for one thing, we know very little of the dockets of courts in the Principate. Therefore the impulses to law provided by forensic discussion cannot be studied empirically but must rather be hypothesized on the basis of the law which they helped to generate. In order to circumvent this difficulty, I have resorted to the "theory of interests" developed as part of their "sociological jurisprudence" by Roscoe Pound and Julius Stone.[18] The theory of interests was de-

(1974); and on Cicero's *Pro Murena*, A. Bürge, *Die Juristenkomik in Ciceros Rede Pro Murena* (1974), with D. Nörr, *SZ* 92 (1975) 290-293.

[17] Specifically, the reasoning used to explain and justify decisions; for the distinction, see G. Schubert, *Human Jurisprudence* (1975) 333-335. For bibliography on the distinction between juristic and rhetorical *interpretatio*, see M. Kaser, *RPR*² I 214 and II 8; add G. Kennedy, *The Art of Rhetoric in the Roman World* (1972) 88-90. This is a controversial matter, of course; the researches of (especially) Dieter Nörr have uncovered many links between rhetoric and "juristic reasoning." In general, see F. Wieacker, *SZ* 94 (1977) 27-29 (and 13-38, on "offene Wertungen").

[18] On interests, see especially J. Stone, *Social Dimensions of Law and Justice* (1966) 164-198; drawing in part on R. Pound, *Outline of*

signed in part to explain how a body of law develops, in relation to society, within an essentially stable and relatively slowly evolving case-law system, where the principal law finders (whether jurists or judges) have and are conscious of having nearly exclusive control of the nonstatutory law, but lack access to detailed and authoritative information on their social system. As such, the theory of interests is well suited to explaining the social basis of case law within modern systems of Common Law; and (*mutatis mutandis*) it seems to me also well suited for explaining much of Roman juristic law. As applied to modern law finders, sociological jurisprudence has received much justified criticism because of its inadequacy for a planned economy and a welfare state;[19] but its deficiencies and dangers would be much less significant in the simpler Roman world, where centralized planning was unknown and in any event all but impossible.[20]

When law is interpreted through interest theory, interests

Jurisprudence (5th ed. 1943). For evaluations, contrast E. W. Patterson, *Jurisprudence* (1953) 518-527, with G. Geis, *Kentucky Law Journal* 52 (1964) 267-293; and cf. G. Sawyer, *Law in Society* (2d ed. 1965) 150-165; E. B. McClean, *Il Politico* 41 (1976) 5-34; C. R. Ducat, *Modes of Constitutional Interpretation* (1978) 116-129. This Anglo-American theory differs in important respects from the *Gesetzgeber*-oriented and gap-filling "Interessenjurisprudenz" of the early twentieth century, on which see K. Larenz, *Methodenlehre der Rechtswissenschaft* (3d ed. 1975) 53-64; on it and Roman law, compare M. Kaser, *RPR*² 1 212, and F. Wieacker (cited n. 17) 6-7.

19 Cf. N. Luhmann, *Rechtssoziologie* (1972) 324-325, 332; compare, with specifics, D. L. Horowitz, *The Courts and Social Policy* (1977), and cf. T. B. Marvell, *Appellate Courts and Lawyers* (1978), esp. 184-185; see also K. A. Ziegert, *Zur Effectivität der Rechtssoziologie* (1975) 75-76, and R. Girtler, *Rechtssoziologie: Thesen und Möglichkeiten* (1976) 141-145, with good European overviews and further literature. It is doubtful, however, whether a case-law system can aspire to much more than a sociological jurisprudence; see, in this connection, B. A. Ackerman, *Private Property and the Constitution* (1977) 185-189.

20 This emerges clearly enough from F. Millar, *The Emperor in the Roman World* (1977), who emphasizes the *ad hoc* character of imperial decision making.

are taken as having for law finders the epistemological status of facts.[21] For them interests are neither legal concepts nor legal institutions; they are not like "rights," they are not created by law nor can they be removed by law. Rather, interests are the typified embodiment of demands actually advanced upon the law by men living in a historical society; it is the claimants themselves, and not the law finders, who define the content of these interests. Within the historical context of a given society, interests mainly serve to organize undifferentiated wants and desires,[22] to give them power and make them persuasive to others. Individuals, either singly or in groups, put forward "their interests" in order to defend or enhance some aspect of their own position within their society; through "their interests," individuals call upon the law to provide to them, by means of legal rules and procedures, specific sorts of protection.

In relation to the upper-class Roman rental market and the body of law that came to govern it, the exact nature of the interests advanced by landlords and tenants must remain, given the state of our evidence, largely hypothetical—a suppositional stratum beneath the law as we have it. Yet there can be little doubt that such a stratum is legitimately inferred; trials involving urban lease law obviously did occur with some frequency, and in these trials interests will have come to be enunciated relatively clearly under the pressure of competing advocacy. Further, by way of a check, since Rome's upper-class rental market shares many points of similarity with modern rental markets, it is not difficult for us to imagine what these interests must have been. Literary and archaeological sources provide a further check. All we

[21] Cf. R. Pound (cited n. 18) 96; J. Stone, *Social Dimensions* (cited n. 18) 167-168.

[22] Compare e.g. H. D. Laswell and A. Kaplan, *Power and Society* (1950) 23: "An *interest* is a pattern of demands and its supporting expectations"; and, from a sociological viewpoint, L. M. Friedman, *The Legal System* (1975) 148-160. The persuasive character of interests links them directly to discussion in courtrooms.

need do beyond this is to believe that the jurists listened when laymen spoke of what they wished the law to do. And what possible reason is there for us to deny this proposition?

Precisely how did these interests influence the emerging urban lease law? I have already suggested[23] that the rules of this law represented at the very least a *de facto* choice by the jurists among the interests advanced by typical litigants. Even if we assume that the jurists took only this relatively passive attitude, a description of Roman lease law in terms of the interests it protected is of considerable value. In the first place, interest theory allows us to consider an area of law as a complete entity, encompassing the whole pattern of interests contained in it; thus, we can avoid a possibly biased judgment, made on the basis of isolated rules, as to the social intent of lease law as a whole.[24] Interest theory brings out a complex pattern of many competing interests; it shows how these interests were accorded varying weight in different situations and at different times; and it thereby demonstrates what aspects of lease law were a source of difficulty or concern for the jurists. Finally, interest theory provides a way of considering legal rules without detracting from any of their formal claim to coherence within the larger structure of their legal system; and where (as is usually the case) these rules are not logically entailed by that system, then interest analysis provides a way of assessing both the flexibility of the legal system in adapting itself to

[23] In Chapter V, at nn. 6-7.

[24] Particularly to be avoided are analyses that speak of the bias or "one-sidedness" of urban lease law, on the basis of single juristic decisions or isolated themes (such as the landlord's right to expel or preclude at any time, or his retention of possession). Illustrative of such evaluations is M. Kaser, *RPR*² I 186, 563, 567. Contrast K. Llewellyn, *The Bramble Bush* (2d ed. 1951) 49: "no case can have a meaning by itself!" There is, I think, no evidence that in general social bias influenced the jurists' decisions on lease law; however, their rules may have had some class-related effects in diverting scarce resources away from lower-class housing.

specific social needs and the concomitant degree of free maneuverability retained by the jurists.

In this chapter, however, I want to argue for a much greater degree of influence on Roman lease law by the interests expressed in forensic discussion. I want to advocate our complete penetration of the "illusion of timelessness,"[25] or so at least in this one specific area of Roman private law. My thesis is the following:

(1) That, in the course of arriving at each of their decisions, the jurists undertook, as a constituent and fundamental part of their decision-making process, something which can be called (or can be reduced to) a "weighing" of the interests expressed in litigation on either side of a particular legal problem, with the object of obtaining the most socially practicable solution of the problem;[26]

(2) Further, that the result of these "weighings" was their creation of a lease law which, in terms of the relevant interests, would have had certain clearly foreseeable effects

[25] On the relationship, within maturing legal systems, of legal rules to time, and above all to a planned future, see N. Luhmann, *Rechtssoziologie* (cited n. 19) 344ff., an important discussion. In general, the issues at stake were well brought out by B. Rüthers, *Die Unbegrenzte Auslegung* (1968); Rüther's concept of *Richterrecht* (esp. pp. 457-476) is analogous to a familiar Anglo-American view of judges, which finds classic expression in K. Llewellyn, *The Common Law Tradition: Deciding Appeals* (1960). Compare W. F. Murphy, *Elements of Judicial Strategy* (1964).

[26] Such balancing emerges as the explicit purpose of private law in Ulpian, D. 1.1.1.2 (= *Inst.* 1.1.4), a passage today often considered genuine, cf. M. Kaser, *RPR*² 1 197 n. 34; *idem, Meth.* 56 n. 103; on G. Longo, in *Atti Perug.* (1971) 155-227, see R. Wittmann, *SZ* 93 (1976) 485-487. An instrumental conception of law, whereby law is a goal-oriented activity intended to alleviate problems of social life, is familiar in ancient philosophy (e.g. Diog. Laert. 10.150-153, from Epicurus), commonplace in ancient rhetoric (e.g. Arist. *Rhet.* 1.6.1ff.; Cic. *Inv.* 2.156, 168-169), and presumed by (e.g.) the juristic doctrines of *utilitas*, cf. M. Kaser, *RPR*² 1 185, 212, and compare T. Honsell, *SZ* 95 (1978) 93-137, with bibliography. On balancing of interests, see T. M. Benditt, *Social Theory and Practice* 3 (1975) 321-342.

on the existing social structure of the Roman rental market, which was presumably intended to have such effects, and which apparently did have such effects;

(3) Finally, that to this extent (at least) the jurists may be said to have used Roman lease law as an instrument of social control.[27]

It should be noted that, while my thesis supposes for Roman lease law a considerably higher degree of "social consciousness" than most modern Romanists have asserted for Roman private law as a whole, nonetheless this degree is much lower than that in any modern system of law. I am not arguing that the jurists undertook any specific kind of social engineering, that they (for instance) aimed either at the systematic alteration of the rental market and its major social institutions, or at the deliberate support of one group within the market against another. All that I am arguing is that, through the mechanism of their decision making and to the extent that the social character of actual litigation made this possible (Chapter III), the jurists sought in a general way to guide the rental market toward ends which they considered socially desirable, and that in this way they sought to change the market by slow stages with due allowance at every stage for the subsequent reassertion of competing interests. Finally, I should also stress that juristic rules, unlike the rules of modern legal systems, were not generally created in a courtroom context where rule-finding

[27] As I hope is already clear, this hypothesis provides no explanation for the entire juristic decision-making process. Problem-solving behavior in law is described with extraordinary clarity by W. Twining and D. Miers (cited n. 12) 75-81; my formulation evades the intricate problem of compliance, which is almost impossible to deal with for Roman law. On social control, see M. Janowitz, *The Last Half-Century* (1978) 3: "Social control is . . . the obverse of coercive control. Social control refers to the capacity of a social group, including a whole society, to regulate itself. Self-regulation must imply a set of 'higher moral principles' beyond those of self-interest." On social control and the law, cf. *ibid.* 364-365; compare K. Llewellyn, *Jurisprudence* (1960) 399-411.

was required by the exigencies of a case; my thesis should rather be understood as explaining how, within the context of *on-going* litigation, the jurists received the stimulus for legal change and then went about achieving it.

If my thesis is correct, then it ought to be possible to confirm it through two kinds of empirical observation. First, it should be possible to reconstruct the interests which *over the long run* the jurists tried to protect, and to arrange them in a way that suggests the general social ends which the jurists promoted. This subject was treated at length in Chapter V above, where it was argued that "the rules of Roman lease law reflect discernible patterns in the balancing of interests."[28] The priorities of Roman lease law "would seem clear: first and foremost, to encourage Roman property owners to exploit their property through rental to the upper classes; second, to encourage the upper classes to avail themselves of the opportunity to rent. These priorities seem to remain remarkably stable over time."[29]

Second, it should also be possible to discover within the jurists' decisions, despite their brevity, evidence that in the process of decision making the jurists had been sensitive *in the short run* to discussions of urban lease at the working level. And there is in truth an abundance of such evidence.

The juristic decisions on urban lease law by and large confine themselves to significant questions of law which can easily be imagined as having arisen in actual disputes. Many traces remain of original *responsa*;[30] by contrast, there are no logical puzzles or "limiting cases" merely designed to explore the extremes of a rule's interpretation. Decisions do

[28] Above, Chapter V, after n. 39.

[29] Above, Chapter V, after n. 38; the success of this policy is discussed just after n. 39.

[30] Cf. *Coll.* 12.7.9 (controversy on tenant's vicarious liability for slaves; the response is suppressed in D. 9.2.27.11); D. 6.1.59 (accession of fixtures to dwelling); D. 19.2.15.8 (liability of pseudo-procurator for lease concluded by him); D. 19.2.27.1 (abandonment due to fear); D. 19.2.30 pr. (expulsion due to the building's demolition). Rescripts: esp. D. 19.2.9.1; C. 4.65.3, 5.

not turn on rigid or excessively technical points of analysis, nor do they seem to rely on concepts and categories which are obscure or misleading from a social viewpoint; on the contrary, they are usually readily understandable on the forensic level even if one disagrees with the result. The choice between analytical alternatives seems sometimes to have been resolved through reference to patterns of interests.[31] Often the jurists showed considerable subtlety at "building-in" some accommodation for interests which had ostensibly lost under their decisions.[32] To this extent, the jurists preferred to tolerate a higher degree of analytical complexity, rather than to sacrifice valid interests so as to preserve simplicity.[33] Important reinterpretations of existing law may seek to increase the power of one party so as to provide a context for securing the interests of the other.[34] At times, this preference even led the jurists to construct rules which may have been difficult to defend on an analytical level, but which were entirely natural within their social setting.[35] In at least one case, juristic recognition of an

[31] E.g. Ulpian's effort to limit middleman's damages when the principal lessor lacked the right to lease (cf. D. 19.2.7-8, with Chapter IV at nn. 60-63). Compare the argument (largely suppressed in the *Digest*) as to the most effective means of securing a tenant's interest in removing his furnishings (Chapter IV at nn. 224-226).

[32] E.g. the possible requirement of a *denuntiatio* when the landlord seeks to repair a dwelling (Ulp. D. 43.17.3.3, with Chapter IV at nn. 77-79); the allowance of alternative housing where the tenant is expelled without the landlord's fault (Ulp. D. 19.2.9 pr.; cf. Labeo D. 19.2.60 pr.); the requirement that the landlord safeguard the tenant's furnishings for a period after preclusion (D. 39.2.34, cf. D. 19.2.56).

[33] *Contra* G. Longo, *Ric.* 523-570, who sought to strip Roman lease law of most of its "corresponsive obligations."

[34] Thus, the late classical increase in legal mechanisms for expulsion probably shows that they were trying to bring expulsion under State control (Chapter IV at n. 88); Ulpian's reinterpretation of the pledge relationship between an owner and his subtenant probably shows a willingness to grant the subtenant an interdict *de migrando* against the owner (D. 13.7.11.5, with Chapter IV at n. 170).

[35] E.g. the legal implication that the tenant had tacitly agreed to a

interest resulted in a trial-and-error experiment until a satisfactory means of securing it was discovered.[36] Many texts indicate that the jurists were willing to reconsider their decisions, and often such reconsideration is readily comprehensible as the consequence of social dissatisfaction with the original rule. Reconsideration seems to have underlain instances where the jurists disagreed among themselves,[37] or allowed an awkward rule to slip into obsolescence through disuse,[38] or progressively modified a general rule by making provision for exceptions.[39] Where such reconsideration is attributable to social dissatisfaction, it implies the existence of at least rudimentary attempts by the jurists to evaluate the social consequences of their rules.

Evidence for the jurists' sensitivity to the forensic expression of competing interests is extremely important; for, within the Roman judicial system, juristic sensitivity on this point may fairly be considered the essential prerequisite for the establishment of law as an instrument of social control.

---

pledge of his furnishings (Nerat. D. 20.2.4; *et al.*). This fiction is so extreme that Pomponius drops it when extending the pledge to cover damage through *culpa* (D. 20.2.2.).

[36] Cf. the process that led to the establishment of a tenant's vicarious liability *ex conducto* (Chapter IV at nn. 205-209).

[37] E.g. Proculus' disagreement with Sabinus about a tenant's contractual liability for his slaves (*Coll.* 12.7.9 and D. 9.2.27.11, with Chapter IV at nn. 205-206); Nerva's argument that slaves could be manumitted even after preclusion (D. 20.2.9); the disagreement about the tenant's ability to get a *cautio damni infecti* from his building's owner (Chapter IV n. 106).

[38] That is probably the significance of the silence which overtook Proculus' position on the tenant's pro-noxal contractual liability (Chapter IV at n. 206).

[39] E.g. the limitations imposed on the rule in D. 19.2.27.1 concerning tenant's abandonment due to fear (Chapter IV at nn. 99-109); Ulpian's limitation on the rule that the tenant inform his landlord before abandoning (D. 19.2.13.7); the modification of the pledge of furnishings to exempt the property of guests (D. 20.2.5 pr.; 43.32.1.3) and contractual partners (D. 43.32.1.5, 2), tenant's furnishings essential to his life (cf. Chapter IV at n. 137), and the value of his burial expenses (Ulp. D. 11.7.14.1).

As Julius Stone has written: "On such a view one irreducible minimum requirement of justice is in a broad sense procedural. It is that society shall be so organised that men's felt wants can be freely expressed; and that the law shall protect that expression, and provide it with channels through which it can compete effectively for (though not necessarily attain) the support of politically organised society. . . . Free expression is basic to the self-improvement, as well as to the stability in change, of a mature society."[40]

So much, then, for my thesis as to the genesis of Roman lease law. I have tried to provide, through this discussion, an idealized model, an explanatory mechanism by which certain important features of lease law's origin can be elucidated. In using this model, I have hoped to broaden the landscape of Roman legal history, but in certain relatively well-fixed directions; for while the "stratum" of interests in lease law remains hypothetical, it is no more improbable, I think, than some of the elaborate conceptual schemata imposed on Roman law in modern times. In brief, my general view of Roman lease law is that analytical and forensic discussion are complementary aspects of a complete historical consideration; analytical discussion aimed and aims to achieve for law a binding logical order, while forensic discussion aimed and aims to demonstrate or to advance law's social acceptability and utility.[41] In legal history, the tension

[40] J. Stone, *Social Dimensions* (cited n. 18) 794 (Stone's footnotes omitted); compare *Human Law* (cited n. 15) 382, 341. In Parsonian terms, analytical discussion is concerned mainly with integration and pattern maintenance, much less with adaptation and goal gratification; in forensic discussion the emphasis is reversed and free expression of interests therefore becomes paramount. For this terminology, cf. e.g. T. Parsons, in *Theories of Society* vol. I (ed. Parsons *et al.*, 1961) 36-41.

[41] The dichotomy here presented is often found in "realistic" writings, and is still overly simplistic in that it presupposes an essentially organic society; cf. G. Schubert (cited n. 17) 335-338. In any event, let me be clear: I have no faith in any schema that rigidly distinguishes "fachinterne" and "ausserjuristische Argumente," especially if the only evidence is the summary justification a jurist

between these two levels of discussion should be considered as essentially creative. In the case of Roman law, we can date this from the moment when Ser. Sulpicius Rufus recognized that urban lease was not merely an indistinguishable form of *locatio conductio*, but rather a special kind of contract requiring rules of its own; and similar creativity continued throughout the long history of Roman jurisprudence, until that system finally withered and died away.

Three final points remain to be made concerning the feasibility of this general view of Roman private law. First, urban leasehold was in one sense a "good" area for Roman jurisprudence. The average parties to an upper-class Roman lease were, if not always social equals, then at least not far apart. Each side therefore had a reasonable opportunity to defend itself in a court of law; each side had ready access to the Roman courts and to judicial authority at Rome, each side was likely to possess the financial means and social influence required to elicit help from jurists and orators, each side was capable of presenting a "good face" before a *iudex*. Furthermore, the problems of upper-class urban leasehold were also problems with which the jurists themselves were likely to be familiar from both sides, at least at second hand if not personally. Since there was nothing remote about urban leasehold, the jurists could visualize its problems as a whole, secure that no side of them remained unknown. They could predict with some accuracy the social implications of their decisions within this specific context. Compared with urban leasehold, there were many "bad" (difficult or awkward) areas in Roman jurisprudence, as for example labor law,[42] or for that matter the law directed toward lower-class

---

chances to offer for a particular decision; nor is such a justification an X-ray of his mind at the moment of decision. In my opinion, *all* legal decisions tend to involve both levels of discourse, and it is the work of legal history to recreate the ambiance of decision. For a discussion, cf. F. Wieacker (cited n. 17) 1-10.

[42] The researches of F. M. de Robertis have made Roman law's poverty in this area notorious. However, it is dangerous to draw

tenants in their lodging houses. The law of urban leasehold is easily distinguishable from such areas, above all by the richness of its thought.

Second, there is need to emphasize once again the considerable flexibility of analytical doctrine in many areas of Roman law.[43] As was observed above, urban leasehold is in Roman law one of the three principal forms of lease of an immoveable. The other two are strikingly dissimilar. Lease of a storeroom in a *horreum* had the main consequence of imposing on the *locator* a *custodia*-liability with regard to things left by the lessee in the storeroom; this duty arises from the plain sense of the transaction between the parties, and it is symptomatic only of a modern dogmatic rigidity that such a liability should ever have been considered a basis for denying the appurtenance of this contractual form to *locatio conductio rei.*[44] Farm lease is even more dissimilar. Examples are the tenant farmer's duty to cultivate (failure to cultivate constituted not only grounds for expulsion but also *culpa*), his duty to keep the premises in repair, his tacit pledge of the fruits (and the absence of a tacit pledge of furnishings), the differences in *reconductio tacita* after the

---

social and economic conclusions from this fact, cf. D. Nörr, *SZ* 82 (1965) 67-105, esp. 86ff. T. Mayer-Maly, *Recht der Arbeit* 20 (1967) 281-290, attempted to isolate the principles of Roman labor law; but his later article, in *La Formazione Storica del Diritto Moderno* vol. III (1977) 1321-1345, clearly demonstrated the far greater subtlety and complexity of medieval canon law.

[43] The close relationship of Roman law to its economic base is increasingly recognized by Romanists: e.g. M. Horvat, in *Antologia Giuridica* I (1968) 213-222, *contra* A. Steinwenter, *Fundus cum Instrumento* (1942) 99-101, on the law relating to *fundi*; J. Hammerstein, *Die Herde* (1975) 63-64, on the economic nature of a *grex*. A bibliography of recent (mainly Italian) scholarship is in M. Kaser, *RPR*² II 569 (to nn. 13, 14); on "ideology," cf. F. Wieacker (cited n. 17) 8-10, and compare *idem* (cited n. 3) 356-358. Modern scholars have often proceeded from unrealistic understandings of Roman society.

[44] But so C. Alzon, *Location des Entrepôts* (1966) 208-214. A balanced discussion now in G. Rickman, *Roman Granaries* (1971) 194-209, who clearly demonstrates the importance of the economic base.

lease's term expired, the tenant farmer's ability to obtain recompense for "useful" improvements, the landlord's warranty against latent defects affecting cultivatability, the tenant farmer's right to obtain rent remission in the event of catastrophic damage to the crops, and so on.[45] In the case of urban lease, it is to my mind questionable whether the jurists began by recognizing *any* legal consequence, save for the tenant's nonpossession of the leasehold, as being inevitably entailed by the mere fact of the lease's existence.[46]

Third, Roman juristic law is (from a sociological perspective) strikingly different from any modern type of law finding.[47] During the classical period, which was in other

[45] These differences are all observed in Chapter IV above; cf. also this chapter, n. 7. A detailed consideration of the legal position of the *colonus* in the early Empire is still lacking. The article on tenant farming by M. Finley, in *Studies in Roman Property* (ed. Finley, 1976) 103-118, shows how helpful such a study could be for historians.

[46] To some extent, indeed, urban leasehold might better be thought of as the exchange of money for certain services from the landlord, and not just for a place (*res*); this view is consistent with the landlord's warranty that conditions prevailing at the lease's outset will continue, and also with his right to offer equivalent housing in some circumstances. Compare "Javins v. First National Realty Corp.," in *Federal Reporter* 428 (1970) 1071-1083, esp. 1074-1075 (U.S. Court of Appeals, D.C. Circuit; Wright, J.): "The city dweller who seeks to lease an apartment . . . has little interest . . . even in the bare right to possession within the four walls of his apartment. When city dwellers, both rich and poor, seek 'shelter' today, they seek a well-known package of goods and services. . . ." The court then implied a "warranty of habitability," though on somewhat different grounds.

[47] The ensuing paragraph follows in the main A. Schiller, *An American Experience in Roman Law* (1971) 148-160 (who owes much to Max Weber); for additional bibliography, see F. Wieacker (cited n. 1) 11 n. 33. I am claiming, of course, that the "style" of Roman jurists itself took on functional significance; compare L. M. Friedman (cited n. 22) 216, on late nineteenth-century American judicial opinions: "Conceptual jurisprudence was another defence against the threat to legal independence. . . . These cases are boring to read, but this vice is a virtue. The cases made no dangerous claims to innovation. They treated law as a realm unto itself; the judges merely discovered and announced pre-existing principles of law."

political domains a time of gradually increasing absolutism, the aristocratic jurists were nonetheless for all practical purposes the sole depositaries, furtherers, and transmitters of a living legal tradition; and their tradition was (at least to the mid-second century A.D., and probably later) also formally independent of the Roman court system. Within the court system, juristic decisions took on normative force by virtue of their source, and not because of the reasoning offered in their support; for the most part, these decisions were not intended to persuade and hence not even supplied with a token of adequate supporting argumentation. Inside the narrow circle of jurists, free discussion and disagreement were not uncommon, but we have no evidence that disagreement ever resulted in lengthy exchanges of written argument. To a large extent, therefore, the jurists exercised the privilege and the discretion of concealing the precise reasons for their decisions behind a veil of personal authority (the "illusion of timelessness"). Thus a certain ambiguity of motivation always attended the position taken by a particular jurist, his disagreement with a colleague, and the ultimate prevalence among jurists of one view over another. From the modern viewpoint of a law whose means and ends are mainly defined by public policy, such ambiguity in the formation of law has both its advantages and its disadvantages.[48] It is important, however, that the advantages not be entirely overlooked; for they are not likely to have remained unknown to the jurists. Was such a weapon ever forged to lie rusting in its sheath?

It is my hope that the general view in this chapter will

[48] The main disadvantage is that the social purpose of the resulting rule is indefinite, even in relation to the specific case under discussion; therefore it does not teach effectively. But in truth the gulf that divides us from the Romans in this matter is very great; the extended written decision serves a wide variety of social and legal functions within modern legal systems. The Roman "failure" in this regard is rightly emphasized by J. P. Dawson, *Oracles of the Law* (1968) 113-119. The "failure" was somewhat mitigated when law was created in the rhetorical ambiance of litigation.

help legal historians to find their way out of a dilemma that has plagued modern scholarship, and stems from the modern feeling that Roman private law must be discussed in much closer connection to its social context. But it is not yet clear how such discussion should be conducted. For instance, some scholars have supposed that the jurists in effect only acted in simple reflex to economic or social pressures when they formed their rules.[49] By contrast, Alan Watson recently expressed the view that private law normally "does not progress in a rational way, and that the divergence between law and the needs or wishes of the people involved or the will of the leaders of the people is marked."[50] It is not easy to steer a course between these extreme views until a way can be found to identify even hypothetically "the needs or wishes of the people involved," and to show how these "needs or wishes" were communicated to the jurists and how the jurists responded to them.

In order to resolve this dilemma, I have resorted to an approach which is frankly modernistic, and specifically "realistic" as that word is understood in American jurisprudence.[51] Its utility lies in its ability to explain the evidence without forcing or distorting it; the jurists are seen as responsive to the forensic expression of interests which arise naturally out of the social institutions underlying the law.

[49] E.g. B. Vonglis, *La Lettre et l'Esprit de la Loi* (1968) 200-201; cf. L. Lombardi, *Saggi sul Diritto Giurisprudenziale* (1967) 36-54.

[50] A. Watson, *Society and Legal Change* (1976) 6; Watson discusses Roman law in his Chapters 2-4.

[51] On "America's dominant philosophy of law," see e.g. R. S. Summers, *Harvard Law Review* 92 (1978) 433-449, a eulogy for Lon Fuller. I have adapted this position to match my material. My own views closely resemble those of R.B.M. Cotterell, *Anglo-American Law Review* 4 (1975) 386-411, e.g. 406: "A truly realistic view of law in its social setting requires the analysis of both [its] conceptual and behavioural aspects and the examination of their interrelationship." Therefore the two "aspects" are thought of and considered first separately (above, Chapters IV, V) and then together (Chapter VI). This view is hard to apply only because we must be so vague about the uses to which juristic rules were put after their creation.

This approach requires testing in relation to other areas of law, where it may prove to be helpful only in special circumstances when (as was evidently the case in urban lease law) the station and wealth of average litigants allowed the jurists a fuller control of law's social content. But even if my approach proves to be exaggerated or wrong, there is still a need within legal history to pay a more sustained attention to interests; for surely it is improbable that the jurists ignored altogether the expression of contemporary demands upon the law.

On the other hand, if it should prove to have a degree of general application, the discussion of interests would help considerably in clarifying both how and why the jurists operated in the High Roman Empire. I do not underestimate the barriers, both practical and theoretical, to such further research; but the potential gain is also great. The gain would come from a new way of looking at Roman private law. The jurists did not live exclusively in their tiny enclave of law and legal thinking; they were also functioning participants in the complex flow of their social system, at times bending to the flow and at other times channeling it. Within its society Roman juristic law had both possibilities and limitations as a means for social control; in doing what they were capable of doing, the jurists sometimes succeeded and sometimes failed. No doubt the jurists were involved, as individuals, in the political and cultural events of their time, as well as in the underlying social struggles and "ideologies," and we can expect their involvement to have left its mark on their work; but on another level there is a portion of their work that is not in this sense derivative, but instead comprises their contribution, *not as individuals but as jurists*, to the directing of their society. Discussion of interests can assist us in illuminating these aspects of Roman legal science. And I suspect that, in the end, a surprise may yet await us: we may discover that the jurists' invention and employment of juristic methods, rather than leading them most often into a sterile formalism, instead repaid them handsomely by generating a substantial increase in law's instrumental power.[52]

The potential service of a discussion of interests, at least in "good" areas of law like urban lease law, lies in its capacity to fill out the shadowy space between social institutions on the one side and the naked legal rules on the other—to demonstrate the reciprocal lines of calculation which can bind law to society and society to law. If such realism means that we come to see Roman jurisprudence more firmly anchored in its time and place, then, or so I think, this result is in one respect eminently desirable: we shall at last claim for Roman jurisprudence no more than the jurists themselves sought to achieve for their law.

[52] With this last sentence, compare P. Selznick, in *International Encyclopedia of the Social Sciences* vol. IX, s.v. "Law: The Sociology of Law" (1968) 50-59, at 56 (on Common Law); and N. Luhmann, *Rechtssystem* (cited n. 3) 15-23.

Appendix A: An Egyptian "Eviction Notice"

A RECENTLY published Oxyrhynchite papyrus (P. Mich. Inv. 1355) contains a Greek private letter written sometime in the third century A.D. by the tenant of a house to his landlord. (Both their given names are unknown.) The first half of the letter is lost; the papyrus begins as the tenant is recalling his former good relations with his landlord. The translation is by Prof. Youtie:

> . . . and no one knew whether the house was mine or yours because there was no disagreement between me and you. But now I am being subjected to violence by your very own Ptolema, who sent me word to this effect: "Give up the house. Otherwise, your household furnishings will be put out." I ought not to have been subjected to these things. For I have assurances (from you) for the period from the Amesysia to the Amesysia, and the god willing I owe you nothing on the rents except for the present semester only. I pray for your good health.

This is the only ancient document purporting to give, in direct discourse, the words of an "eviction notice." Note the notice's extreme abruptness, with no allowance for even a temporary delay; furthermore, the notice itself does not indicate the landlord's reason for the expulsion, and the tenant seems taken completely unawares. The Amesysia was a moveable Egyptian feast in midsummer; cf. F. Bilabel, *Neue Heidelberger Jahrbücher* (1929) 29. The tenant's current rental agreement, an oral one, was to run for a year as defined by this festival, and was divided into two six-month payment periods. As regards rent, the sole question involved the payment for the current six months, which was probably payable at the end of the period and hence not yet in arrears. The tenant, in any event, obviously saw no ground here for expulsion. As for the notice, the tenant seems to accept its legal validity, and he may be assumed to have vacated already. His counterstroke consisted in an appeal to the social indignity of the situation (social pressure), on the one hand, and in a firm written complaint about the expulsion's groundlessness, on the other. The latter tactic doubtless prepared his ground in a suit.

In A.D. 214, a situation very similar to this resulted in a petition to the Emperor Caracalla from a certain Flavius Callimorphus. The emperor's reply, which listed the grounds for a justified expulsion, is C. 4.65.3.

Bibliography: H. C. Youtie, *Zeitschrift für Papyrologie und Epigraphik* 30 (1978) 186-190.

Appendix B: Translation of Latin Passages Quoted in the Text

ALL EXTENDED quotations have been translated as emended in my text and footnotes. The translation aims primarily for clarity of statement, and I have made no attempt to duplicate the style of the original. Words or symbols within parentheses indicate editorial comment or supplement. I have not indicated the possibility of interpolation.

CHAPTER II: *The Social Institutions of the Roman Rental Market*

Ulpian, 18 *On Sabinus* (D. 7.1.13.8):

[a] "Equally, if the usufruct of a house is legated, the fructuary ought not to construct spaces for rent there, nor divide the house into apartments; he can indeed lease it out, but he ought to lease it as a house. Nor should a bath be constructed there. As for what (Nerva?) says, namely that he should not construct spaces for rent, understand by that what are commonly called lodging houses or fulling factories."

CHAPTER IV: *The Roman Law of Urban Leasehold*

Reconstruction of the *Actio Locati*:

[a] "Whereas the plaintiff leased to the defendant the farm (*or* the work to be done, *or* his services) under dispute, which transaction is disputed, whatever on account of this transaction the defendant ought in good faith to do for or give to the defendant, let the *iudex* condemn the defendant to pay to the plaintiff its value; if it does not so appear, let him absolve him of liability."

Appendix B

Clause in the Lease of a Warehouse (*CIL* 6.33747):

[b] "Whoever holds space under hire within these warehouses does not have the right to lease it out or to assign the contract."

Clause in the Lease of a Warehouse (*CIL* 6.33747):

[c] "We do not accept responsibility for the safekeeping of things brought into these warehouses. . . . If the lessee of a storeroom leaves his property there and does not entrust it to a guard, the warehouseman will be blameless."

Clause in the Lease of a Warehouse (*CIL* 6.33747):

[d] "In these warehouses things brought in or moved in are pledged to the warehouseman unless security is (otherwise) provided for rental payments."

Clause in the Lease of a Warehouse (*CIL* 6.37795):

[e] "If in these warehouses a lessee builds anything in, he shall have no right to remove it unless this power is accorded him."

Gaius, 10 *On the Provincial Edict* (D. 19.2.25.1):

[f] "When someone has leased to another a farm for his exploitation or as a dwelling, if for some reason he sells the farm or the building, he should provide that through the same agreement, the tenant farmer be permitted by the buyer too to exploit, or the urban tenant to dwell; otherwise he (the tenant), if excluded, will sue him (the lessor) on the lease."

Labeo, 5 of *The Posthumous Writings as Epitomized by Javolenus* (D. 19.2.60 pr.):

[g] "If a house is leased out for many years, the lessor ought to provide not only that the lessee be able to dwell in it from July 1 of each year, but also that during his term of lease he be able, if he wishes, to lease it out to an occupant. And so if this house was under repair from January 1 and remained so on June 1, such that no one can live in it or show it to another, (Labeo says that) the lessee will owe the lessor nothing, so much so that he cannot even be forced to dwell in the repaired house from July 1, except if the lessor be ready to give him a comfortable house to live in."

Rescript of Caracalla, A.D. 214 (C. 4.65.3):

[h] "You say that you have a room under lease; if you pay rent to the owner of the apartment building, it is not right that you be expelled unwillingly unless the owner shows that it is required for his own purposes, or he wishes to repair the house, or you have behaved improperly in the leasehold."

Alfenus, 30 of *The Digests as Epitomized by Paul* (D. 19.2.30 pr.):

[i] ". . . if the demolition was unnecessary, but (he did it) because he wished to improve the building . . ."

Labeo, 4 of *The Posthumous Writings as Epitomized by Javolenus* (D. 19.2.28.2):

[j] ". . . But if the lessor does not furnish the lessee with the power of taking a house under lease, and he (the lessee) then rented a place to dwell in, (Labeo) thinks that as much is owed to him (the lessee) as he (the lessor) would have furnished had bad faith not been present. Yet if he (the lessee) obtained a free dwelling, deduction should be made from the house's lease for this portion of the term."

Ulpian, 32 *On the Edict* (D. 19.2.7):

[k] "If I lease to you another person's apartment building for 50 (coins) and you lease the same building to Titius for 60, and Titius is then forbidden to dwell in it by the owner, the prevailing view is that you ought to obtain 60 in a suit on the lease, since you yourself are liable to Titius for 60."

Tryphoninus, 9 of *The Controversies* (D. 19.2.8):

[l] "Let us examine whether neither 60 nor 50 is owed, but rather as much as it lay in his interest to enjoy the leasehold; and the middleman should obtain as much as he must provide to the one who rented from him, since the profit from the contract, which was concluded for the purpose of a higher rent, raises the sum adjudged. But nevertheless the chief lessor will have a counterclaim for the 50 which he would have received from him if the owner of the apartment building had not forbidden the sublessee to dwell in it. This rule is currently in use."

Marcellus, 8 of *The Digests* (D. 19.2.48.1):

[m] "If a person did not return a hired slave or some other moveable thing, he will be condemned for as much as the oath on the suit is."

Ulpian, 69 *On the Edict* (D. 43.17.3.3):

[n] "When an urban tenant forbids access to the owner who wishes to repair his building, the prevailing view is that the interdict *uti possidetis* properly lies, and that the owner gives a public oath that he prevents the urban tenant not from dwelling in it, but from possessing it."

Paul, 34 *On the Edict* (D. 19.2.24.2):

[o] "If a home or a farm is leased out for payments over a period of five years, and if a tenant farmer abandons cultivation of his farm or if an urban tenant (abandons) his dwelling, the owner can sue them forthwith."

Alfenus, 2 of *The Digests* (D. 19.2.27.1):

[p] "Again, (Servius) was asked whether or not a person owes rent if he moves out because of fear. He answered that if there was reason for him to fear danger, then, even if there really was no danger, he still does not owe rent; but if there was no legally acceptable reason for fear, then he owes rent nonetheless."

Ulpian, 32 *On the Edict* (D. 19.2.13.7):

[q] "At the approach of an army the lessee moved out, with the consequence that soldiers stole windows and other things from their lodgings. If he moved out without giving notice to the owner, he will be liable on the lease; but Labeo says that he is liable if he could resist and did not resist, and his view is correct. But likewise, if he was unable to give notice, I do not think him to be liable."

Ulpian, 22 *On the Edict* (D. 19.2.15.2):

[r] ". . . Servius says that the owner ought to be responsible to the tenant farmer for all force which cannot be resisted, as for example . . . if an enemy invasion occurs; . . . but if nothing out of the ordinary occurs, the tenant farmer bears the loss. The same should be said if a passing army wantonly steals something. . . ."

Ulpian, 84 *On the Edict* (D. 39.2.28):

[s] ". . . Similarly treated is also loss on account of urban tenants' moving out, if this occurred because of a legally proper fear. Aristo quite aptly adds, however, that just as Cassius requires that a legally proper fear furnish a reason for moving out, so too Cassius ought to say the same for the case of one who propped up a building, if he was compelled to prop it up due to a legally proper fear of its collapse."

Ulpian, 53 *On the Edict* (D. 39.2.13.6):

[t] "The question is raised as to whether the owner of a building can provide security to his own urban tenants. Sabinus says that security may not be given to urban tenants; for either they rented a building defective from the outset and have what they sought, or the building fell into disrepair and they can attempt to suit on the lease. This view is the better one."

Ulpian, 42 *On Sabinus* (D. 39.2.33):

[u] "The suit on impending loss is not accorded to an urban tenant, since he can sue on the lease if the owner prevents his moving out."

Gaius, 10 *On the Provincial Edict* (D. 19.2.25.2):

[v] "If a neighbor builds and the windows of an apartment are thereby darkened, (a jurist held) that the lessor is liable to his urban tenant; indeed, there is no doubt that a farm tenant or an urban tenant can abandon the leasehold. Also, if suit is brought against him about the rent, the balance of the off-set should be calculated. We will understand the same to be true if the lessor does not repair doors or windows which are excessively broken."

Ulpian, 42 *On the Edict* (D. 19.2.25.2):

[w] ". . . So also, if any revenue is lost because of the demolition, by the same logic Sabinus wanted it to be recompensed. If, for example, the residents moved out or they cannot dwell in it so comfortably, this can be charged to the builder."

Paul, 3 *On Sabinus* (D. 7.1.30), and Marcellus, 4 of *The Digests* (D.8.2.10):

[x] ". . . a modest light . . . ," ". . . as much as is required for the occupants in the normal course of their daily life . . ."; ". . . it is possible to dwell even in a darkened building . . ."

Ulpian, 73 *On the Edict* (D. 43.32.1 pr.):

[y] "The Praetor says: 'If the person in question is not one of those things concerning which you and the plaintiff have agreed that whatever is moved or brought into the dwelling in question, or originates or is made there, acts as a pledge to you for that dwelling's rent; or if he is one of the things and you have been paid the rent, or security has been provided on this account, or you are responsible for nonpayment: then I forbid the use of force to prevent the person who moved him in on account of the pledge from moving him out.' "

Ulpian, 73 *On the Edict* (D. 43.32.1.3):

[z] "However, if a person has a free dwelling, an analogous form of this interdict will avail him."

Marcianus, *Monograph on the Action of Hypotheque* (D. 20.2.5 pr.):

[aa] "In the thirteenth book of his *Sundry Lessons in Law* Pomponius writes that if the lessee provides me with a free dwelling, my furnishings are not pledged to the owner of the apartment house."

Pomponius, 13 of *Sundry Lessons in Law* (D. 20.2.7.1):

[ab] "One should note that not all furnishings are pledged, but just those brought in to be there; this is the better view."

Scaevola, 5 of *The Responses* (D. 20.1.32):

[ac] ". . . that they be there permanently, and are not suited to the needs of the moment . . ."

Rescript of Alexander Severus, A.D. 223 (C.4.65.5):

[ad] "It is settled as law that things which tenant farmers bring into a farm, if their owners have agreed, are bound by the law of pledge to the owners of the property. But

when a house is leased, the owners' knowledge is not required in the case of things brought in or moved in; for these things too are held by the law of pledge."

Marcianus, *Monograph on the Action for Hypotheque* (D. 20.2.5.1):

[ae] "The same author (Pomponius) says: 'It should be noted that, if its owner wishes, a pledge can be brought in to be obligated for part of a debt.' "

Gaius, 26 *On the Provincial Edict* (D. 43.32.2):

[af] "This interdict is undoubtedly of use to the urban tenant also regarding things which are not his, but were, for example, loaned or leased to him or deposited with him."

Ulpian, 73 *On the Edict* (D. 43.32.1.5):

[ag] "It should be observed that the Praetor does not require that the object be in the lessee's estate (?), nor that it be moved in as a pledge, but 'if it was brought in on the account of pledge.' Therefore if things belong to someone else and if they are such that they cannot be held on the account of pledge, but nonetheless they are moved in on the account of pledge, this interdict is pertinent; for if things were not brought in on the account of pledge, the lessor will also be unable to retain them."

Ulpian, 73 *On the Edict* (D. 20.2.6):

[ah] "Although in the case of urban property we usually accept it as tacitly agreed that furnishings are bound, just as if this had been agreed to for each object, still a pledge of this kind does not stand in the way of freedom —a view approved also by Pomponius; for he says that it is no obstacle to manumission that (a slave was) obligated for the dwelling."

Ulpian, 73 *On the Edict* (D. 20.1.14 pr.):

[ai] "The question arose as to whether, if the due-date of a payment has not yet arrived, it should be allowed to seize pledges even in the middle of a term. I think that seizure of a pledge should be accorded, for I have an interest (in the pledge); Celsus writes the same."

Ulpian, 73 *On the Edict* (D. 43.32.1.1):

[aj] "This interdict is set up for the urban tenant who wishes to move out after his rent has been paid; it does not avail the farm tenant."

Ulpian, 73 *On the Edict* (D. 43.32.1.4):

[ak] "If a rental payment is not yet owed, Labeo says that this interdict fails unless he (the tenant) is ready to pay that payment. Therefore, if he has paid a six-month payment and a six-month payment is outstanding, he will employ the interdict in vain unless he pays also for the following six months; but this is true if a special agreement was made in the lease of a house that it not be permitted to move out for a year or for a specified time. The rule is the same if a person rents for many years and the term has not yet expired. For since pledges are obligated for the entire lease, it follows that the interdict will (not) pertain unless they are freed."

Ulpian, 43 *On Sabinus* (D. 39.2.33):

[al] "The suit on impending loss is not accorded the urban tenant, since he can sue on the lease if the owner prevents his moving out,"

Paul, 10 *On Sabinus* (D. 39.2.34):

[am] ". . . at any rate if he was ready to give security for past rent; otherwise the owner's retention of the pledge would seem to become legally proper. Still, if he (the owner) retains things as pledges and they perish when the neighboring building collapses, one can say that the lessor is liable by the action for pledge if he could have moved these things to a safer place."

Paul, *Monograph on the Duties of the Prefect of the Watch* (D. 20.2.9):

[an] "There is a distinction between things obligated because of a pledge and things which due to an evident agreement are bound on the account of pledge, in that we cannot manumit slaves obligated as a pledge, but we (successfully) manumit (slaves in the latter category) so long as we remain in the dwelling, i.e. before we are locked out

on account of rent. For we will not free slaves retained on the account of pledge. Nerva, the jurist, was mocked when he pointed out that slaves detained for rent can be freed through a window."

Martial, *Epigrams* 12.32.1-5:

[ao] "Vacerra, you disgrace to the First of July / I saw your luggage, I saw it / what was not retained for two years' rent / your wife carried it, she of the seven red hairs / and your white-haired mother with your enormous sister. . . ."

Papinian, 6 of *Legal Problems* (D. 12.6.55):

[ap] "If a possessor in bad faith leases out urban property, what he collects in rent may not be reclaimed from the one who paid it, but is owed to the owner. . . . But if he receives passage money on ships leased out by the owner, or (if he receives) the rental payments from apartment houses, he is liable to him (the payer) for money not owed, and the latter was not freed of his obligation by his payment. . . ."

Ulpian, 28 *On the Edict* (D. 13.7.11.5):

[aq] "It should be accepted that money has been paid not only if it is paid to him to whom the thing is owed, but also if (it is paid) to another by his will, or to one from whom he inherits, or to his procurator, or to a slave he ordered to collect money. Wherefore if you rent a house and then lease a portion of it to me, and I pay a rental payment to your lessor, I can engage you in an action on pledge—for Julian also writes that it can be paid to him; and if I pay part to you and part to him, the equivalent should be true. Obviously my furnishings are bound only up to the amount for which I rented the apartment; beyond doubt it was not agreed that my trifles be bound for the whole rental payment of the apartment house. But what was tacitly agreed upon also with the building's owner was obviously this, that it is not the arrangement of the apartment dweller which advantages the owner, but rather his own (arrangement)."

Paul, *Monograph on the Duties of the Prefect of the Watch* (D. 19.2.56):

[ar] "When their lessees are long absent and pay no rent for this period, and the owners of warehouses or apartment houses desire to open them and inventory their contents, they should be granted a hearing by the officials charged with this (i.e. the Prefect of the Watch). In a matter of this kind a period of two years ought to be observed."

Marcianus, *Monograph on the Action of Hypotheque* (D. 20.2.2):

[as] "In the fortieth book of his *Sundry Lessons in Law* Pomponius writes: 'Furnishings are bound as a pledge not only for rental payments, but also if an urban tenant's dwelling deteriorates through his own fault, on which account a suit on the lease will lie against him.' "

Ulpian, 32 *On the Edict* (D. 19.2.11.2):

[at] "Likewise the lessee should take care lest in any way he worsen the legal or physical condition of the thing (leased), or allow it to become worse."

Rescript of Diocletian (C. 4.65.29):

[au] "Since you assert that the lessee demolished buildings which he took in good condition, the provincial governor will order his heirs to restore them after an assessment of the buildings has been held between you."

Ulpian, 23 *On the Edict* (D. 9.3.5.4):

[av] "A person is liable for this through an action under the Aquilian law; on this ground, Labeo says that when someone is condemned because his guest or a third party threw something from an apartment, he should be granted a specially adapted action against the thrower. This view is correct. Obviously if he was the thrower's landlord he will have an action on the lease as well."

Ulpian, 32 *On the Edict* (D. 19.2.11.4):

[aw] "Lessor and lessee had agreed that no hay be stacked in an urban villa; he (the lessee) stacked hay; then a slave put a fire to it and set it ablaze. Labeo says that the lessee

is liable on the lease, because he himself furnished the cause by bringing in (hay) against the lease."

Hermogenianus, 2 of *The Condensation of Law* (D. 19.2.12):

[ax] "But also if some third party sets the fire, assessment of the loss will be made in a trial on the lease."

Ulpian, 32 *On the Edict* (D. 19.2.11 pr.):

[ay] "Let us examine whether a lessee ought to be responsible for the fault both of his slaves and of whomever he admits. And to what extent is he liable, whether that he surrender slaves noxally or that instead he be liable on his own account? And will he just transfer the suits against those whom he admits, or will he be liable as if for his own fault? My own view is that he is responsible on his own account also for the fault of those he admitted, even if nothing is agreed upon (in the lease), provided that in admitting them he shows fault in that he has such people as members of his household or guests. Pomponius in his sixty-third book *On the Edict* also approves this view."

Paul, 19 *On the Edict* (D. 9.3.6.2):

[az] "The occupant ought to be responsible for his own fault and for that of his household."

Ulpian, 18 *On the Edict* (Coll. 12.7.9):

[ba] "But if some slaves of an urban tenant burn down an apartment house, according to Urseius in Book 10 Sabinus responded that the owner may be sued, on the account of his slaves, by a noxal trial under the Aquilian law; but he (Urseius) denies that the owner is liable on the lease. But Proculus responds that when a tenant farmer's slaves burn down a farmhouse, the tenant is liable either on the lease or from the Aquilian law, with the conditions that the tenant can surrender the slaves noxally, and that if the matter is adjudged in one trial there should be no further suit by the other."

Ulpian, 18 *On the Edict* (D. 9.2.27.11):

[bb] "Proculus says that when a tenant farmer's slaves had burned down a farmhouse, the tenant is liable either on

the lease or from the Aquilian law, with the conditions that the tenant can surrender the slaves noxally, and that if the matter is adjudged in one trial there should be no further suit by the other. This is so if the tenant was free of fault; but if he had blameworthy slaves, he is liable for the wrongful loss (?) as to why he had such people. He (Proculus) writes that the same rule should be enforced also concerning the persons of urban tenants of an apartment house; this view makes sense."

Alfenus, 2 of *The Digests* (D. 19.2.27 pr.):

[bc] "It is not right that occupants immediately deduct from their rent when their use of some part of the apartment is a bit less comfortable. For (Servius responds that?) the occupant is subject to the condition (?) that if something unfortunate (?) occurred, on account of which the owner properly demolished something, he should suffer a little part of the inconvenience, though not to the extent that the owner had opened the part of the apartment in which the occupant has a large part of his use."

Labeo, 4 of *The Posthumous Writings as Epitomized by Javolenus* (D.19.2.28 pr.-1):

[bd] "But if the lessee was not hindered from using his dwelling in a house, he (Labeo) thinks that rent is owed for that part even of a house which had become defective."

Ulpian, 32 *On the Edict* (D. 19.2.19.5):

[be] "If an urban tenant brings a bronze strongbox into a building and the owner then narrows the building's entrance, the better view is that he (the owner) is liable on the lease and (also) by the suit to deliver up, and this whether or not he was aware of it (the problem); the duty falls to the *iudex* that he compel him to furnish to the tenant an entrance and an opportunity to remove his strongbox, this of course at the lessor's expense."

Ulpian, 32 *On the Edict* (D. 19.2.19.4):

[bf] "If an urban tenant adds a door or some other things to the building, what action should lie? The better view is

what Labeo wrote, that an action lies on the lease to permit him to remove it, provided that he gives security for impending damage, so that he in no way worsen the building's condition during the removal, but that he restore the original aspect to the building."

Julian, 6 *From Minucius* (D. 6.1.59):

[bg] "The occupant placed windows and doors into another's buildings; the buildings' owner removed them a year later. My question is whether the person who had placed them can (now) claim them as his property. He (Sabinus?) responded that he could; for things connected to another's buildings belong to these buildings so long as they remain joined, but as soon as they were removed they return at once to their original legal state."

Ulpian, 28 *On the Edict* (D. 19.2.5):

[bh] "If I lease to you a dwelling and then remit a rental payment, the proper action is on lease and hire."

Ulpian, 32 *On the Edict* (D. 19.2.13.11):

[bi] "If a person remained in his leasehold after the term of lease expired, not only will he have apparently rehired it, his pledges also apparently continue to be bound. This is true, to be sure, unless a third party obligated the things on his behalf during the earlier lease; in this case a new agreement will be required. The situation will be identical if properties in the public domain are leased. But as for our view that the tenant farmer seems to rehire through the silence of both parties, this should be understood to mean that they seem to have renewed the same lease for the year when they are silent, but not for subsequent years, and this even if, for example, a five-year lease had originally been provided for the leasehold. But also if nothing to the contrary is done in the second year after the five-year period ends, (I think that?) the same lease was apparently continued in that year; for they seem to have agreed by the very fact that they were silent. And this rule should be observed for each successive year. But for urban properties we employ a different rule, that a

person is obligated for as long as he resides, provided that a fixed term for the hire was not included in the written document."

Ulpian, 73 *On the Edict* (D. 43.32.1.4):

[bj] "If a rental payment is not yet owed, Labeo says that this interdict fails unless he is willing to pay that payment. Therefore, if he has paid a six-month payment and a six-month payment is outstanding, he employs the interdict in vain unless he pays rent also for the following six months; . . ."

Ulpian, 32 *On the Edict* (D. 19.2.9 pr.):

[bk] "If a person leases to me a house or a farm which he has purchased in good faith, and he is then evicted with no bad faith or blame on his part, Pomponius says that he is nonetheless bound on the lease to provide the lessee with the right to enjoy the leasehold. Obviously, if the owner does not allow this and the lessor is ready to provide another dwelling no less comfortable, he (Pomponius) says that the most equitable course is that the lessor be released (from his obligation)."

Labeo, 5 of *The Posthumous Writings as Epitomized by Javolenus* (D. 19.2.60 pr.):

[bl] ". . . except if the lessor is ready to give him a comfortable house to live in."

CHAPTER V: *Recognition of Interests in Roman Lease Law*

Gaius, *Institutes* 4.153:

[a] "We are considered to possess not only when we possess ourselves, but also if another is in possossion in our name even though he is not subject to our power, such as a farm tenant or urban tenant."

Ulpian, 1 of *The Institutes* (D. 1.1.1.2):

[b] ". . . Some things are useful in a public sense, some in an individual sense. . . ."

Paul, 14 *On Sabinus* (D. 1.1.11):

[c] ". . . what is useful to all or to a majority in the State . . ."

Index of Legal Sources

The first reference indicates the principal discussion.

I. Pre-Justinianic Sources

II. Justinianic and Byzantine Sources

Index

Index

Index

General Index

Index

Index

Index

Index

Index

Library of Congress Cataloging in Publication Data

Frier, Bruce W 1943-
Landlords and tenants in imperial Rome.

Includes index.
1. Landlord and tenant (Roman law) I. Title.
2. Law 340.5'4 79-3207
ISBN 0-691-05299-9

www.ingramcontent.com/pod-product-compliance
Lightning Source LLC
LaVergne TN
LVHW011117300926
849160LV00008B/422
9780691615707